Deradicalisation and Terrorist Rehabilitation

The threat of terrorism, if not adequately managed, is likely to increase exponentially. As terrorist groups' influence and networks spread globally, a concerted effort in counterterrorism strategy is critical to mitigating the threat they present. Governments facing the threat of terrorism are typically strengthening their law enforcement, military and intelligence capabilities, but more complex initiatives such as deradicalisation and terrorist rehabilitation are more time-consuming and less attention-grabbing and so tend to be neglected. It is all too easy to 'do' rehabilitation ineffectively or to simply ignore it altogether. This is unfortunate, as an effective rehabilitation strategy can yield dividends over the longer term. Every committed terrorist is a potential recruiter, whether in prison or at liberty, for more terrorists. Even in death, they can potentially be presented as martyrs. Conversely, successfully rehabilitated terrorists can be valuable assets in the public relations theatre of battle.

There is no single, simple solution to the challenges of deradicalisation and rehabilitation, but this book places examples of best practice within a robust but flexible, conceptual framework. It gives guidelines for establishing and implementing a successful deradicalisation or rehabilitation programme, derived from a series of empirical case studies of successful projects around the world. It sets out both the necessary and desirable facets of such a programme, identifying which areas to prioritise and where budgets can be best spent if resources are tight. The authors provide detailed case studies of each step to illustrate an approach that has worked and how best to replicate this success.

Rohan Gunaratna is Professor of Security Studies and Head of the International Centre for Political Violence and Terrorism Research, S. Rajaratnam School of International Studies, Nanyang Technological University, Singapore.

Sabariah Hussin is a Research Analyst at the International Centre for Political Violence and Terrorism Research, S. Rajaratnam School of International Studies, Nanyang Technological University, Singapore.

Routledge Studies in the Politics of Disorder and Instability

This series brings together research on issues involving dissent, disorder, rebellion, revolution and governability at national, regional and comparative levels. Focusing on the political, social and economic causes of these phenomena and analysing case studies from around the world. It aims to develop our understanding of both the details of individual examples and the common characteristics of international trends.

Rebel Recruitment and Information Problems
Kazuhiro Obayashi

International Case Studies of Terrorist Rehabilitation
Edited by Rohan Gunaratna and Sabariah Hussin

Deradicalisation and Terrorist Rehabilitation
A framework for policy-making and implementation
Edited by Rohan Gunaratna and Sabariah Hussin

For the full list of titles in this series, please visit www.routledge.com/Routledge-Studies-in-the-Politics-of-Disorder-and-Instability/book-series/RSPDI

Deradicalisation and Terrorist Rehabilitation

A Framework for Policy-making and Implementation

Edited by Rohan Gunaratna and Sabariah Hussin

LONDON AND NEW YORK

First published 2019
by Routledge
2 Park Square, Milton Park, Abingdon, Oxon OX14 4RN

and by Routledge
711 Third Avenue, New York, NY 10017

Routledge is an imprint of the Taylor & Francis Group, an informa business

© 2019 selection and editorial matter, Rohan Gunaratna and Sabariah Hussin; individual chapters, the contributors

The right of Rohan Gunaratna and Sabariah Hussin to be identified as the authors of the editorial material, and of the authors for their individual chapters, has been asserted in accordance with sections 77 and 78 of the Copyright, Designs and Patents Act 1988.

All rights reserved. No part of this book may be reprinted or reproduced or utilised in any form or by any electronic, mechanical, or other means, now known or hereafter invented, including photocopying and recording, or in any information storage or retrieval system, without permission in writing from the publishers.

Trademark notice: Product or corporate names may be trademarks or registered trademarks, and are used only for identification and explanation without intent to infringe.

British Library Cataloguing-in-Publication Data
A catalogue record for this book is available from the British Library

Library of Congress Cataloging-in-Publication Data
Names: Gunaratna, Rohan, 1961- editor. | Sabariah Hussin, editor.
Title: Deradicalisation and terrorist rehabilitation : a framework for
   policy-making and implementation / edited by Rohan Gunaratna
   and Sabariah Hussin.
Description: Abingdon, Oxon ; New York, NY : Routledge, 2018. |
   Series: Routledge studies in the politics of disorder and instability |
   Includes bibliographical references and index.
Identifiers: LCCN 2018018187| ISBN 9781138602519 (hbk) | ISBN
   9780429469534 (ebk) | ISBN 9781138602526 (pbk)
Subjects: LCSH: Terrorism—Prevention. | Terrorists—Rehabilitation.
Classification: LCC HV6431 .D4657 2018 | DDC 363.325/17—dc23
LC record available at https://lccn.loc.gov/2018018187

ISBN: 978-1-138-60251-9 (hbk)
ISBN: 978-1-138-60252-6 (pbk)
ISBN: 978-0-429-46953-4 (ebk)

Typeset in Galliard
by Swales & Willis Ltd, Exeter, Devon, UK

Contents

List of illustrations vii
List of contributors viii
Acknowledgements xi
Foreword xii

1 **Introduction** 1
   ROHAN GUNARATNA AND SABARIAH HUSSIN

2 **Behind bars: do prison settings hold the key to successful custodial rehabilitation programmes?** 12
   JOLENE JERARD

3 **Countering radical ideology: case studies of religious rehabilitation programmes** 32
   AHMAD SAIFUL RIJAL BIN HASSAN

4 **Economic rehabilitation of terrorists: what can be learned from disarmament, demobilisation and reintegration programmes?** 46
   D.B. SUBEDI

5 **Entrepreneurial rehabilitation: the promise of social entrepreneurship in disengaging religious terrorists** 64
   YANTO CHANDRA

6 **Family and social rehabilitation as a mode of holistic rehabilitation programme** 79
   MUHAMMAD SAIFUL ALAM SHAH BIN SUDIMAN AND NUR IRFANI SARIPI

7 **Psychological rehabilitation for ideology-based terrorism offenders** 95
ZORA A. SUKABDI

8 **Assessment and evaluation of terrorist rehabilitation programmes** 117
MALKANTHI HETTIARACHCHI

Index 137

Illustrations

Figures

2.1	From disengagement to reintegration	14
2.2	Housing of terrorist detainees	22
7.1	Expression of faith	99
7.2	Psychological aspects for counselors	102
7.3	Ten steps in rehabilitating ideology-based terrorism offenders	104
7.4	Internal processes in effective empowerment programs	110
7.5	Natural behavior transformation process	112
7.6	Behavioral transformation process initiated by others	113
7.7	How denial and forgetting mechanisms can intervene in the process of psychological rehabilitation	113
8.1	Counter, manage and innoculate: a three-dimensional approach to prevent radicalization and re-radicalization	118
8.2	Prochaska and DiClemente's wheel of change	124

Tables

7.1	Roles and motives of terrorism offenders in Indonesia	97
7.2	Development methods for religious terrorism offenders	103
7.3	Differences in pedagogy and andragogy	109
8.1	Categorization of detainees and inmates	125

Contributors

Yanto Chandra is Assistant Professor at the Department of Public Policy, City University of Hong Kong. Previously, he was a faculty member at the University of Leeds (UK) and the University of Amsterdam (Netherlands). He received his doctorate from the University of New South Wales (Australia). His book *Social Entrepreneurship in the Greater China Region: Policy and Cases* (Routledge, 2016) is the first official book on the subject in the region.

Rohan Gunaratna is Professor of Security Studies and Head of Singapore's ICPVTR at the RSIS, Nanyang Technological University (NTU), Singapore. He received his doctorate from the University of St Andrews, Scotland where he was British Chevening Scholar. The author of 18 books including *Inside al Qaeda: Global Network of Terror* (Columbia University Press, 2002). He is a specialist of the global threat environment, with expertise in threat groups in Asia, the Middle East and Africa.

Ahmad Saiful Rijal Bin Hassan is a senior analyst with the ICPVTR, at the RSIS, the NTU, Singapore. He is also a member of the RRG Secretariat and an RRG counselor. He graduated with a Bachelor's degree in Islamic Jurisprudence from Al-Azhar University and a Master's degree in International Relations from RSIS.

Malkanthi Hettiarachchi is a chartered clinical psychologist. She has worked extensively in community, inpatient and forensic settings (prisons and detention and rehabilitation centres) in Sri Lanka, the UK and Australia. She was instrumental in building rehabilitation and reintegration capabilities in Asia, Africa and the Middle East and was a trainer for Interpol, the United Nations Interregional Crime and Justice Research Institute and other organisations. She holds MSc in Clinical Psychology from RMIT, Melbourne, Australia and MSc in Mental Health from Kings College, University of London and PhD in Policing Intelligence and Counter Terrorism from Macquarie University, Sydney, Australia.

Sabariah Hussin is a research analyst at the ICPVTR, at the RSIS, the NTU, Singapore. She is also a member of the RRG Secretariat, Singapore. She graduated with an Executive MBA in International Marketing from Berne

University of Applied Sciences and holds an MSc in International Relations from RSIS.

Brian Michael Jenkins pioneered the study of terrorism when, in March 1972, as a new analyst at the RAND Corporation, the former Special Forces officer alerted the US government to the rising threat of international terrorism by writing a memorandum forecasting growing terrorist incidents and the policy problems this would create for the United States and the international community. The spectacular terrorist incidents that followed his forecast, culminating in the Munich massacre, prompted then President Nixon to create the Cabinet Committee to Combat Terrorism, which, in turn, asked Jenkins to initiate a research effort on its behalf. One of Jenkins' first steps was to create a database of terrorist incidents that would eventually enable researchers to carry out quantitative analyses of patterns and trends. Jenkins currently serves as Senior Adviser to the President of the RAND Corporation. He is also an adviser to a number of government departments and agencies and often testifies before the US Congress.

Jolene Jerard is Deputy Head and a research fellow at the ICPVTR, at the RSIS, the NTU, Singapore. She was a visiting research fellow at the Centre for Conflict and Peace Studies in Kabul, Afghanistan. She received her PhD in International Relations from the University of St Andrews, Scotland. She has co-edited several books including *Terrorist Rehabilitation and Counter-Radicalisation: New Approaches to Counter-Terrorism* (Routledge, 2012); *Countering Extremism: Building Social Resilience through Community Engagement* (Imperial College Press, 2013) and *Resilience and Resolve: Communities against Terrorism* (Imperial College Press, 2015).

Nur Irfani Saripi is a counsellor with the RRG, Singapore. She has counselled female individuals and youths who are radicalised by extremist ideologies and imbued universal values in their rehabilitation journey. She graduated with a Bachelor's degree in Islamic Jurisprudence from Al-Azhar University and a Master's degree in Strategic Studies from RSIS.

D.B. Subedi is an adjunct lecturer in the School of Humanities at the University of New England, Australia. He is also a senior fellow at the Centre for Security Governance in Canada. He holds a PhD in Peace and Conflict Studies from University of New England, Australia. He is an author of variety of journal articles, book chapters, policy briefing papers and a co-editor of *Cultivating Peace: Contexts, Practices and Multidimensional Models* (Cambridge Scholars Publishing, 2014).

Muhammad Saiful Alam Shah Bin Sudiman is an associate research fellow at the ICPVTR, at the RSIS, the NTU, Singapore. He is a member of the RRG Secretariat and an RRG counsellor. He is also a member/advisor of United Nations Counter-Terrorism Centre with special expertise on religious rehabilitation. He graduated with a Bachelor's degree in Islamic

Theology from Al-Azhar University and a Master's degree in International Relations from RSIS.

Zora A. Sukabdi is a forensic psychologist and researcher at the Centre for Forensic Behavioural Science, Swinburne University of Technology, Melbourne, Australia. She is also the founder and executive director of the Global Center of Well-Being. She is a doctorate candidate at Swinburne University of Technology. She developed *'MIKRA' Risk Assessment and Treatment Management to Terrorist Offenders*, a manual for the Indonesian National Anti-Terrorism Agency.

Acknowledgements

We would like to express our gratitude by thanking Ambassador Ong Keng Yong for his steadfast support for terrorism research. As the Executive Deputy Chairman, S. Rajaratnam School of International Studies (RSIS) at the Nanyang Technological University in Singapore, Ambassador Ong understood the importance of integrating academic theory into practice. We are grateful to many in government both past and present for their unwavering support for research into terrorist rehabilitation that made this compilation possible.

We also would like to thank the Ministry of Home Affairs of Singapore especially the leaders for their vision. They fostered a treasured multi-partite cooperation between the government, community organisations and academia. In particular, our deepest appreciation goes to Mr Benny Lim for his visionary leadership in the formative years of these initiatives. These partnerships have enabled the International Centre for Political Violence and Terrorism Research (ICPVTR) to embark on off-shore capacity building in terrorist rehabilitation and community engagement. This led to a deeper contribution to the literature on counter-radicalisation and deradicalisation, and to public policy initiatives globally. We are thankful to the Religious Rehabilitation Group (RRG) Co-Chairs, Ustaz Ali Haji Mohamed and Ustaz Mohd Hasbi Hassan, and Vice-Chair of the RRG, Ustaz Dr Mohamed bin Ali, for their leadership.

We wish to express our appreciation to a Fulbright Specialist Professor Richard J. Chasdi and RSIS Research Fellow Dr Mahfuh Haji Halimi for reviewing the manuscript. We are indebted to their contribution and the work of our colleagues Irene Tan, Neo Wee Na and many others at the ICPVTR in one way or another to make this compilation a reality. This book is dedicated to making terrorist rehabilitation and community engagement a global imperative.

Foreword

Following the commencement of US military operations against those held responsible for the 9/11 terrorist attacks, al-Qaeda's cadre and its jihadist allies continued a worldwide terrorist campaign, with major attacks in Pakistan, India, Tunisia, Yemen, Indonesia, Kenya, Saudi Arabia, Morocco, Turkey, the Philippines, Spain, Egypt, the United Kingdom, and Jordan between 9/11 and the end of 2005. None these attacks approached the complexity or scale of the multiple hijackings on 9/11—a reflection of the jihadists' limited operational capabilities as their networks were being destroyed—but more than 1,000 people were killed and more than 5,000 were wounded in the bombings and armed assaults. In addition, authorities uncovered and foiled numerous jihadist plots.

The global counterterrorist campaign was filling jails with terrorist suspects, but no one was under the illusion that al-Qaeda's leaders would abandon their struggle or that the jihadist movement they inspired could be entirely destroyed. It was not possible to shoot all the jihadists, and imprisonment offered only a temporary solution.

Most of these early jihadist operations were suicide attacks in which the perpetrators died. Most of those who were arrested had played supporting roles, although some were plotting new attacks. They would be sent to prison, generally for a short period of time, where they were likely to be further radicalized or could radicalize others, multiplying their number and eventually emerging as even more-determined adversaries. Authorities looked for ways to turn those in custody away from their commitment to this violent ideology while dissuading others from following in their original path.

In my book, *Unconquerable Nation: Knowing the Enemy, Strengthening Ourselves*, I argued that authorities had to look for ways to break the cycle of jihadism from entry to exit.[1] This cycle begins with the radicalization of eager acolytes and often ends only with their death. I still accept the premise that measures to counter violent extremism and deradicalization efforts aimed at those who turn to terrorism are useful, indeed necessary, although I have become less sanguine about the ability of government to identify and divert potential terrorists.

The United States has tended to pound on the operational portion of this cycle, from the moment where jihadist recruits, or self-recruited acolytes, manifest intentions to carry out attacks to the moment of their interception. This narrow tactical focus was understandable in the immediate shadow of 9/11 when the United States was driven by fears of further 9/11-scale terrorist attacks or worse. Killing or capturing terrorists took priority—their eventual rehabilitation was not a concern. But, as the world has learned since, captivity, however long, does not necessarily diminish the jihadists' commitment.

This volume describes the attempts of various nations to deradicalize and rehabilitate terrorists in custody. Singapore, Sri Lanka, Saudi Arabia, and other countries developed sophisticated strategies and invested in highly structured programs aimed at rehabilitating terrorists. More recent efforts have been motivated by concerns about the exodus of volunteers who traveled to the so-called caliphate created by the Islamic State (IS). Would witnessing—and, for some, participating in—IS atrocities and exposure to the death and destruction that attended the reduction of the IS transform returnees, including women and children, into psychologically damaged, permanently rewired future threats to society?

The discussion also reflects how much has been learned since 2001 about radicalization and deradicalization. Apart from brainwashing and re-education camps—primitive techniques of psychological coercion unacceptable in democratic society—there are few historical examples of deradicalization techniques. Psychological operations aimed at inducing insurgents to defect and Italy's efforts to turn incarcerated Red Brigades operatives offered some precedents, but pioneers in the field had to blaze new trails, learning from experience and each other.

Understanding why some jihadists decided to engage in violence was a prerequisite. Terrorism is not simply the endpoint of increasing radicalization. Only a tiny percentage of those expressing radical views become terrorists. Extremism alone does not propel people to terrorism. The decision to engage in violence is complex, involving other psychological factors and individual circumstances.

Rehabilitation efforts have proved to be equally complex, involving more than a sermon from an appropriate imam pointing out the error of the subject's ways. Rehabilitation requires intense interaction at the individual level and includes religious guidance, psychological counseling, financial assistance, improving education, family and community engagement, even marriage, all aimed at achieving a permanent transformation of behavior. The chapters compiled by Rohan Gunaratna and Sabariah Hussin suggest common principles but illustrate diverse approaches. What is appropriate and works in one society might not be suitable in another.

Deradicalization and rehabilitation are broadly defined and may mean different things. The various approaches described in the volume take place under different circumstances and have different objectives: reconciliation and reintegration of combatants following a long civil war; religious education aimed at discrediting jihadist interpretations of the Koran; and repudiating violence. Are deradicalization and rehabilitation programs aimed at transforming fundamental beliefs, instiling new values, diverting violent-prone extremists into more satisfying lives with job training and marriage, and therefore more acceptable societal norms, or submission to legitimate governmental authority and obedience to the law? Advocates of deradicalization and rehabilitation might respond, all of the above, but these are different goals.

The paramount objective must be somehow eradicating the urge to violence. Absent an X-ray for the human soul, we cannot measure sincerity. The only metric is whether the subjects reengage in violent pursuits. Intensive rehabilitation efforts such as those implemented by Singapore, Sri Lanka, and Saudi Arabia are generally viewed as successful, although the circumstances of the target population in each country vary, as do the metrics. Saudi Arabia claims a success rate of 80 percent for its deradicalization program. Malaysia claims a success rate of 95 percent. These would seem to be extraordinary results. Based upon incomplete and imperfect data, worldwide recidivism rates for ordinary criminals run from between 20 and 59 percent two years after release to between 55 and 72 percent five years after release.[2] As of 2017, more than 35 percent of the jihadist detainees released from the US Detention Facility at Guantanamo Bay, where there are no deradicalization efforts, are known or suspected to have returned to the ranks of active jihadists.[3]

Political ideologies may be abandoned more easily than causes derived from religious beliefs. While jihadist organizations have shown remarkable resiliency, individual jihadists have shown remarkable persistence in their commitment. Some of those engaged in recent jihadist attacks in Europe first came to attention of the authorities years before. They had been repeatedly arrested, spent time in prison, and, when not incarcerated, were often under some level of surveillance in the outside world. Even when some jihadist plotters knew or suspected that they were being watched, they continued with their plans, undeterred by the prospect of arrest. Those willing, even eager, to die are not easily diverted.

To be sure, this group portrait of tenacious true believers reflects the fact that the population being examined comprises only those who come to our attention because attacks and arrests frame the subject. How many jihadists change their mind and permanently drop out of the armed campaign is unknown—there are some. Examples also exist of individuals edging toward violence who veer off to another path only to later reengage. Does deradicalization require continuous booster shots? Lifetime monitoring? And is that possible only in certain societies that are more willing and able to control their citizens' behavior?

Is it also possible that deradicalization programs are not much different from well-funded court-supervised supervision, with its mixture of monitoring, limitations on movement and social interaction, drug and psychological treatment, the obligation to hold a job, and the threat of being returned to prison for failure to abide by the conditions of release? In other words, are deradicalization programs successful to the extent they continue to exert physical and psychological control over the subject?

It would seem that lessons learned in the case studies of rehabilitation programs described in this book should be applicable to dissuading people from embracing violence. Experience in deradicalization surely must increase understanding of the dynamics that led one to becoming a terrorist in the first place.

But diverting would-be terrorists and deradicalizing them after they have become terrorists pose different challenges. Deradicalization is a behavioral task; diverting would-be terrorists poses a targeting problem.

The targets of deradicalization are easily identified—they are in custody where they also are a captive audience. Identifying who might be at risk of becoming a terrorist and therefore needing attention is a more difficult task. Even without official intervention, only a small fraction of those holding radical views go on to become terrorists. Community programs aim at communities, not individuals, and may not reach those of greatest concern.

Some countries have invited members of the community to identify persons of concern. Others have established formal procedures to ensure that any hint of radicalization will be recognized and passed on to the authorities. Response will meet demand. Apart from the Orwellian aspects of creating a society of informants looking for signs of radicalization, or the stigma it inevitably attaches to anyone whose name is submitted, practically speaking, the volume of referrals brought to the authorities' attention can easily overwhelm their capacity to intervene in any meaningful way. A name goes into a file, followed perhaps by a superficial inquiry, and a cursory interview. Repeat the process thousands of times—the United Kingdom had to deal with 4,000 referrals in 2015 alone. Most of the subjects identified in this manner are unlikely to ever become terrorists, but the greater the investment made to keep them on the right path, the greater the temptation will be to count them as 'preventions.'

New terrorist recruiting techniques further obviate the notion that terrorist violence is the last stop of radicalization. IS advertises its atrocities to a broad audience on social media. Volunteers are not recruited into a terrorist organization, but exhorted to action, which brings recognition and membership after the fact. Some who respond seem to be motivated as much by the violence as by the beliefs, and it appears that a significant percentage has histories of aggression, substance abuse, and mental-health issues.

The United States is conspicuous by its absence from these case studies. The country has taken a different course. The 9/11 attacks pushed US authorities to intervene before attacks occurred. New laws enabled prosecution for an intention to commit terrorist crimes, creating a criminal predicate for early intervention, but this was still done within the framework of crime. Countering violent extremism (CVE) could be viewed as an effort by the authorities to push further upstream to the frontier of thought, although in a seemingly more benign way not involving prosecution. CVE efforts are still tentative.

The United States favors a traditional law-and-order approach to terrorism in which the primary task of the police is to apprehend criminals and gather evidence for their prosecution. Americans accept the necessity of domestic intelligence efforts, but remain suspicious of government and are sensitive to potential infringements of their rights. Programs to disrupt those opposed to US institutions or policies conjure up memories of prior abuses by federal investigators as they battled with the New Left and antiwar groups in the 1960s. It is simply politically more acceptable to deal with terrorism as with any other form of violent crime, although investigators and prosecutors have been given additional tools to ensure their success.

The United States has yet to think seriously about deradicalization and rehabilitation. Prisons at one time were concerned with the rehabilitation of criminals, but this is less the case now and anyway would not apply to terrorists who are generally considered to be not just ordinary lawbreakers but are seen in the light of their actions to be inherently evil. The escalation of terrorism, the exaltation of atrocity by the more recent cohorts of jihadist ideology, and the evolution of terrorist targeting toward 'pure terrorism'—completely random violence simply to demonstrate commitment—impede any notion that terrorists can (or should) be turned around and rehabilitated.

Terrorist-related offenses carry long mandatory sentences—15 years or more, with life sentences not infrequently imposed. And in most federal cases, the full sentence must be served. Putting release well beyond the horizon reduces any imperative to deradicalize or rehabilitate. The US legal system allows rewards for cooperation during trial, but tends to discourage deal-making after conviction—no rewards are offered for renouncing jihad.

As of 2017, almost all of those who participated in or plotted to carry out terrorist attacks in the United States since 9/11 remain in jail. Of 178 jihadists who plotted or carried out terrorist attacks, 11 were killed during or shortly after the attacks. Of the remaining 167, only 9 have been released. Several of these received short sentences because they played only a minor role, cooperated with authorities, or lied to investigators to protect a relative. One served a longer sentence and was then deported. The rest remain in prison. And conditions in maximum-security prisons do not lend themselves to rehabilitation. No one reengages because no one is released.

This is, in my view, a wasted potential resource. Not all inmates currently serving long sentences may remain so devoted to the cause. Remaining sentences could be reduced to elicit cooperation in discouraging terrorist recruiting, much like the Italian government did in the repentant program. Determined to reduce the number of IRA members in its prisons, British authorities compiled evidence to justify the release of those individuals whose family or community backgrounds suggested that they could be moved away from violence. This reduced both the population of detainees and the alienation in the communities from which they came. However, if repentance brings rewards, why not make the same offer to other categories of offenders?

The United States seems unlikely to fundamentally alter its approach. Generally speaking, political motives bring special status to inmates only when the violence they collectively represent is seen to pose a significant threat to society and therefore requires a broader political strategy. With fewer than 200 jihadists plotting or participating in terrorist attacks in the 16 years since 9/11, in a nation of 320 million people with over 3 million Muslims, this is a very small number. They have killed fewer than 100 people—a needless loss of life, to be sure, but an average of six a year in a country with an annual average of 15,000 criminal homicides. The long sentences they receive are intended as a deterrent to others contemplating violence. Whether the tiny turnout of violent jihadists in the United States reflects effective suppression or simply indifference among America's Muslims to jihadist exhortations is not known.

The absence of large numbers of jihadist terrorists in the United States, however, argues against special attention. Jihadist terrorism comprises only a tiny sliver of violence in America, which is a more serious problem of vast proportions. There is too little terrorism to merit it being treated as any other form of criminal violence.

As should be apparent from the reflections in this foreword, readers will have much to think about as they read this important volume.

Brian Michael Jenkins
2017

Notes

1 Brian Michael Jenkins, *Unconquerable Nation: Knowing the Enemy, Strengthening Ourselves*. Santa Monica, CA: The RAND Corporation, 2006.
2 Seena Fazel and Achim Wolf, 'A Systematic Review of Criminal Recidivism Rates Worldwide: Current Difficulties and Recommendations for Best Practice,' *PLoS One*, June 18, 2015. www.ncbi.nlm.nih.gov/pmc/articles/PMC4472929/ (accessed May 8, 2018).
3 Office of the Director of National Intelligence, *Summary of the Reengagement of Detainees Formerly Held at Guantanamo Bay, Cuba*. Washington, DC: US ODNI, March 2017 release. www.dni.gov/files/documents/Newsroom/GTMO-Reengagement-Summary-for-March-2017-Release.pdf (accessed May 8, 2018).

1 Introduction

Rohan Gunaratna and Sabariah Hussin

Terrorism, extremism and exclusivism present major security challenges in the world today. They are interlinked and present a growing threat to social stability. Exclusivism as an extension of extremism is the belief or doctrine of believing that only one interpretation of the religious texts is right thereby excluding the possibility of others interpretations. It often manifests in the form of religious-politico-social rhetoric and behaviour that rejects diversity.[1] These phenomena are detrimental to social harmony and could threaten the existing international order. If governments fail to address terrorism, these conflicts could escalate, evolving into full-fledged insurgencies and even spread to neighbouring countries beyond the conflict zones.

Over the years, government agencies and their partners, such as the European Union and the United Nations (UN), have constructed a counterterrorism toolkit that provides guidance in addressing issues of terrorism. This toolkit covers three principal counterterrorism approaches: (1) strategic counterterrorism; (2) operational counterterrorism; and (3) tactical counterterrorism.

Strategic counterterrorism, also known as countering violent extremism (CVE), is designed to shape and influence the threat environment. It covers both the preventive and corrective aspects of countering ideologies. Its objective is to create a hostile environment for terrorist operatives and an unfriendly environment for their supporters. The strategic counterterrorism initiatives consist of community engagement measures to help prevent extremism from developing as well as to build social resilience rehabilitation and reintegration programmes to deradicalise terrorists and extremists.

While community engagement is the tool to prevent exclusivism and extremism, rehabilitation attempts to disengage terrorists and insurgents from violent action by addressing radical ideologies and misunderstood concepts, instilling appropriate defence mechanisms in the detainees and imparting universal values to prevent manipulation by terrorist organisations.

Conversely, operational and tactical counterterrorism aims to kill or capture terrorists and dismantle their operations. It is, therefore, essential that the tactical and operational counterterrorism measures be complemented with strategic counterterrorism approaches to provide a holistic counterterrorism approach.

As such, this book will serve as a guide to creating and implementing a rehabilitation programme. It will outline and detail the necessary steps required in creating a successful rehabilitation programme and this will be further demonstrated by case studies from various countries. It must also be noted that there is also a companion book *International Case Studies in Terrorist Rehabilitation* that readers may find useful. This book aims to provide a theoretical framework supported by case studies. The companion book goes further into detail and builds upon the theoretical framework introduced in this book. It has thrice as many country-based case studies on deradicalisation and rehabilitation programmes, presenting real-life experience with implementing rehabilitation programmes in various settings. The companion book serves to reinforce the framework established in this book and give a better understanding of the challenges encountered in translating theory into practice. In essence, both books aim to send the message that idealistic solutions may not exist when crafting a rehabilitation programme. Instead, each programme will need to be tailored to its specific setting. With the tailoring, it provides an expansion of ideas for those who desire to design and implement rehabilitation programmes.

The context

After al-Qaeda had attacked America's iconic landmarks on 11 September 2001, the Bush Administration (2001–2009) announced the global war on terror and invaded Iraq on 20 March 2003. The action caused a segment of Muslims worldwide to be angry about the suffering of Iraqis as a result of the invasion. The insurgents, terrorists and extremists who sought to build global support for a fight against the US and its allies exploited the situation. Thereafter, as a strategy to engage Muslim communities and prevent violent radicalisation, the US adopted CVE during the Obama Administration (2009–2017).

In contrast, the Trump Administration (2017–current) returned to the kinetic and lethal approach adopted by the Bush Administration. In President Trump's new counterterrorism policy, the White House counterterrorism team perceives CVE as ineffective, and succumbs to the use of hard power. The return to the target-centric approach and abandoning the population-centric approach is likely to increase public support for terrorism, extremism and exclusivism in the coming years. Thus, President Trump and his followers are determined to replace the term CVE.

It is true that tactical and operational counterterrorism can detect, disrupt and degrade terrorist operations. However, the reality is that an understanding of the human terrain, through the perspectives of anthropology, sociology, political science, regional studies and linguistics, is extremely important in countering terrorism. This is where strategic counterterrorism comes in, either by preventive methods or correctives ones such as engaging and influencing the public. It is essential to stabilise local, national, regional and global contexts with initiatives to counter extremism and promote moderation (*wassatiyah*). The US under President Barack Obama understood strategic counterterrorism and his team embraced CVE as the cornerstone of US counterterrorism strategy. However, while the US supported rehabilitation and community engagement efforts overseas, its reception in the US homeland was limited. For instance, there was no effort to build a rehabilitation programme in Guantanamo Bay and military force remained the dominant strategy. This is not to say that the prevalence of the hard option of military force meant that the US did not develop some capabilities in strategic counterterrorism. However, despite this progressive approach in the Obama years, with the advent of the Donald Trump era, it would appear that the future of counterterrorism, at least for the foreseeable future, looks to be set for a return to lethal and kinetic operations. Although a target-centric strategy is essential to prevent and pre-empt attacks, a population-centric strategy is key to mitigating the threat and defeating terrorism.

Background

Initially, it appeared that the military might of the United States and its allies would lead them to win the wars in Iraq and Afghanistan with ease and achieve their stated objective of reducing terrorism. However, looking more closely, it would appear that the decision to adopt a singular hard power approach was misguided at best, since it alienated the local populace and resulted in a spike in radicalisation, providing terrorists with fertile recruiting grounds. This ensured that al-Qaeda got more of an opportunity to entrench itself in Afghanistan and Pakistan, as well as ensuring the rise of Abu Musab al-Zarqawi's group in Iraq, which was the precursor to the Islamic State (IS).

In contrast to the Bush Administration, the Obama Administration realised the need for a softer approach and focused on enlisting the participation of Muslim leaders and communities. To take on the terrorists and manage extremism in their communities, President Obama engaged Muslim leaders and empowered Muslim communities. There was limited support for CVE. The American sense of justice advocated punishment for both the misguided and wrongdoers. Even though religion is confined to the private space in America, the US government was courageous in seriously embracing community engagement or rehabilitation.

One major fault was the US Administration's miscalculation of the developments in Afghanistan and Iraq. In Afghanistan, US forces downsized, causing the return of the Taliban, and in Iraq the US advocated a total withdrawal thinking that Iraqi forces could contain the threat. In both these theatres, the insurgents returned with a vengeance threatening the fragile governments that the US put in place. Without eliminating the threat and stabilising Iraq, President Obama withdrew US forces, thereby creating conditions for the rise of IS.

Understanding the threat

Global Islamic extremist groups emerged during the multinational, anti-Soviet Afghan Mujahidin campaign (1979–1989), a by-product of the proxy war the

West and its allies fought during the Cold War period. This effort was led by Maktab al-Khidamat, the predecessor of al-Qaeda, which invited Muslims worldwide to join its fight. After the withdrawal of the Soviets, Western sponsorship ended and al-Qaeda transformed into an anti-Western movement. By painting a conspiracy like a scenario of global Western hostility towards Muslims and Islam, al-Qaeda initiated the 'Global Jihad' movement.

This movement can be roughly distributed into three phases. Global Jihad 1.0, the first phase, emerged after al-Qaeda attacked the US on 9/11 and attracted dozens of militant groups in Asia, Africa, Middle East and the Caucasus regions. Global Jihad 2.0, the next phase, emerged after Abu Bakr al Baghdadi declared a caliphate and announced the formation of IS on 29 June 2014. Currently, the world is witnessing the third phase, which includes the global expansion of IS. With its battle space shrinking in Iraq and Syria, IS has continued to create more *wilayats* (provinces) in its stronghold of power in the Middle East, Africa, the Caucasus and Asia to be used as launching pads to mount terrorist attacks. Despite the loss of territorial space, IS continues to invest heavily in social media to create networks, cells and personalities to fight and garner support for its cause.

As the 'pioneering vanguard', al-Qaeda instilled the belief among other Muslim threat groups that it will lead the way for future violent episodes. By staging an iconic attack on US landmarks using commercial airliners, al-Qaeda inspired and instigated other threat groups to fight against the superpower. The suffering of Muslims in Iraq galvanised a segment of the Muslim population worldwide to support Global Jihad. Until then, Muslim support for violence had been peripheral. Unfortunately, the US and Britain failed to recover weapons of mass destruction, and this was seen as an unclear cause to wage war. With a million civilian deaths in Iraq and the resultant media and public outrage, the proportion of Muslims that supported the West's fight against the threat groups contracted. Meanwhile, the segment of Muslims that support exclusivist, extremist, terrorist and insurgent ideologies grew.

Both al-Qaeda and IS present a growing global peril today. An incarnation of al-Qaeda, IS can be considered as a vicious by-product of the Afghan, Iraqi and now Syrian conflicts. Both IS and al-Qaeda are multinational global movements, but the scale, magnitude and intensity of IS threats are more severe. While IS represents the higher order threat, the threat posed by al-Qaeda persists. Should IS and al-Qaeda join forces, the threat to the world will escalate drastically. Their key strength resides in their abilities to reach out to Muslim communities in Asia, Africa, the Caucasus, the Middle East and migrant and diaspora communities in the West. Both armed groups rely heavily on social media, especially the use of encrypted instant messaging applications as their propaganda machinery to politicise, radicalise, recruit and militarise their communities. IS fighters' mastery of social media enabled its narratives to spread worldwide, drawing fighters from 121 countries.

The situation now calls for states to address the threat and effect of the returnees. Foreign terrorist fighters (FTFs) pose a grave threat to their respective homelands due to their military training and hatred-filled ideology. Thus, countries are witnessing a phenomenon where FTFs leave their conflict zones and choose to either return to their home or travel to a third country with the intention of joining other conflicts. This 'blowback effect' has seen the spread of violence to different regions. The *American Political Science Review* indicated that the returnees' lethal capacity doubled due to their battlefield experience compared to before they went to the conflict zones. The number of IS FTFs has been assessed at over 40,000, coming from 121 states. The challenge is so massive that a global response to the FTF phenomenon was adopted by the UN Security Council through its Resolution 2178, which provided a roadmap to tackle the FTF problem. Data from START United States plots revealed that 28 per cent of FTFs participated in a plot and 60 per cent of FTFs became involved in a terrorist plot. The challenge thus doubled for states to manage the FTFs as well as home-grown terrorists.

Managing the threat

Western nations led by the US have advocated the use of a military-centric strategy to defeat insurgency and terrorism. The use of overwhelming kinetic and lethal force reduced the threat in the immediate-term (1–2 years) but caused it to grow in the mid-term (2–5 years). Although effective in Afghanistan in the initial phase to weaken al-Qaeda and its host the Taliban, the Global War on Terror failed to contain the threat from spreading beyond the initial conflict zones.

The effects of the international community's mismanagement of Iraq and Syria radicalised segments of Muslim communities worldwide. Both battlefield and off-the-battlefield (lone wolf) attacks demonstrate that the threat has spread worldwide in the long-term (5–10 years). Targeted governments and their partners need a comprehensive strategy to control and manage the threat. While security forces are capable of fighting insurgency and terrorism, the affected government should increasingly build partnerships with community organisations to manage exclusivism and extremism.

Emerging strategies

In its fight against IS, the world is confronted with six challenges. First, multiple coalitions divided by geopolitics must work together to contain, isolate and totally eliminate IS in its heartland of Iraq and Syria. Second, it needs to address the group's creation of *wilayats* in the global south, acting as bridgeheads to expand quietly and stage surprise attacks. Third, the world is still reeling from trying to address IS' ideology of extremism, terrorism and insurgency, which presents a long-term security threat to communities, societies, nations and the international system. Fourth, it needs to manage and regulate social media, which IS uses to further its cause. Fifth, it must address and attempt to stem the financing of terrorism. And finally, sixth, it should attempt to resolve root causes such as the marginalisation of Sunnis in Iraq, repression in Syria and misgovernance in Afghanistan etc.

As the threat evolves, it is essential to refine and retool to operate both in the physical and virtual spaces. The newest frontiers in strategic counterterrorism are in digital rehabilitation and online counter extremism. Currently, various institutions are undertaking research on these frontiers to confirm their effectiveness.

The threat, therefore, should compel governments to review the way they operate since they are confronted not with threat groups but threat networks. Governments need to shift from counterterrorism cooperation to collaboration. Governments need to exchange personnel, build common databases, conduct joint training and operations, and share experiences, expertise and resources. With the globalisation of IS, a multipronged, multidimensional, multiagency, multijurisdictional and a multinational approach is central.

Smart power, not hard or soft power!

To guarantee victory for governments, states must develop a full-spectrum response alongside non-state actors. Governments also need to enlist the support of and work with a range of partners – community organisations and the private sector. To fight the threat, they need to build a wide range of capabilities upstream, midstream and downstream. Upstream, the capabilities needed include the prevention of community radicalisation through community engagement and vigorous counter-ideology efforts; midstream, the rehabilitation and reintegration of terrorists and extremists; and downstream, the use of kinetic and lethal action to catch, kill or disrupt terrorist operations.

At the heart of winning the fight is the integration of hard power with soft power and the production of smart power. The strategy is not only to conduct focused operations employing hard power to fight the insurgents and terrorists but also to apply soft power to engage the extremists and exclusivists. With the threat spreading beyond the battlefield, the government and its partners must have the capacity to generate sufficient smart power, which is vital to eliminate the threat. While tactical and operational counterterrorism is essential, strategic counterterrorism is the key to ultimate success. Even if a government has built the finest tactical and operational counterterrorism capabilities, strategic counterterrorism cannot be ignored. Depending on the theatre, all three capabilities should be applied to produce the best outcome.

This book aims to understand rehabilitation since it is the least understood strategy, especially in the Western world. The importance of rehabilitation was alluded to when Mitt Romney, the US Presidential candidate, stated: 'We can't kill our way out of this mess' and 'We don't want another Iraq, we don't want another Afghanistan.' He advocates for the US to have a comprehensive strategy to reject extremism.

Rehabilitation

With the growing severity of the evolving terrorist threat, more governments are realising the need to address the threat proactively. Due to the large influx of returning FTFs and the fear of consequent radicalisation of local communities, governments are working with community partners to address these threats. Nonetheless, the number of governments that has invested in preventive measures or community engagement and corrective measures such as deradicalisation and rehabilitation is still inadequate. Although there are greater awareness and interest on the part of governments to build both community engagement and rehabilitation programmes, compared to the threat, the government–community partner efforts to seed new programmes and upgrade existing programmes is limited.

Most countries have visions for rehabilitation but no real rehabilitation programmes. A few countries have developed ad-hoc and unstructured rehabilitation programmes, for example China, Germany and Iraq. Fewer countries still offer comprehensive rehabilitation programmes, among them are Singapore, Saudi Arabia and Sri Lanka. Under the leadership of the United Nations Interregional Crime and Justice Research Institute (UNICRI), the good practices from these programmes have helped start new ones or improve existing programmes. Although IS has recruited from 121 countries, less than a fifth of these countries has programmes for rehabilitation of terrorist and extremists. Countries such as the US, Bangladesh and the Maldives do not have structured deradicalisation programmes in place.

The current wave of sustained terrorism has caused scholars and practitioners to begin referring to rehabilitation as a crucial aspect of countering terrorism. However, the number of books on the subject covering approaches or modes of rehabilitation is a handful.[2] While the previous studies are useful, this work updates readers on the current and emerging developments in rehabilitation.

Terrorist rehabilitation is defined as the action to restore a person to normal life through training, counselling and therapy after imprisonment or a period of detention. The objectives of the rehabilitation programmes must be clearly outlined. This is because rehabilitation works best when there is a willingness to participate and detainees are open to this idea. The objectives can focus on changing the detainee's fundamental beliefs, or getting the detainees to denounce the use of violence and related violent extremism issues, or providing psychological support; the design has to be tailored to each case of detention for it to be an accurate fit as a remedy of great efficacy.

In this context, rehabilitation of terrorists is carried out through seven modes. They are:

1   social rehabilitation, where family and community play a role in the detainee's journey to reintegrate into the community;
2   psychological rehabilitation, where detainees work with psychologist to re-establish their capacity to function in society and achieve self-efficacy, which lead to positive behaviour transformation;
3   religious rehabilitation, as religion has been used to justify violence that the detainees perpetrated and the fact that terrorist groups used ideologies that are religious in nature, where religious clerics extricate these misunderstood concepts and impart correct teachings of these ideologies;

4 educational rehabilitation, which provides the detainees the opportunities to gain academic qualifications or gain entrepreneurship knowledge to be economically independent;
5 vocational rehabilitation, which allows detainees to acquire new skills or upgrade current skills to gain employment upon release;
6 creative arts therapy rehabilitation, which uses art themes for therapeutic interventions and transformative journey to reintegration into the community; and
7 sports and recreational rehabilitation, which is employed to channel detainees' energy to perform physical sports activities to improve their self-esteem.

The varied rehabilitation modes are employed by governments and agencies around the world depending on the recommendations, availability of resources and acceptance by the implementing bodies. Opportunity for utilising rehabilitation should be made available at different times. A rehabilitation programme can be prescribed as part of a prison sentence or an alternative to incarceration; this restrictive condition can be determined through a risk-assessment approach.

Building rehabilitation capabilities requires leadership, a legal framework, a dedicated organisation, infrastructure and expert resources. Increasingly the world has started to understand that no single agency can develop and implement a comprehensive criminal or terrorist rehabilitation programme. Rehabilitation is an enterprise where the government, the private sector, community organisations and academia must work together in collaboration. There is recognition that the prison responsible for institutionalising incarceration is the body responsible for holding the offender. Although prisons are identified as the custodial setting, they often lack the knowledge and skills to transform those they hold.

Only a few countries have the resources to build their prisons with the expertise to return those who abandoned family and society back to mainstream living. They rely on the private sector for resources, the community for support and academics for assessment. Under corporate social responsibility, the best private companies devote significant resources to equip those affected for employment and after release recruit them as beneficiaries. Similarly, community leaders and institutions – social, religious, cultural, educational – pave the way and build bridges to bring the beneficiaries back to the mainstream. In community settings, the private sector and community organisations can support the beneficiaries' families too. There should be an exchange of ideas and skills by different groups of religious scholars, social and family workers, teachers, vocational instructors, artists, bankers, sports instructors, counsellors and psychologists in order to work in prison and community settings. In addition, the security and intelligence practitioners, the institutions of higher learning and think tanks can develop and refine the assessments to measure the degrees of radicalisation and deradicalisation.

Under the different modes of rehabilitation, diverse partners come together to develop different approaches to intervention. To develop and sustain these multiple interventions, visionary leadership is central. At all levels, a goal-oriented leader will be more effective than a rule-oriented one. At the heart of collaboration, creative and innovative leadership will produce holistic programmes that are relevant and applicable while minimising the risk of recidivism. Rehabilitation is a risk but a risk worth taking as it works for the common good of the individual, the family, the workplace and the community.

As pathways to transformation are unique, leaders should draw expertise and resources from different sectors to chart and sustain the beneficiaries' journeys to change. Success depends on drawing from multiple sectors and relevant partners, and the ability to hold them together to achieve a common goal, which is a transformed person able to reintegrate into the wider community. The beneficiaries are best transformed in settings where they believe that they can and will lead a better life. They come from all walks of life from government sectors to private sectors. The classic detention and prison are not the ideal settings for embracing change for the better. Punishment to deter reoffending and rehabilitation to prepare for release from day one should be the twin goals of all prisons and detention facilities. Community engagement programmes will enable governments and their partners to counter the ideological threat and treat the affected and influenced communities.

To win the fight against exclusivism, extremism and terrorism, a full-spectrum response is needed. No longer can the threat be mitigated only through tactical and operational counterterrorism. Beyond the kinetic and lethal capabilities, governments together with their partners need to build structures to counter threat groups and their ideologies. If ideology is the main driver of threat, the game changer in the fight against terrorism is rehabilitation in both custodial and community settings.

Today, rehabilitation is a global imperative. For rehabilitation to succeed, it should be an enterprise. Multiple agencies must come together to deliver effective rehabilitation services to affected and influenced populations. This book seeks to share the global experience in terrorist rehabilitation. It focuses on approaches to rehabilitation and the varied experiences of countries of fighting the current and emerging threat using strategic approaches.

The future

With the enduring threat of IS and its global expansion, the field of rehabilitating terrorists and extremists is changing rapidly. Unlike al-Qaeda-centric groups that operated discretely, IS operates openly. As a large movement with mastery of social media, the scale, magnitude and intensity of radicalisation are appreciable.

With the global expansion of IS, those in custody for participating, supporting and advocating for IS will grow exponentially. Many governments and their community partners have been working to deter terrorist recruitment and radicalisation. Nonetheless, the appeal and seductive power of IS has made many vulnerable individuals susceptible to indoctrination and recruitment. To transform the lives of those mainstream society could not carry with it requires rehabilitation programmes. Without rehabilitation, prison will not prepare them to reject exclusivism and extremism and embrace coexistence and moderation.

To summarise, most countries have a vision for rehabilitation but without the corresponding rehabilitation programmes. A few countries have developed ad-hoc and unstructured rehabilitation programmes. Fewer still offer comprehensive rehabilitation programmes. These include Singapore, Saudi Arabia and Sri Lanka. Under UNICRI leadership, the good practices from these programmes have helped start new programmes or improve existing ones. Although IS recruited from over 100 countries, less than one-fifth of these has programmes for rehabilitation of terrorist and extremists.

About the book

Complex as it seems, there is no definitive solution to preventing and countering violent extremism. Thus, this task has emerged as a major policy concern and has challenged states in their counterterrorism efforts. The chapters in this book have demonstrated that progressive states and agencies have expended a milieu of soft and hard CVE strategies that include disengagement, repression and rehabilitation as part of the approach to reintegrate radicalised individuals into society. The choice of a framework for a deradicalisation programme is by no means straightforward. It is intricate and requires a deep study on an array of factors that will positively impact the overall rehabilitation and reintegration programme.

In Chapter 2, Jerard explores the relatively under-discussed notion of accommodation or living arrangements of terrorist detainees and explores the possible impact that this has on the rehabilitation and reintegration programmes. It is time for governments to re-evaluate their strategies and consider the inclusion of terrorist rehabilitation as part of their CVE strategies. The multitude successes, seen through the examples in the chapters of this book, have also employed the different modes of rehabilitation, namely social, psychological, religious, educational, vocational, creative arts therapy and sports and recreational. The empirical evidence attached to the studies done through these modes have assisted psychologists to assess the participants' level of violence or propensity to perform an attack.

Amidst the new terrorism landscape, terrorist organisations construct ideologies and use religion as a platform to justify their acts of violence. In Chapter 3, Hassan deconstructs these misconstrued ideologies with appropriate religious teachings through three innovative approaches while addressing radical ideologies through religious rehabilitation programmes.

A critical component for ex-detainees to succeed in their reintegration programmes will be in building their economic capabilities. Subedi, in Chapter 4, engages in a discussion of economic rehabilitation, in which the participants gain economic independence while facilitating their re-entry into society.

Showcasing the use of creativity while maintaining a cost-effective tool to help former religious terrorists return to normalcy, Chandra (Chapter 5) unfolds the key success factors in developing social intervention mechanisms that successfully disengage terrorists and help them pursue a post-release career in the service industry.

The community, specifically family, plays a pertinent role in establishing cooperation between the detainees and the rehabilitation programmes. Sudiman and Saripi in Chapter 6 focus on family involvement as part of the social rehabilitation component. Commitment to the family has been the main pillar for the detainees to want to denounce violent extremism. The effort to re-establish human capacity and function in society can be achieved when the detainees have a peaceful state of mind and favourable attitudes towards life.

Sukabdi, in Chapter 7, focuses on character building and well-being in rehabilitating ideology-based terrorism offenders through a comprehensive psychological rehabilitation thus realising behavioural transformation.

Crucial to the success of any rehabilitation programme is assessment and evaluation. Established rehabilitation programmes have grappled with these challenges for almost a decade. Hettiarachchi, in Chapter 8, uses various assessments from the least complex to the more complex methods of measurement within rehabilitation programmes and prisons to assess violent extremism and radicalisation as well as group-based violence.

Notes

1 Some of the prominent works include *Understanding Deradicalization: Methods, Tools and Programmes for Countering Violent Extremism* by Daniel Koehler (Routledge, 2017); *Terrorist Rehabilitation: A New Frontier in Counter-terrorism* co-edited by Rohan Gunaratna and Mohamed bin Ali (World Scientific Publishing, 2015); *Terrorist Rehabilitation: The U.S. Experience in Iraq* by Ami Angell and Rohan Gunaratna (CRC Press, 2011); and *Terrorist Rehabilitation and Counter-radicalisation: New Approaches to Counter-terrorism* by Rohan Gunaratna, Jolene Jerard and Lawrence Rubin (Routledge, 2012).
2 Modes of rehabilitation refer to the engagement of all the facets and faculties of a detainee in custody. See Ami Angell and Rohan Gunaratna (2011). *Terrorist Rehabilitation: The U.S. Experience in Iraq*. Boca Raton, FL: CRC Press: 351.

Bibliography

Bruce, George (1968). *The Stranglers: The Cult of Thuggee and Its Overthrow in British India*. New York: Harcourt, Brace & World.
Chasdi, Richard J. (2018). *Corporate Security Crossroads: Responding to Terrorism Cyberthreats, and Other Hazards in the Global Business Environment*. Santa Barbara, CA: Praeger.
Fannin, Leon F. (1989). 'Thuggee and Professional Criminality'. *Michigan Sociological Review*, (3): 34–44.
Koehler, Daniel (2017). *Understanding Deradicalisation: Methods, Tools and Programs for Countering Violent Extremism*. Abingdon, Oxon, NY: Routledge.
Obama, Barack (2016). Remarks by the President at Islamic Society of Baltimore, Baltimore, Maryland, 3 February.
Yalcinkaya, Haldun (2016). 'Turkey's Struggle against the Foreign Terrorist Fighters of Daesh', in *Panorama Insights into Asian and European Affairs: Countering Daesh Extremism European and Asian Responses*. Singapore: Konrad Adenauer Stiftung/RSIS.

2 Behind bars

Do prison settings hold the key to successful custodial rehabilitation programmes?

Jolene Jerard

> Stone walls do not a prison make, nor iron bars a cage.
>
> (Richard Lovelace)

Named after the one-hundred-eyed Greek giant Argus Panoptes – 'the all-seeing one', English philosopher and social theorist Jeremy Bentham created an architectural design known as the Panopticon at the end of the eighteenth century. The unique and revolutionary design of the Panopticon epitomised the aspiration to create an institutional building that would enable a single watchman to observe all the inmates without the inmates themselves being able to tell that they are being watched. The nature of the design helps to minimise the manpower needed to ensure the security of the complex. By extension, almost unequivocally the centrality of power visually rests in the hands of the authority, as observers, and the effect on the residents within the building is the sense of being observed. Perhaps even more disdainful to some is the expected norm amongst the inmates – the perception of being monitored by a bureaucratic overlord, stripped of privacy and personal space. The 'central guiding idea that of arranging prisoners in a circle, watched by an all seeing eye at the centre' (Stedman 2007: 3) came to epitomise the characteristic of the Panopticon:

> The panoptic mechanism arranges spatial unities that make it possible to see constantly and to recognize immediately. In short, it reverses the principle of the dungeon; or rather of its three functions – to enclose, to deprive of light and to hide – it preserves only the first and eliminates the other two. Full lighting and the eye of a supervisor capture better than darkness, which ultimately protected. Visibility is a trap.
>
> (Foucault 1977: 195–228)

In the present politico-religious wave of terrorism that is sustained through pervasive violent extremist ideologies, the Panopticon has loosely over time come to be understood analogously with the notion of being under constant watch. It is this conceptual notion of space and its important yet underemphasised implications for rehabilitation and reintegration programmes that frame this chapter.

Whilst both practitioners and observers are analogous to the watchman in the tower, the enduring challenge is the seeming emphasis given solely to the types of programmes and the measures to classify the detainees that have been put in place. An element that is tied to the classification of detainees and yet has an enduring impact on the eventual success of the programmes initiated as well as the levels of recidivism is the living space or accommodation that the detainees are provided with. This has been under-emphasised or swept under the carpet as a perennial challenge that has to be accepted. The watchman looks through a rose-tinted lens in the attempt to monitor the activities and ensure that the detainee adheres to the rule of law whilst in the facility. Paradoxically, aware that they are being watched, detainees at times project the veneer of observance of the rules of law, fully cognizant that in the process they might be able to escape watchful eye of the watchman. It is in part this challenge to definitively gauge one's complete recanting of radical extremist ideology without a shadow of doubt that has inadvertently led to the questions surrounding the veracity of rehabilitation programmes.

Through the looking glass: clarification and assumptions

In response to an evolving terrorism threat landscape and the arrest of terrorists and extremists, the milieu of disengagement, rehabilitation, deradicalisation and reintegration collectively emerged as a strategic response to manage radicalised individuals that were incarcerated. 'The alchemy of strategy hence refers to the art of a nuanced and calibrated plan that is both calculated and intentionally positioned to manifest itself with the creation of maximum impact on the ground' (Jerard 2016). Custodial rehabilitation was as such positioned as a means through which to mitigate future threat. In writing about why punishment inherently fails, Giligan (2012) notes that the 'only rational purpose for a prison is to restrain those who are violent, while we help them to change their behavior and return to the community'. If it is solely for the purpose of revenge and punishment then we have failed to achieve the strategic end game of working towards a society that is safe and secure, even before we have started. This is very much in contrast to the more punitive measures that were taken in the US from the 1970s.

Navigating the terms and terminology

The conceptual notions of disengagement, rehabilitation, deradicalisation and reintegration are laden with intellectual minefields (Figure 2.1). Often used interchangeably, the lack of clarity in the conceptual understanding between and amongst these terms adds to the fog of misunderstanding. Peeling away the layers, the process begins when a radicalised individual disengages from violence; thereafter the individual undergoes a battery of modes or approaches to facilitate the course of rehabilitation. The individual then achieves a state of deradicalisation prior to be being reintegrated into society.

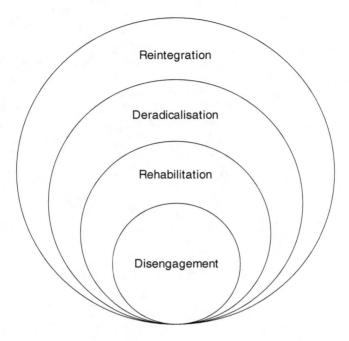

Figure 2.1 From disengagement to reintegration

To some extent the level of complexity of understanding and accessing these programmes is compounded by the differentiated measurements of success that the programmes are held against. While the strategic end game that countries are working towards are broadly the same – a society that is safe and secure – measures of success of the programmes are differentiated against the parameters within which states govern. This is especially the case with regards to the role of religion within the confines of state and governance. Countries either choose to work towards an individual's or a group's disengagement from violence or go further and work towards engaging the individuals ideologically thereby working towards deradicalisation. Ashour (2009: 5) defines deradicalisation as a 'process of relative change' wherein 'a radical group reverses its ideology and de-legitimises the use of violent methods to achieve political goals, while also moving towards an acceptance of gradual social, political and economic changes within a pluralist context'. Lynch (2000: 45) defines rehabilitation as 'any discourse or practices that speak to transforming or normalizing the criminal into a socially defined non-deviant citizen, including psychological programs, drug treatment programs, educational and work training programs, work and housing placement assistance, and half-way houses' (cited in Aggarwal 2015: 137). Whilst Lynch's experience stems from the mould of criminal rehabilitation, there is gravitas in the manner in which the lessons are gleaned.

Rehabilitation vs deradicalisation

At the crux is the differentiation that is drawn between *cognitive* and *behavioural* change. The process of deradicalisation as defined above has an added scope of a *cognitive* element through efforts made to debunk extremist ideology while disengagement refers to the *behavioural* element individual's interest to disengage from violence but still harbour extremist thought. Often the role of the *cognitive* element of the programme involves the use of religious doctrine to debunk religiously motivated terrorism. This may not be the case when the terrorist group does not adhere to a religiously inspired ideology. In this instance the ideological drivers that may be ethno-nationalist focused would be addressed via bringing on board other approaches to help debunk the misconstrued understanding.

Rehabilitation and reintegration programmes both encapsulate this very process bearing in mind the strategic end game sought. These programmes have the added notion of engagement at some level on the reasons behind an individual's choice to conduct acts of violence and terrorism. The inability to differentiate these layers convolutes attempts to understand and appreciate the process as whole and the reciprocal impact that it has on strategic policies of countries in the management of terrorist detainees.

The European Commission (2006) refers to radicalisation as the 'phenomenon of people embracing opinions, views and ideas that could lead to acts of terrorism'.[1] The pathway of radicalisation differs amongst individuals. A fundamentalist person refers to individuals who have literalist interpretations of religious doctrine. An extremist would refer to an individual who holds fundamentalist values, sympathises with violence but refrains from engaging in violent acts. The central difference between the fundamentalist, extremist and terrorist or violent extremist would be the use of violence to further their cause for radical political change. The process from (ideological) extremist to terrorist (violent action), in this case, would be referred to as radicalisation. It is this shift from cognitive to behavioural that epitomises this journey of an individual to violent action (Jerard 2015).

Terrorist rehabilitation – neither new nor revolutionary

The assumption that terrorist rehabilitation and reintegration is a concept that is new, revolutionary and innovative is a fallacy. As an inspired idea, the process draws from lessons learned from decades invested in the study of criminal rehabilitation. It too emerged out of necessity to manage the security implications when those who have been radicalised returned back to society after a period of incarceration. It was understandably similar fears and thought processes that had, in turn, dominated the seeking of ways to manage the impact of terrorism. The hope is that those who were incarcerated on acts of terrorism would, through engagement, realise their errors, recant their violent extremist ideologies and reintegrate back into mainstream society. Perhaps, at the present time, a more accurate description is that it is an under-utilised method of managing the threat of terrorism. The ongoing efforts made are, however, not without implicit challenges and underlying scepticism.

To an extent, the malleability of human nature is at the crux of this argument. In his seminal work, Francis Allen (1978) – the proponent of 'the decline of the rehabilitative ideal' – points to the 'vibrant faith in the malleability of human beings' and the development of 'a workable consensus on the goals of treatment' that forms the cornerstone of a programme aimed at rehabilitation.

Social theorist Michel Foucault's theory of surveillance and visibility highlights the peculiar power dynamic within the prison system. Foucault (1977) noted that, for an inmate: 'He is seen, but he does not see; he is the object of information, never a subject of communication.' Are individuals more *malleable* when they think that are being watched? That is an assumption that is often made and it, in turn, results in the creation at times of a uniquely psychologically restrictive environment even after an individual is released and reintegrated back into society. It is, paradoxically, the return to the Panopticon where individuals, whether they are watched or otherwise, still perceive that they are being watched. Thereby even at an eventual point of time where freedom is given and they are no longer detained, there is a sense of imprisonment despite being free.

Are the modes of rehabilitation outmoded?

As a process, countries around the world have embarked on various methods of rehabilitation of criminal detainees over time. Research in general points to several modes or approaches that can be used in the process of terrorist rehabilitation namely 'religious, social, vocational, educational, creative and psychological'[2] (Angell and Gunaratna 2011: 351). While in principle the modes of rehabilitation represent a crucial starting point to consider, it is mendacious to assume that a successful terrorist rehabilitation programme is hinged on the quality of the methods or modes used in a rehabilitation programme alone.

The modes of rehabilitation can perhaps be best thought of as a necessary but insufficient element in the entire process of rehabilitation and reintegration. Furthermore, the modes ascribed above are based on approaches used in existing rehabilitation programmes. While they can be used as general guidelines, the challenge here is to step away from the cognitive silos of assuming that these modes of rehabilitation represent the all-encompassing solution to the formation of rehabilitation programmes globally. Assuming that the modes or approaches of rehabilitation are limited to those that were crafted by particular countries would be counterproductive and limiting in the overall quest to develop future modes or approaches that could yield considerable success.

Most modes of rehabilitation cannot function unilaterally. They are dependent on assessments made of the level of radicalisation of the terrorist inmates and their concomitant willingness to participate in the deradicalisation programmes. The choice of the modes of rehabilitation used is dependent on the access to specialised resources such as psychologists, social workers or religious clerics as well as limitations and constraints imposed by space.

Rehabilitation programmes that have seen considerable levels of success are accompanied by an array of accompanying factors. These factors point towards ensuring not only the sustenance of the programmes but also eventually help reify the conceptual process of rehabilitation. They stem from a broader question for countries where incarceration is seen as either punishment and deterrence or rehabilitation. What carefully calibrated rehabilitation programmes offer instead are mechanisms to increase understanding behind the fallacies created by the misinterpretation of religious texts and mechanisms for the individual to cope with an environment that can be pervasive to radicalisation. The level of innovation of a programme stems from the manner in which these programmes are crafted and, in turn, the detainee's eventual response to them.

It seems almost counter-intuitive that the success ascribed to a terrorist rehabilitation and reintegration programme may begin to come down to the very place that rehabilitation and reintegration experts try so hard to remove those in custody from. Be it punitive or pastoral, the approaches undertaken during the course of the terrorist rehabilitation programme form the collective gamut of approaches that is used in the engagement of the detainee.

Highly individualised process

Scholars over time have agreed on the notion that 'radicalisation is a complex and highly individualised process, often shaped by poorly understood interaction of structural and personal factors' (Vidino and Brandon 2012: 169). Compounding the problem is the fact that there is 'no grand theory of radicalisation and no common terrorist profile, [and as such] there is no single explanation for why people de-radicalise or disengage from a militant group' (Vidino and Brandon 2012: 169). This has then led several policy-makers to question both the necessity and veracity of ongoing programmes on rehabilitation. It then begets the age-old question – *should we or shouldn't we?*

On one hand, policy-makers and practitioners can choose to either initiate a process of rehabilitation or, on the other, they can choose incarceration without rehabilitation with the hope that incarceration will offer both the punitive measure and the deterrent effect that is sought. In a peculiar way, countries that have chosen the path of rehabilitation have done so with the hope of ensuring that the notion of deterrence extends beyond the time that the terrorist is incarcerated in prison. Whether one choses to see the glass as half full or half empty, what remains consistent is that countries have steadfastly prized the securing of communities as the end game. Efforts at rehabilitation and reintegration can be seen in the same light.

Albeit often spoken of almost as a monolithic concept, the success of a rehabilitation and reintegration programme comprises two parts of one puzzle. The success of rehabilitation programmes is dependent on both (1) the effectiveness and efficacy of the various approaches undertaken in the creation of programmes for rehabilitation and reintegration and (2) the ability for the rehabilitation programme to ultimately lead to successful reintegration of a terrorist detainee. The rehabilitation programme does not end with the detainee's time in prison albeit it plays an essential role towards ensuring the success of a rehabilitation and reintegration programme.

Broad-ranging emphasis over that last decade has been placed on discussions and deliberations on the creation of terrorist rehabilitation programmes in general or perhaps more specifically various modes of rehabilitation[3] that would comprise a larger rehabilitation programme. Substantive discourse has revolved around the critiques on level of impact of the rehabilitation programme and questions on the level of success of terrorist rehabilitation. The detainee population is not monolithic. A lesser-deliberated milieu is the notion of the place of incarceration, (more often than not) the site and conditions in which these rehabilitation programmes take place and the importance they in turn play vis-à-vis terrorist rehabilitation. It might be high time we make space for a discussion on space given the role it possibly plays towards the eventual success of a terrorist rehabilitation programme.

This chapter will explore the accommodation or living arrangements of detainees and the impact that this has on the rehabilitation and reintegration programme of terrorist detainees. A majority (if not all) of terrorist rehabilitation programmes takes place within prisons or places wherein the individual is incarcerated. *Can potential successes of a terrorist rehabilitation programme be undermined by the very nature wherein these programmes are conducted? To what extent do present processes and assumptions need to be critiqued to ensure a calibrated response for the future?*

Panopticon: detention and the ingenious cage

Carceral geography at its crux explores the geographical perception of incarceration. It dovetails with other parallel disciplines that include prison sociology, psychology and criminology. We ask the quintessential question in this chapter, *could what makes a prison, eventually make or break a terrorist rehabilitation programme?* Undoubtedly a complex dynamic that governments today grapple with is the management of terrorist detainees. This has become an ongoing challenge for governments given the nature of the terrorist landscape. More than the placing individuals behind bars, the current challenge that governments have is in engaging terrorist detainees; the need for highly effective management of prisons and other related custodial institutions is at its highest. While a fair amount of time and energy has been devoted to the creation and improvement of modes of rehabilitation, there are several unfortunate potholes in the journey that could halt or regress any positive effort made.

Detention in the context of counterterrorism has fuelled debates ranging from judicial legislation to the treatment of terrorist detainees. Preventative detention acts as 'a prophylactic measure against terrorist threats' (Waxman 2008: 11). The incarceration of an individual too has a ripple effect spinning off when an individual is taken off the streets over a period of time, preventing further acts of violence. Procedural protection of the individual and institutional reforms of prisons have been raised consistently. Despite the ongoing debates within the disciplines of criminology and human rights, these conversations have seldom made substantive headway into framing the impact detention in it of itself has on the eventual success of terrorist rehabilitation programmes. It is this presupposition that this chapter explores.

Form and function

A secure prison in form and a benevolent corrections system in function is the ideal that countries aspire to work towards with the aim of a programme that has pastoral values as its foundation. 'Functional corrections systems are also a prerequisite to efforts to tackle "new" global threats, such as violent extremism and transnational organized crime, which are affecting an increasing number of conflict and post-conflict settings' (United Nations Department of Peacekeeping Operations 2015). '[D]espite their heterogeneity, at the cornerstone of each of these [rehabilitation] programs is the idea that terrorists can be engaged such that there is a subsequent reduced risk of re-engagement in terrorism upon release' (Horgan and Bradock 2010: 268). Ideally, for convicted terrorists, the custodial rehabilitation system should 'prevent further radicalisation of prisoners, prevent terrorist activities from being directed or supported from within the prison system, and provide for the de-radicalisation and reintegration of prisoners into society where possible and thereby reduce recidivism' (Global Counter-Terrorism Forum 2012).

Saudi prisoner Ghassan Abdullah al-Sharbi at his periodic Review Board meeting told his board: 'You are 100 per cent right, there is a strong deradicalisation programme, but make no mistake, underneath there is a hidden radicalisation programme' (Osborne 2016). As much as there is wonderful work being done, the challenge is to ensure these programmes refrain from unwittingly reinforcing the very ideology that they aim to debunk. These efforts at reformation need to go hand in hand. The need to 'reform national legal frameworks and penitentiary systems to ensure the security of inmates, personnel and facilities and establish procedures to prevent and counter radicalisation in prisons based on human rights and the rule of law' (United Nations General Assembly 2015) is a necessary inclusion to the rehabilitation measures that are put in place. This has been an element that is hard to manage in varied prisons settings globally. The challenge may arise not from the programmes implemented but from the inability to yield substantive returns due to the regressive impact that the spatial constraints have at times inadvertently had on positive gains made.

Space and security

Even prior to its official declaration, the Islamic State (IS) has been championing the release of prisoners. In a 2012 audio statement, 'Destroying the Gates', Abu Bakr al-Baghdadi noted: 'We remind you of your top priority, which is to release the Muslim prisoners everywhere, and making the pursuit, chase, and killing of their butchers from amongst the judges, detectives, and guards to be on top of the list.' The 'Breaking of the Walls' campaign by al-Baghdadi then began on 12 September 2012 with the release of 100 prisoners from Tikrit.

While there have been a number of instances of prison breaks in Indonesia in 2013, they were not conducted by IS. They were in part due to overcrowding and mismanagement of prison security. On 11 July 2013 at the Tanjung Gusta, Medan, 200 people escaped during a prison riot including Fadli Sadama, who was later caught in Malaysia. Fadli, a courier for Noordin Mohammed Top, was a member of Kumpulan Militant Indonesia. Subsequently, on 18 August 2013 in North Sumatra 80 people escaped from prison. Thereafter, on 20 August 2013 in West Aceh's Meulaboh Prison 9 prisoners escaped after they sawed through the prison bars. Moving ahead, lax prison security coupled with an increase in calls for freeing prisoners both online and in the real world could push forward efforts at prison population reduction.

Similar efforts have been seen most recently in the Philippines by IS. On 27 August 2016, a jail break took place at the Provincial Jail Compound, Marawi City, Lanao del Sur, when approximately 20 armed men forcibly entered the jail bringing with them four RPGs on-board eight vehicles. The incident resulted in the escape of 30 prisoners. Securing prisons will continue to be a challenge where understaffed and overcrowded prisons generally contribute to a permissive environment for both recruitment and radicalisation. In this instance, space and elements of security work hand in hand.

Key areas of prisons management, crisis management and standard operating procedures of inmate supervision, detainee classification and discipline within the prison facility are just the tip of the iceberg. At times, these pre-existing challenges are seen as opportunities for governments to undertake efforts to improve on existing systems, but such efforts only serve to obscure more deeply the critical relationships between prison architecture and protocol, and prisoner cognition and behaviour. In a study of the perception of Dutch prisoners of their relationships with prison staff, Beijersbergen et al. (2014) noted that building styles, floor plans and other design features do indeed have a significant impact on these perceptions. While emphasis has been placed on the nature of programmes and the various modes of rehabilitation, *how important is distance between people in the prison facility in impacting behaviour?* A carefully calibrated programme can regress if any good work done by the programme is undone as soon as the detainees retire back to their respective cells at the end of the day.

Thriving subculture of extremist thought and radicalisation

The notion of space begs yet another question. How much do spatial constraints and distance between inmates facilitate the proliferation of an environment that is predisposed to higher levels of radicalisation? A majority of (if not all) terrorist rehabilitation and reintegration programmes consists of prison-based rehabilitation intervention programmes that are conducted within the custodial settings of prison facilities:

> Police efforts to combat terrorism can be undermined by poor prison management. A successful counter-terrorism strategy must go beyond arresting violent extremists. It must also include addressing important incarceration issues, such as where to hold terrorist convicts and how to deal with them in custody . . . Prison rehabilitation must be an integral part of any counter-terrorism strategy, so why these individuals become involved in terrorist

operations in the first place and their experiences in the prison system are crucial matters for policymakers.

(Ungerer 2011: 1–20)

The importance of the prison facility has a stake and inadvertently influences the level of success ascribed to the programme. In many prisons there is a thriving subculture: 'The inmate subculture is comprised of a peculiar language and a distinctive set of informal norms, attitudes, beliefs, values, statuses, and roles that give prisoners a different perspective from people on the outside' ('Prisons: Prisoners – Inmate Subcultures and Informal Organizations' n.d.). The proximity between detainees, as well as the nature of those who are detained in particular, creates a unique subculture.

In Australia, the debate ensues on whether minors should be kept alongside high-risk inmates, given the nature of the crime. Junaid Thorne, in an interview with ABC Australia, after his release shed light on the prison dynamics inside Australia's super maximum-security prison. He noted:

> Anyone in jail can tell you that there's ways around any restriction. While the classical way would just be by shouting under the door, through the backyard through the cages in the backyard that's pretty much the easiest way. It is very well organised in there by the brothers, by the inmates themselves.
> (Rubinsztein-Dunlop 2016)

In referring to the the inmates at the super maximum-security prison, Junaid further added that, in his opinion, he 'wouldn't call them serious convicted terrorists. They just seemed like real normal people that had a sound or strong belief in faith' (Rubinsztein-Dunlop 2016). Cognitive biases work both ways. Just as it affects the manner in which counterterrorism practitioners and scholars broach the notion of rehabilitation, for the terrorist detainees their cognitive biases resonate just as much as they attempt to make sense of their surroundings. The thriving subculture of extremist thought and action in this instance was further facilitated by the inmates' ability to circumvent the limitations of space, which had led to secret codes and notes being sent in and around the prison facility.

Location impacts outcome

Generalisations of whether inmates should be housed separately from the general prison population or housed together with the general prison population partially outlines with broad brushstrokes only the broad spectrum of ideas surrounding the management of terrorist detainees within a custodial setting. The reality instead is much more nuanced. Be it housed separately or together with the general prison population, at each of these categories, the impact of the housing arrangements of the terrorist detainees can be further differentiated when the terrorist detainees are concentrated, dispersed or placed in isolation, respectively (Figure 2.2).

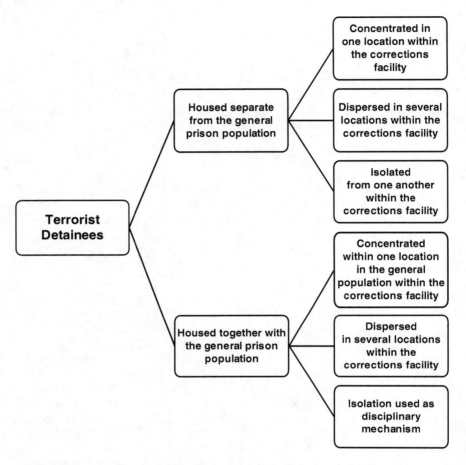

Figure 2.2 Housing of terrorist detainees – concentrated, dispersed and isolated

Broadly the decision that is made in the first instance is for terrorist detainees to be either housed separately or housed together with the general prison population. This decision is sometimes made out of choice or purely by circumstance, given the governing state of affairs. Principle 20 of the Council of Europe's Guidelines for prison and probation services regarding radicalisation and violent extremism notes:

> Regardless of whether prisoners sentenced for terrorist-related crimes are kept in separate prisons or wings or are dispersed across the prison system, the risk they may pose, including the risk of radicalising other prisoners, shall be evaluated individually before their allocation is defined and shall be reviewed at regular intervals.
> (United Nations Office on Drugs and Crime 2016a: 47)

Tied to the concept of space, as noted in the Council of Europe's Guidelines, is that of detainee classification efforts. The use of a comprehensive detainee classification that works hand in hand with departments helps to categorise detainees. Presently, countries have attempted to classify terrorist detainees by means of three criteria namely, the severity of crime, length of sentence and levels of radicalisation.

The dominant discourse on terrorist rehabilitation points towards separating terrorist detainees from the general prison population. The underlying rationale is that if the terrorist detainees are housed with the general prison population, there is an increased propensity for the radicalisation of the general prison population. It is pertinent to bear in mind that while a prison

> restricts a terrorist's ability to orchestrate acts of violence, but it is not necessarily an effectively enforced 'time out' from radical activism. Rather, when the prison gate swings shut behind them, it opens a new door in front of them for spreading their message and methods.
>
> (Wilner 2010: 10)

Conversely, there is also an increased risk of terrorist detainees being exposed to criminal tradecraft.

Possible advantages and disadvantages of concentration

The advantages and disadvantages of concentration differ when an individual is housed either away from or together with the general prison population. The impact rendered from the *concentration* of terrorist detainees in one wing or block differs in both these instances.

When housed away from the general prison population and concentrated within a separate wing or block within the corrections facility, while the terrorist detainees are concentrated in their sleeping quarters, during the course of their daily interaction they would be interacting with other terrorist detainees. In this instance, there is no contact with others from the general prison population.

The underlying assumption is that with a smaller group to monitor (given that terrorist detainees naturally form a smaller subset), it would be comparatively easy to keep tabs on the terrorist detainees in general. This would translate positively to increased attention being given to detainees and calibrated efforts undertaken to ensure the standards of security would be met, if not surpassed. When effort is made to arrange for terrorist detainees to be housed separately, resources are poured in to increase the security measures of the facility. The security alone does not prevent radicalisation. Instead, the proper management of the facility would yield greater dividends. If improperly managed, the terrorist wing or block can facilitate further radicalisation of the (already radical) inmates. New bonds can be easily forged and old networks revived during their independent interactions, this in turn increasing the levels of risk when inmates eventually leave the facility.

When undergoing various programmes, if housing arrangements are maintained as the status quo, that condition will pose a challenge given the environment incarcerated extremists return to on a daily basis might retard or impede any positive headway made towards disengagement from violence or having prisoners recant their ideology. Yet another challenge is the almost unspoken level of camaraderie amongst the detainees, as for some being placed within the facility is seen as a badge of honour. In Thailand the terrorist detainees, or security detainees as they are known there, are segregated from the general population and housed in a separate wing – an area cordoned off. In the case of Thailand, this has resulted in the entrenched notion amongst the detainees that the 'Muslims' are not only disenfranchised but also targeted. This results in a stronger in-group dynamic that in turn creates bonds of friendship and familial ties that are even harder to break.

When housed together with the general prison population and concentrated within a separate wing or block within the corrections facility, in this instance, while the terrorist detainees are concentrated in their sleeping quarters, during the course of their daily routine they would be interacting with the general prison population. In this instance, contact with the general prison population remains. Some countries in the attempt to initiate the process of separating terrorist detainees from the general prison population opt for this. This is especially prevalent in medium-level security facilities in Indonesia. Here the terrorist detainees have the best of both worlds.

Possible advantages and disadvantages of dispersal

The advantages and disadvantages of *dispersal* differ when an individual is housed either away from or together with the general prison population. The impact rendered from the *dispersal* of terrorist detainees in one wing or block is almost similar in both these instances with much of the positive and negative traits shared in condition where terrorist detainees are concentrated together.

When incarcerated extremists are housed away from the general prison population and dispersed within a separate wing or block of the corrections facility across few concentrated pockets, this can help dilute the strong in-group dynamics present when terrorist inmates aggregate together. This is an expensive proposition for even if enacted, responsibility for success or failure may fall squarely onto the system and how terrorist detainees are classified. On occasion, these small pockets of concentrated inmates can be created across a few corrections facilities. This attempt is made to ensure that inmates are much more manageable for the staff of the corrections facility.

Prison staff working with both detainees who are concentrated within a corrections facility or dispersed either across either one or several facilities are sometimes assumed to be more specialised at managing terrorist detainees in general. While to some extent this is true, it additionally opens with it a greater propensity for the radicalisation of prison staff given their close and consistent proximity of to the detainee population. The prospect of corruption such as efforts to facilitate the detainees' access to contraband is just one example of ways that management of the prison facility can go awry. In several countries staff rotation is done over a short period of time to ensure that there is a limit to the personal bonds created between inmates and prison personnel. In this instance, the disadvantages seen in the concentration of detainees within a corrections facility will be generally applicable in instances where the detainees are dispersed across the corrections facility.

Whether housed together with the general prison population or dispersed within a separate wing or block within the corrections facility as with the earlier example, the issue at hand in this case lies with the terrorist detainees' continued interaction with the general prison population. The challenges raised, including the propensity for staff radicalisation, resonate in this instance as well.

In the Philippines, the New Bilibid Prison, commonly known as the Muntilupa, houses terrorist inmates with the general prison population. In an innovative strategy to enforce a level of control and maintain the balance of power between criminal gangs and radical extremists within the Muntilupa, terrorist inmates are housed with the mainstream prisoners and distributed among 12 different gangs within the broader Muntilupa facility. To break the power structures created when the terrorist detainees are concentrated in a given environment, the gang leaders offer a counter balance to the power structures that have been built.

Possible advantages and disadvantages of isolation

The advantages and disadvantages of *isolation* differ when an individual is housed either away from or together with the general prison population. The impact rendered from *isolation* totally differs based on the means used within the context of isolation or general population strategies.

In the context of prison management of terrorist detainees when housed away from the general prison population, being *isolated* from one another within the corrections facility can broadly be understood beyond the typical parameters of solitary confinement. In this instance, the terrorist detainees are kept separate from other detainees. Being kept separate will as such address the concerns of the possible spread of radical ideology between inmates as well reduce the impact that interaction with other detainees may have for setbacks to efforts made at rehabilitation and eventual reintegration.

However, in the face of a typical challenge of resources and spatial constraints, this is often regarded as being much harder to achieve. When used in a well-structured manner, a tailor-made approach can be adapted to suit the needs of each detainee; in this instance, the use of isolation can yield considerable benefit. In Singapore, terrorist detainees are kept isolated from other inmates held on charges of terrorism. Visits are only permitted from their families, social workers and counsellors. This would enable tailor-made programmes for terrorist detainees to be crafted with greater precision.

The use of *isolation* is differentiated when a detainee is housed together with the general prison population. The use of isolation in this instance refers to solitary confinement and in this instance is seen as a punitive measure. Sharon Shalev, an international expert in the field of solitary confinement and seclusion 'recommends that the use of seclusion, segregation and all forms of restraints should be significantly reduced, and reserved for the most extreme of cases, and then used only for a very short time' (Shalev 2017). Having conducted an independent review on the use of seclusion and restraint in a number of detention settings in New Zealand, Shalev opines that solutions can be sought outside the confines of physical isolation. Solitary confinement is often used to enforce discipline within a corrections facility. While drawing up the process to craft the strategic use of isolation as a disciplinary function, 'it is of utmost importance that [the general] housing [of] prisoners in cells should not amount to isolation' (United Nations Office on Drugs and Crime 2016b: 53).

Housed together out of circumstance or choice?

In most countries, the housing of terrorist detainees together with the general prison population arises from a continuation of the general state of affairs. Any efforts and attempts to house the terrorist detainees separately from the general prison population are often met with a stumbling block, namely in the form of a lack of options to even enact a change of this scale given the spatial and financial constraints. A central differentiation to be made would be whether the terrorist detainees are housed together out of necessity or by choice. In most instances they are housed together with the general prison population out of necessity.

Going against the grain, some countries have purposefully initiated attempts to house their terrorist detainees with general population out of choice. In Morocco, it was the increased solidarity and strength observed by prison officials when the terrorist detainees were concentrated together that resulted in the decision to house the terrorist detainees with the general prison population. While some countries take this course of action due to spatial constraints, in the case of Morocco it was a deliberate strategy to ensure security within the corrections facility. The strategy undertaken was as a means to dismantle the power structures amongst the terrorist detainees that in turn made it difficult for authorities to manage these inmates. This is against the dominant school of thought and the fears of increased radicalisation when detainees are housed together with the general prison population. However, according to the Moroccan authorities, this calibrated strategy has in turn yielded dividends for them, as they were able to break the power structures within the facility where the terrorist detainees were housed.

In most countries there is not one well-defined solution. Often enough, decisions about how to deal with incarcerated extremists are challenging – yet the capacity to find an optimal combination of present systems in one country remains elusive. Any cogent argument made that there are attempts to find a uniform solution when it comes to housing terrorist detainees is met with the same ethereal ardour that these are nothing but parochial statements.

Conclusion

In broaching the subject of rehabilitation and reintegration there are resonant limitations that have to be embraced in the process of working on the subject. The challenge has been to convince governments to re-evaluate their strategies and to consider the inclusion of terrorist rehabilitation as part of strategies that have been undertaken. Often, the challenges raised in this section impede the concretisation of efforts on terrorist rehabilitation and reintegration.

Necessary limitations

The entrenched challenges of the field have to be embraced. One resounding critique is the lack of published scientific data. Despite the compendium of studies on rehabilitation and reintegration, the undeniable challenge is that as a whole terrorism

> is a study area which is easy to approach but very difficult to copy within a scientific sense. Easy to approach – because it has so many angles, touching on all aspects of human behavior. Difficult to cope with – because it is so diverse.
> (Merari 1978: 167–175)

A central challenge that has in turn afflicted the field, as it has with terrorist rehabilitation and reintegration, is the notion that the field of critical terrorism studies looks upon the genre as being underdeveloped and embryonic (Horgan 1997) and, to a large extent, 'impressionistic, superficial and often pretentious, venting far reaching generalizations on the basis of episodic evidence' (Schmid and Jongman 1988: 77).[4] This challenge has resonated in the field of terrorist rehabilitation and reintegration.

Intuitively, countries that have been exploring the notion of the rehabilitation of terrorist detainees would have conducted assessments that in turn guide their programmes. Nonetheless, there have been critiques that rehabilitation and reintegration have been 'under-researched' (Bhui et al. 2012: 2) and that 'despite their popularity, data surrounding even the most basic facts of the programmes are limited' (Horgan and Bradock 2010: 267). Horgan and Bradock (2010: 269) also note there is lack of a 'framework for guiding the development of future such initiatives that draw lessons from effective programmes'. Understandably, the need for evidence based assessments is key. The frustration of the academic community needs to be nuanced given the affiliated sensitivities surrounding nature of the subject matter. In the case of terrorist rehabilitation, the challenge that cannot be dismissed is that there is a lack of open-source published data as opposed to no research at all.

A second limitation is that in several countries the rehabilitation and reintegration efforts are neither synchronised nor streamlined. They, in turn, take place during the post-surrender, post-detention and post-conviction phases of incarceration (Clutterbuck 2015). The the underlying assumption is that terrorist rehabilitation efforts are initiated after an individual is placed within the prison facility after sentencing. In reality this may not be the norm. Rehabilitation programmes do not begin only after sentencing takes place. At present, in the Philippines, the Metro Manila District Jail, which segregates its terrorist inmates from the mainstream prisoners, comprises of 1,344 different types of prisons and jails. As of 2016, there are approximately 555 terrorist inmates. Several of the inmates while undergoing trial have been engaged in processes of rehabilitation and this has resulted in a complex vignette of ad-hoc programmes.[5]

A third limitation that is sometime lesser spoken of is the question of who runs the prison facility. Recently, in a 2016 article by *Time* magazine on privately run prison facilities, the argument raised by Joseph Margulies (2016) highlights the perennial dilemma, the fear governing reasons behind why 'justice should not be administered through the prism of profit' as well as the fear that 'companies that build and run private prisons have a financial interest in the continued growth of mass incarceration'. The role played by terrorist rehabilitation and reintegration will be impacted by the manner by which prisons are run. With private-sector prison administration, the release of detainees has the potential to be tied to possible loss of financial gain and, as such, impede the desire to craft a possible way forward. Contingent on the ability to make rehabilitation and reintegration programmes an imperative, is the subject's willingness to participate, and for-profit prison systems might dampen participation enthusiasm.

The conceptual notion of dynamic security underlies 'knowing what is going on in a prison, in addition to providing a safe and secure background against which the whole range of activity making up the life of a prison takes place' (United Nations Office on Drugs and Crime 2015: 30). In an interview with incarcerated extremists, Feisal, the former leader of JI's Mantiqi 3, who was arrested in Philippines, noted his participation would be contingent on both the nature of programmes as well as the possibility of release in the near future.[6] Given the bleak possibility of release, Feisal noted the futility associated with his participation.

Great promise for great reward

Terrorist rehabilitation and reintegration form a necessary part of larger efforts within counterterrorism. The reciprocal effect that they have when successful and the inadvertent loss incurred in the absence of such programmes in the long run seem too great to incur. Given the governing realities, the potential successes of a terrorist rehabilitation programme can be undermined by the very location wherein these programmes are conducted. The way to move forward with an effective terrorist rehabilitation programme will be to ensure that a measured and calibrated strategy is undertaken to re-evaluate effectively the present processes and governing assumptions of existing programmes. While the present sentiment is that we should encourage terrorist rehabilitation and reintegration programmes, the challenge will lie in a greater understanding of the benefits of reciprocal effectiveness of terrorist rehabilitation programmes to terrorists, their families and acquaintances, and to society. These programmes, as highlighted in this chapter, form a subset of the larger rehabilitation and reintegration process. To a large extent, what makes a prison could eventually make or break a terrorist rehabilitation programme. The impact of distance and proximity has a long-standing impact on the how the terrorist rehabilitation and reintegration programmes eventually unfold.

The paradox of the Panopticon that was detailed at the start of the chapter presents a thoroughly uncomfortable reality. While it might have been named after the one-hundred-eyed Greek giant Argus Panoptes, it is impossible to be all-seeing and all-knowing. To a large extent thus far, successful efforts at reintegration could hinge directly on the perceived notion of being watched by others around them or even by an overzealous sense that the newly reintegrated former detainees feel they are being watched. The irony is that, despite the proclivity for platitudes, space and the perception of space have an intrinsic part to play in the both the process of terrorist rehabilitation and successful reintegration strategies.

Notes

1 See also Michael Emmerson (2009) *Ethno-religious Conflicts in Europe: Typologies of Radicalisation in Europe's Muslim Communities*. Brussels: Centre for European Policy Studies.
2 Modes of rehabilitation refer to the engagement of all the facets and faculties of a detainee in custody. See Ami Angell and Rohan Gunaratna (2011) *Terrorist Rehabilitation: The U.S. Experience in Iraq*. Boca Raton, FL: CRC Press: 351.
3 Modes of rehabilitation have come to be broadly understood as the pathways or strategies undertaken to rehabilitate approaches to facilitate the course of rehabilitation. The individual then achieves a state of deradicalisation prior to be being reintegrated into society.
4 See also Kris Christmann (2012) *Preventing Religious Radicalisation and Violent Extremism: A Systematic Review of the Research Evidence*. London: Youth Justice Board for England and Wales: 8. Available at: https://assets.publishing.service.gov.uk/government/uploads/system/uploads/attachment_data/file/396030/preventing-violent-extremism-systematic-review.pdf (accessed 11 May 2018).
5 Clarke Jones, Philippine Update: 2–3 August 2016, School of Regulation and Global Governance Australian National University Accessed At: http://asiapacific.anu.edu.au/sites/default/files/Clarke-Jones-Shared-Governance-Philippine-Prison-System.pdf
6 Interview conducted on 30 July 2015 with Ahmad Faisal Bin Imam Sarijan alias Zulkifli alias Donnie Ofracio alias Badrudin alias Jol alias Jabbar alias Bro in Manila, Philippines.

Bibliography

Aggarwal, Neil K. (2015) *Mental Health in the War on Terror: Culture, Science, and Statecraft*. New York: Columbia University Press.
Allen, Francis A. (1978) 'The Decline of the Rehabilitative Ideal in American Criminal Justice'. *Cleveland State Law Review*, 27(2): 147. Available at: http://engagedscholarship.csuohio.edu/clevstlrev/vol27/iss2/3 (accessed 11 May 2018).
Angell, Ami and Rohan Gunaratna (2011) *Terrorist Rehabilitation: The U.S. Experience in Iraq*. Boca Raton, FL: CRC Press.
Ashour, Omar (2009) *Votes and Violence: Islamists and the Process of Transformation*. London: The International Centre for the Study of Radicalisation and Political Violence.

Beijersbergen, Karin A., Anja Dirkzwager, Peter Laan and Paul Nieuwbeerta (2014) 'A Social Building? Prison Architecture and Staff-Prisoner Relationships'. *Crime & Delinquency*, 62(7): 843–874.

Bhui, Kamaldeep S., Madelyn H. Hicks, Myrna Lashley and Edgar Jones (2012) 'A Public Health Approach to Understanding and Preventing Violent Radicalisation'. *BMC Medicine*, 10(16): 2. Available at: http://dx.doi.org/10.1186/1741-7015-10-16 (accessed 11 May 2018).

Clutterbuck, Lindsay (2015) 'Deradicalization Programs and Counterterrorism: A Perspective on the Challenges and Benefits', in *Understanding Deradicalization: Pathway to Enhance Transatlantic Common Perception and Practices* (series). Washington: Middle East Institute. Available at: www.mei.edu/content/deradicalization-programs-and-counterterrorism-perspective-challenges-and-benefits (accessed 11 May 2018).

European Commission (2006) 'Terrorist Recruitment: Commission Communication, MEMO/05/329', in *Terrorist Recruitment: a Commission's Communication Addressing the Factors Contributing to Violent Radicalisation*. Available at: europa.eu/rapid/press-release_MEMO-05-329_en.pdf (accessed 11 May 2018).

Foucault, Michel (1977) 'Discipline and Punish, Panopticism', in Alan Sheridan (ed.) *Discipline & Punish: The Birth of the Prison*. New York: Vintage Books: 195–228. Available at: https://foucault.info/doc/documents/disciplineandpunish/foucault-disciplineandpunish-panopticism-html (accessed 11 May 2018).

Giligan, James (2012) 'Punishment Fails. Rehabilitation Works', *New York Times*, 19 December. Available at: www.nytimes.com/roomfordebate/2012/12/18/prison-could-be-productive/punishment-fails-rehabilitation-works?mcubz=0 (accessed 11 May 2018).

Global Counter-Terrorism Forum (2012) 'Rabat Memorandum on Good Practices for Effective Counterterrorism Practice in the Criminal Justice Sector'. *Good Practice*, 11: 11–12. Available at: www.thegctf.org/Portals/1/Documents/Framework%20Documents/A/GCTF-Rabat-Memorandum-ENG.pdf?ver=2016-09-01-115828-653 (accessed 11 May 2018).

Horgan, John (1997) 'Issues in Terrorism Research'. *The Police Journal*, 50(3): 193–202.

Horgan, John and Kurt Bradock (2010) 'Rehabilitating the Terrorists?: Challenges in Assessing the Effectiveness of De-radicalisation Programs'. *Terrorism and Political Violence*, 22: 267–291. Available at: www.start.umd.edu/sites/default/files/files/publications/Derad.pdf (accessed 23 April 2017).

Jerard, Jolene (2015) 'Terrorism in Indonesia: An Examination of 10 Radical Groups'. Doctoral dissertation in St Andrews Research Repository, University of St Andrews, Scotland.

Jerard, Jolene (2016) 'Daesh and the Alchemy of Strategy: Southeast Asia Threat and Responses by the Region and ASEAN', in Rohan Gunaratna et al. (eds) *Panorama: Insights into Asian and European Affairs Countering Daesh Extremism – European and Asian Responses*. Singapore: KAS Panorama. Available at: www.kas.de/politikdialog-asien/en/publications/46739 (accessed 11 May 2018).

Lynch Mona (2000) 'Rehabilitation as Rhetoric: The Ideal of Reformation in Contemporary Parole Discourse and Practices'. *Punishment & Society*, 2: 40–65.

Margulies, Joseph (2016) 'This Is the Real Reason Private Prisons Should Be Outlawed', *Time*, 24 August. Available at: http://time.com/4461791/private-prisons-department-of-justice/ (accessed 11 May 2018).

Merari, Ariel (1978) 'A Classification of Terrorist Groups'. *Terrorism: An International Journal*, 1: 167–175.

Osborne, Samuel (2016) 'Saudi Arabia's terrorist rehab actually "secret radicalisation programme," Guantanamo prisoner claims', *Independent*, 1 December. Available at:

www.independent.co.uk/news/world/middle-east/saudi-arabia-terrorist-rehab-secret-hidden-radicalisation-programme-guantanamo-prisoner-claim-a7449191.html (accessed 11 May 2018).

'Prisons: Prisoners – Inmate Subcultures and Informal Organizations' (n.d.) Anonymous JRank article. Available at: http://law.jrank.org/pages/1796/Prisons-Prisoners-Inmate-subcultures-informal-organizations.html#ixzz4rdspcmzy (accessed 10 May 2018).

Rubinsztein-Dunlop, Sean (2016) 'Counter-terrorism Officials Fear Supermax Prison Further Radicalizing', *ABC Australia*, 12 October. Available at: www.abc.net.au/7.30/counter-terrorism-officials-fear-supermax-prison/7920266 (accessed 11 May 2018).

Schmid, Alex and Albert Jongman (1988) *Political Terrorism: A New Guide to Actors, Authors, Concepts, Data Bases, Theories, and Literature*. Amsterdam: Transaction Publishers.

Shalev, Sharon (2017) 'Thinking Outside the Box? A Review of Seclusion and Restraint Practices in New Zealand'. *International Corrections & Prisons Association*. Available at: http://icpa.ca/thinking-outside-the-box-segregation-and-restraints-in-new-zealand/ (accessed 11 May 2018).

Stedman, Philip (2007) 'The Contradictions of Jeremy Bentham's Panopticon Penitentiary'. *Journal of Bentham Studies*, 9: 1–31. Available at: http://discovery.ucl.ac.uk/1324519/1/009_Steadman_2007.pdf (accessed 11 May 2018).

Ungerer, C. (2011) 'Jihadists in Jail: Radicalisation and the Indonesian Prison Experience'. *Australian Strategic Policy Institute*, 40: 1–20.

United Nations Department of Peacekeeping Operations (2015) *Prison Support in United Nations Peace Operations*. Ref. 2015.11. Available at: https://peacekeeping.un.org/sites/default/files/prison_support_policy_1_september_2015.pdf (accessed 11 May 2018).

United Nations General Assembly (2015) *Plan of Action to Prevent Violent Extremism – Report of the Secretary-General*, A/70/67, 50(f).

United Nations Office on Drugs and Crime (2015) *Handbook on Dynamic Security and Prison Intelligence*. New York: United Nations. Available at: www.unodc.org/documents/justice-and-prison-reform/UNODC_Handbook_on_Dynamic_Security_and_Prison_Intelligence.pdf (accessed 11 May 2018).

United Nations Office on Drugs and Crime (2016a) *Handbook on the Management of Violent Extremist Prisoners and the Prevention of Radicalisation to Violence in Prisons*. New York: United Nations. Available at: www.unodc.org/pdf/criminal_justice/Handbook_on_VEPs.pdf (accessed 11 May 2018).

United Nations Office on Drugs and Crime (2016b) *Handbook on the Management of High-Risk Prisoners*. New York: United Nations. Available at: www.unodc.org/documents/justice-and-prison-reform/HB_on_High_Risk_Prisoners_Ebook_appr.pdf (accessed 11 May 2018).

Vidino, Lorenzo and James Brandon (2012) 'Europe's Experience in Countering Radicalisation: Approaches and Challenges'. *Journal of Policing, Intelligence and Counter Terrorism*, 7(2): 169.

Waxman, Matthew (2008) 'Administrative Detention: The Integration of Strategy and Legal Process', *Counterterrorism and American Statutory Law*, Working Paper, Georgetown University Law Center and the Hoover Institution. Available at: www.brookings.edu/wp-content/uploads/2016/06/0724_detention_waxman.pdf (accessed 11 May 2018).

Wilner, Alex (2010) 'Prison Radicalisation in the West', in *True North in Canada Pubic Policy*, October 2010. Canada: Macdonald Laurier Institute of Public Policy. Available at: www.macdonaldlaurier.ca/files/pdf/FromRehabilitationToRecruitment.pdf (accessed 11 May 2018).

3 Countering radical ideology

Case studies of religious rehabilitation programmes

Ahmad Saiful Rijal Bin Hassan

Introduction

Up to the present time, many countries have proved to be successful in operational counterterrorism, but not strategic counterterrorism. However, to achieve complete success, the operational hunt for terrorists must be accompanied with the correction of their misled ideologies. Investing in religious rehabilitation is one of the vital strategies in pursuing a holistic approach in a terrorist rehabilitation programme. This is because many terrorists of today commit acts of violence under the guise of religion.

Every religion advocates peace and harmony. However, there are certain concepts in religion that have been used to provide justification for acts of violence. Although many major religions of the world promote compassion, tolerance and moderation, there are those individuals or groups who have misused religion to convince people to commit atrocities. Over the past two decades, the world has witnessed terrorism coming from the deviant forms of Hinduism, Judaism, Christianity, Buddhism, Islam and Sikhism (Gunaratna 2009). One of the remedies is for the religious teachers and scholars from the respective religions to rectify the deviance by replacing the wrongful interpretations and teachings of religion with the right ones.

This makes having qualified speakers of the faith engaging with terrorists who are being detained a necessity. This will ensure that once terrorist detainees are released, they will have already developed the capacity to resist straying back to their old path, which in turn will help them reintegrate back into the society. This chapter will focus on countries that include religious aspects of rehabilitation in their terrorist deradicalisation programmes. This chapter will first mention the rationale of implementing religious rehabilitation programmes followed by descriptions of the programmes in different countries. The chapter will then conclude by highlighting the challenges faced by religious rehabilitation programmes that are being put into practice and some approaches that can be implemented by practitioners.

Background

Terrorists of today commit atrocities in the name of religion, particularly those who belong to groups such as the so-called Islamic State of Iraq and Syria (ISIS), al-Qaeda and its affiliates such as Jemaah Islamiyah (JI) and Boko Haram. These groups commit violence and mass murder in the name of Islam. By the skilful manipulation of Islamic concepts such as *jihad*, martyrdom and *Sharia* law that many Muslims hold dear, these terrorists are slowly making inroads into the hearts and minds of the Muslim masses particularly among Islam's youth in some parts of the world.

The job of these terrorists is made easier by the continuous conflicts in many Muslim communities worldwide, particularly in Afghanistan, Syria and Iraq where terrorists portray their ideology and movement as the defender and saviour of oppressed Muslims everywhere. Thus, the biggest challenge is to provide a viable alternative interpretation of these concepts that can be accepted by the masses.

Religious ideology is important and all-encompassing in terrorist organisations as it permeates the structure, aids the viability of the organisation and helps to gain support from the masses. There are many paths to terrorism, and its causes are complex and often multi-factorial. However, ideology is a uniting force for many terrorists. Irrespective of how individual terrorists come into a terrorist organisation, ideology allows them to share a common goal, gives a sense of camaraderie and provides meaning (justification) for their struggle. This is particularly true for an ideology that has deep religious undertones.

Yet another crucial point to note is that ideology is formed in the realm of a person's mind, and therefore, the 'capture or kill' strategy alone will not be enough to reduce the threat. Although we can physically imprison a terrorist in the highest security prison or detention centre, we cannot imprison the mind. If we destroy the physical body, there are many more who are infected with the ideology and will come forth to take up the struggle.

In terrorist groups and movements, ideology plays a significant role. First, ideology is the organising principle of the terrorist organisations. It provides a motive and framework for their actions. Second, as demonstrated by ISIS and other like-minded groups, ideology provides justification for their acts of violence. Third, ideology is a language of mass mobilisation. Calling for *jihad* in the garb of performing an Islamic duty has enabled terrorist groups to indoctrinate and recruit terrorist members continuously. Fourth, in the guise of a social programme, ideology can generate Muslim public support whether as supporters who provide financial and logistical assistance or as sympathisers who do not morally condone these acts but show signs of sympathy towards the cause of terrorist groups. Finally, over time, the ideology will further radicalise Muslim communities by indoctrinating them into a culture of violence and radical interpretations of Islam.

Thus the best form of medicine is that which targets the diseased organ – in this case, the mind. A deradicalisation process or religious rehabilitation is needed to deconstruct the ideology that is being misconstrued by terrorists and that can only be addressed by religious scholars. This process is defined as the process of 'changing an individual's belief system, rejecting the extremist ideology, and embracing mainstream values' (Rabasa et al. 2010: xiii). To achieve this, religious scholars must challenge the negatively imbibed ideology and replace it with the proper understanding of Islam by exemplifying Prophet Muhammad's teachings on the values of mercy and compassion, at the same time protecting the sanctity of Islam from being tainted by terrorist groups.

Saudi Arabia

Saudi Arabia's counterterrorism strategy is commonly known as 'PRAC', which stands for Prevention, Rehabilitation and Aftercare. The Prevention programme acts as a preventive measure where activities are conducted to educate the public about the dangers of extremism in order to prevent it from taking place. The Rehabilitation programme is in the form of intensive counselling programmes for inmates who have been detained for terrorist activities; through religious debates and psychological counselling they are rehabilitated/deradicalised. The Aftercare programme consists of various initiatives to help the detainees reintegrate back into the society. In this programme, the detainees are addressed as 'beneficiaries' because they are considered as individuals who stand to benefit from the programmes (Boucek 2008). Another reason for this is because prison officials do not want them to feel that they are being punished for being misguided in learning religion but to correct their thoughts and bring equilibrium to their thinking.

Under the religious component of the rehabilitation programme, there are approximately 150 clerics, scholars and university professors. They engage directly with the detainees in dialogues and debates as well as general Islamic education. Clerics were approached individually on a personal basis and asked whether they could meet with the detainees. These clerics will be instructed not to simply give lectures to the detainees, but to engage them in a dialogue and treat them 'like his own brother'. If a cleric is found to be ineffective in his counselling style, another cleric will be selected to replace him. This is to ensure that detainees will benefit fully from engaging with the cleric. Scholars keep in touch with the detainees after their release as they continue to help them (Boucek 2008).

During the initial stages, dialogue sessions were conducted on a one-on-one basis. After some time, detainees will go through a series of study sessions in a group of up to 20 students. The sessions comprise six weeks of group study conducted by two clerics and a social scientist. As many as ten subjects are covered including topics such as *jihad*, *walaa'* (loyalty) and *bai'ah* (pledge of allegiance). Detainees also go through the tutorial on how to avoid 'misleading' and 'corrupting' books and influences (Boucek 2008).

Scholars are receptive towards the idea of religious rehabilitation as they fear the danger posed to both the Islamic faith and the Saudi state by the misinterpreted religious concepts and therefore are motivated to help guide the detainees back to the correct path. The names of these scholars are not released to the public although some individuals have declared that they are involved in the programmes. However, most of the scholars chose to work quietly. It could be because they are doing this for God's sake or they are afraid of being attacked by terror groups outside for working with the government (Boucek 2008).

Yemen

The Religious Dialogue Committee conducted religious rehabilitation in Yemen. The Committee was founded by the Minister of Endowment and Guidance of Yemen, Judge Hamoud Al-Hitar in September 2002. The Committee was seen as the pioneer in undertaking religious rehabilitation programme efforts post-9/11. The programme was deeply rooted in a religious dialogue that aimed to correct the detainees' misconstrued beliefs and to alter their radical, militant understanding to a moderate and peaceful understanding of Islam. The programme, however, faced many challenges and was often at the focal point of political scuffles. As a result, the programme ceased to operate in 2005 (International Centre for Political Violence and Terrorism Research 2010).

The religious dialogues performed in Yemeni prisons are based on a certain set of rules and principles. The set of rules and principles is discussed first before each dialogue can take place. Topics will be selected prior to the dialogue and detainees have ample time to prepare their arguments. All arguments must be substantiated with accurate referencing to the Quran, *Sunnah* (prophetic traditions) and opinions of authenticated religious scholars (International Centre for Political Violence and Terrorism Research 2010). To establish equality in the dialogue, both detainees and clerics had to take an oath on the Quran to speak the truth and to respect each other's opinions. This swearing on the Quran was considered to be fundamentally important to legitimise the dialogue process (Beg 2010).

Initial dialogue with the detainees was on the issue of Yemen as a non-Islamic state and the government as pro-Western. The clerics responded by providing copies of the Constitution and the penal law for the detainees to inspect. However, the detainees could not find any evidence that the country's constitution and penal law speaks against the *Sharia*. Instead, they are in line with Islamic principles. Another important topic for the dialogue was on the permissibility of killing non-Muslims. The detainees sought to justify their acts of killing on the premise that the victims were *kafir* or infidels and such action against them was allowed by the Quran. The cleric would then explain to the detainees that the Quran states that killing can only be justified with a rightful reason related to the circumstances of war or oppression where people are prevented from practising their religion and are driven out of their homes (Beg 2010).

In the beginning, there were only four religious clerics in the Committee as many other clerics declined to join the Committee for fear of antagonising the fundamentalists and endangering their lives. However, as the news of the Committee's success spread, other scholars joined. Altogether, a total of 58 clerics had volunteered to participate in the Dialogue Committee. The dialogue sessions between the clerics and detainees were usually held two or three times a week, and some 400 detainees took part in the programme. Many of them who are committed to the programme subsequently renounced violence and returned to normal life after their release. They had their sentence reduced and were granted amnesty by the judge for displaying good conduct while in prison.

However, there were still some recidivists among the detainees who were released (Beg 2010). It might be due to the lack of aftercare support and, for some, they could not find a sustainable livelihood pushing them to return to their old path in order to survive.

Religious scholars saw the short-lived religious rehabilitation programme as a successful initiative albeit with many criticisms to the contrary. Several observers opined that the dialogue sessions were moving towards the detainees' acceptance on the legitimacy of the Yemeni government and gaining assurances from them not to commit violence within Yemen. For example, Osama bin Laden's former bodyguard, Nasser al-Bahri claimed that the dialogue was all the while a pretense and no 'complex dialogue took place' (Rabasa et al. 2010: 53). He explained that there was no serious exchange of views between detainees and clerics and that the authorities were only interested in securing the detainees' recognition of the Yemeni government as the legitimate authority.

Egypt

Religious rehabilitation efforts in Egypt began in the early 1990s. The programme was more of a collective deradicalisation programme targeted at the militant Islamist groups such as al-Gama'a al-Islamiyya (IG) and Egyptian Islamic Jihad (EIJ). The government deployed intermediaries including scholars from the Al-Azhar University and, at other times, clerics from the Muslim Brotherhood to convince the radical Islamists in prison (Blaydes and Rubin 2008).

The Egyptian religious rehabilitation model proved to be a success when IG leaders wrote several books to denounce the previous actions committed by the group and repudiating their ideology. Finally, in 2003, the Egyptian government released thousands of IG prisoners as a result of the group's deradicalisation (Ashour 2007: 624). The same goes for the EIJ; the government facilitated meetings between the leaders and the followers in prison to reach a compromise that they would be released in return for attending the deradicalisation programme. There are, however, some EIJ members who joined al-Qaeda (Ashour 2007: 105).

The question of why the IG leadership revised their previous interpretations and understandings of Islam remained unanswered. One possible explanation is that the leaders may have seen their lack of success as divine proof that they were doing something wrong. The leaders then 're-educated' the rank and file through prison tours and a series of dialogue. This 're-education' period consisted of intense 15-day sessions every six months. Detainees were free to ask any questions on any subject they wished (Rubin 2011: 30).

Iraq

Task Force 134 of the US forces is the unit in charge of overseeing detainee operations in Iraq. Under the leadership of Major General Douglas Stone, the US-run detention facilities implemented a rehabilitation programme in 2007.

The hardcore insurgents or – irreconcilables – were separated from those prisoners who could be rehabilitated. The irreconcilables were those who were likely to take up arms because they opposed the new situation in their country. For the religious rehabilitation component, local imams volunteered to conduct religious discussions for the detainees (Stone 2011: 103).

The imams contributed significantly to the programme to the extent that they created a database of radical arguments and prepared counter narratives supported by credible Islamic references. Religious courses were offered to the detainees. For detainees who completed the religious courses, they were granted family visits and were considered for early release. Between January and September 2008, about 10,000 detainees were released. In an attempt to minimise potential recidivism, detainees scheduled for release were made to take up an oath to abide by the law. A guarantor, usually a family member or a local tribal leader, will be liable to uphold this promise in exchange for a detainee's freedom (Rabasa et al. 2010: 79).

The religious education programme began in 2007 and was called the Religious Enlightenment Programme. It was later changed to Islamic Discussion Programme (IDP). It comprises three types of programmes. First, a four-day programme that focuses on the basic tenets of Islam for the moderate detainee population. Second, a three-week programme aimed at those who had already been exposed to radical teachings and/or had links with extremist organisations. Third, a six-week programme that was aimed at the most extreme detainees – those who have been involved with and/or committed terrorist activities and were devoutly extreme in their ideology. The overall objectives for these three IDPs were to increase detainees' understanding of the Quran, to assist in conducting discussion and reflection in a safe place and, most importantly, to prevent the allure of terrorist activities (Angell and Gunaratna 2011).

Each of the IDPss comprised two components: the religious component and the social component. All of the programmes had six hours of discussion a day except for Friday. Days were broken into three hours taught by a religious cleric and another three hours taught by a social worker. All clerics and social workers took part in intensive training programmes before commencing any sessions with the detainees. A guidebook was prepared and given to them as assistance in discussions, role-playing and other activities. The IDPs proved to be a vital component in terrorist rehabilitation in Iraq. So much so, some former detainees who went through the programmes have requested to return to prison and help the other detainees and work with prison officials (Angell and Gunaratna 2011).

Sri Lanka

The '6+1' rehabilitation model developed in Sri Lanka drew on the Singaporean experience but evolved with practice and components created to mirror aspects that the terrorist group Liberation Tigers of Tamil Eelam (LTTE) had previously manipulated. The six components included: (1) educational rehabilitation;

(2) vocational rehabilitation; (3) psychosocial and creative therapies for rehabilitation; (4) social, cultural and family rehabilitation; (5) spiritual and religious rehabilitation; and (6) recreational rehabilitation. The '+1' refers to community engagement, which involves working with various partners such as family members of the detainees and rehabilitation centre staff. In addition, members of the LTTE diaspora and the local community also play a significant role in the community engagement part of the programme. Like Saudi Arabia, Sri Lanka terms its detainees as beneficiaries (Dharmawardhane 2013).

The spiritual and religious component of the programme comprises several acts of worship including yoga and meditation sessions that were conducted by the Brahmi Kumari spiritual group from India. These yoga and meditation sessions sought to relax the mind and nurture a healthy balance between inner and outer worlds. Another type of meditation, which is called *Goenka Vipassana* (mindfulness training), was offered to beneficiaries. This training involves developing self-awareness of emotions and thoughts. Those beneficiaries trained in mindfulness encouraged others to practise the method of meditation. Religious leaders from various religions including Hindu, Sathya Sai and Christian organisations also conducted religious ceremonies, rites and rituals for the beneficiaries (Hettiarachchi 2013).

These programmes have an effective impact in helping beneficiaries to emotionally and morally reconcile with their past and develop a state of inner peace, to prepare them psychologically for the future.

Malaysia

Malaysia's experience in dealing with terrorism was in the mid-1940s, during the communist insurgency. Intermittently, from the 1960s to the 1980s, there had been threats arising from religious extremism. These threats arose due to misinterpretation of Islam, which was connected to each group's interests and struggles. After the communist insurgents surrendered in 1989, Malaysia faced security threats that stemmed from the revival of religious extremist and terrorist groups. Al-Ma'unah, the Kumpulan Mujahidin Malaysia and JI were some of the groups that posed security threats to the nation.

The rehabilitation programme in Malaysia is mainly headed by the Department of Islamic Development (JAKIM) in collaboration with the Prisons Department. The programme heavily involves religious dialogue led by JAKIM clerics. The programme has four main objectives. First, it aims to rehabilitate the detainees by correcting their misconstrued Islamic teachings. Second, it aims to identify the detainees' level of awareness based on an assessment of their understanding and approach towards Islamic teachings. Third, it aims to instil awareness of the roles and responsibilities as Malaysian citizens regardless of race or religion. Finally, it aims to explain to the detainees that their actions were against Islamic teaching.

The religious rehabilitation component started with a basic programme called *Tafaqquh Fiddin*, a monthly meeting where detainees received Islamic studies from JAKIM clerics. For those who did well in these sessions, they were enrolled into a special rehabilitation programme, which is an intensive programme that lasts for about five to seven days and is catered to a smaller group of five to ten detainees. Religious discussions usually revolved around the legitimacy of Malaysia as an Islamic nation. Detainees were educated on the system of governance that the Malaysian government is adopting, which is the implementation of *Sharia* alongside the secular legal code. This is an attempt for them not to preach violence in order to implement the *Sharia*. JAKIM is responsible for the bi-annual evaluations and monitoring of those who have gone through the programmes though the criteria for their release remain unclear.

There is also a special programme catered for the families of the detainees. JAKIM officials visit them and distribute their publications. Religious counselling sessions are also provided for them to discuss Islamic issues. The Malaysian authorities claimed 97 per cent success rate as they have deradicalised/rehabilitated 289 detainees from 2001 to 2012, of which 7 went back to the path of militancy (Zolkepli 2017).

Indonesia

The Indonesian approach to terrorist rehabilitation operates on an ad-hoc basis. It aims first to develop an intelligence network and second to return detainees to society. The religious rehabilitation component involves counselling sessions with the detainees although it does not have a huge influence other than cultural and psychological rehabilitation. Detainees are not willing to engage with religious clerics. Even the most prestigious scholars have little credibility in their eyes because they are seen as part of the government establishment that fails to establish Islamic law in Indonesia (Rabasa et al. 2010).

The religious counseling programme focuses on equipping detainees with the correct understanding of Islam. The main thrusts of the programme include refuting radical ideas, imbuing detainees with the rightful concepts of Islam. Thus far, the Penitentiary of the Indonesian Ministry of Law and Human Rights, along with the special counterterrorism unit Detachment 88, has been collaborating in calling clerics to counsel the detainees. Ex-terrorist members, such as Nasir Abas, a former JI leader, were also called in to assist the authorities in counselling programmes.

Before the rehabilitation process, assessments were carried out based on factors such as the position of the detainee within the terrorist network and his or her level of ideological conviction and mental state. This will help the authorities to assign what level of rehabilitation the detainees need. For instance, those with less involvement in a terrorist group would likely undergo rehabilitation process in group settings while the hardcore members go through it individually.

Detainees' families were provided with religious counselling as they could support the detainee upon his or her release by forging a common understanding of their religion.

Singapore

Singapore, a vibrant city state, was not spared from domestic terrorist threats. Singaporean authorities made their first arrest of 13 JI members in December 2001 and a second arrest of 18 JI members in August 2002. It was reported that this group had planned series of bomb attacks in Singapore that would have had a devastating outcome (Singapore Ministry of Home Affairs 2003). Aside from these group arrests, there were also individual arrests that took place.

A group of voluntary *ulama* or Islamic scholars are the ones who bear the responsibility in providing religious counselling to the JI detainees. The group is called the Religious Rehabilitation Group (RRG). It was formed after the government sought advice from two well-respected *ulama* in Singapore, namely Ustaz Ali Haji Mohamed and Ustaz Mohamad Hasbi Hassan. Both saw the need to come forward and address JI's deviant ideology and hence the formation of the group. The group performs counselling on a voluntary basis. RRG members come from varied educational backgrounds including both those who were trained locally and those who studied at renowned institutions such as the Al-Azhar University in Egypt, Madinah University in Saudi Arabia and the International Islamic University in Malaysia. While the male clerics perform counselling sessions to the detainees, the female clerics help to counsel the wives and children of those who are in detention.

In the early formation period, the RRG carried out extensive research before writing its own counselling manual. Two manuals have been written so far. These manuals serve as guidelines for the counsellors carrying out the religious counselling. The manuals address three major themes – understanding the present reality, correcting misunderstanding of Islamic concepts and managing hatred and anger (Hassan 2010).

It was not smooth sailing for RRG during its initial stage. RRG members were accused of being 'agents of the government' and 'hypocrites of Islam' by the detainees and some in the Muslim community viewed them with suspicion and second-guessed their intentions ('Sterling work against lure of terror', 2014). Nevertheless, RRG continued to strive to correct the JI detainees' distortion of Islamic teachings and assist them in reintegration. The counselling sessions were later extended to self-radicalised and pro-ISIS individuals. The hard work paid off. Together with social and psychological as well as religious rehabilitation, more than two-thirds of those who were detained since 2001 for terrorism-related activities have been released (Heng 2013).

RRG has made continuous efforts to demystify ideas that advocate segregation, hatred and violence, and replace them with messages of peace, tolerance and mutual understanding and the respect that Islam propagates. Beyond counselling, RRG also conducts seminars and community forums. The objective of reaching out to the community is for members of the public to have a clear perspective of Islam's position when it comes to extremism and violence, as well as to ensure that online terrorist propaganda does not sway them. For this, RRG has set up a website and a Facebook page to take the counter-narrative efforts online and to prevent the vulnerable from being led astray.[1]

Challenges

There are several challenges in initiating and sustaining religious rehabilitation programme. First, the authorities should understand that religion is being exploited to justify acts of terrorism. Religion is not the main reason why terrorism occurs; instead religion has been misinterpreted and misrepresented to legitimise violence. As such, dismantling the concepts of hate and bloodshed rests on the shoulders of religious scholars and clerics.

Second, implementing religious rehabilitation must also include other vital components of rehabilitation such as vocational rehabilitation. Once the detainees are released, they can immediately find a job to sustain their livelihood. Detainees who were indoctrinated to a 'lesser degree' might not require a stringent process of religious rehabilitation. Perhaps other modes of rehabilitation might be suitable for this group of detainees, for they might be motivated to conduct acts of terror based on emotional or financial reasons.

Third, prison personnel must be equipped to handle terrorist detainees through formal training. There are prison staffs who allow terrorist detainees free access in the prison to mix with other criminal detainees. These terrorists might indoctrinate other criminal detainees who will, in turn, join the terrorist network upon their release. Thus prison management and adequate training for staff is of the utmost importance.

Fourth, there is a lack of willingness on the part of some governments to facilitate clerics to engage with detainees. For example, in the Yemen the government was less interested in actual ideological engagement and more interested with political expediency. There was no post-release programme put in place, causing some of those who had been released to return to their old paths.

The list is not exhaustive as there might be other challenges that prevent some countries from establishing religious rehabilitation programmes. For some governments, identifying rightful scholars is a difficult task. As such, religious clerics must come forward and take on the responsibility of guiding the detainees to the right path. To introduce religious rehabilitation in prisons, due consideration must also be given to the conduciveness of the facility, be it regarding security or convenience.

Approaches to religious rehabilitation

The focus of religious rehabilitation is to counter the warped understanding of religious beliefs advocated by radicalised individuals. Through religious counselling, scholars attempt to familiarise them with traditional Islamic heritage and to introduce a positive understanding of mainstream religious concepts. The following are some of the approaches that practitioners may consider in conducting religious rehabilitation for radicalised individuals.

The teacher–student approach[2]

This approach entails the religious counsellor acting as a teacher to his or her student in a top-down hierarchal environment where teachings are articulated and followed without question by the radicalised individual. Counselling sessions are treated as student-centred religious learning sessions where the focus is on the student's learning rather than the teaching or counselling imparted by the teacher.

As a teacher/counsellor, he or she must be able not just to transmit 'declarative religious knowledge' (religious knowledge that can be communicated orally or in writing) but also to focus more on transmitting 'functioning religious knowledge'. This method emphasises that the students/counsellees should understand, apply, analyse, evaluate and create based on the religious knowledge gained.

This process stimulates a functioning approach especially when the teachers/counsellors encourage the students/counsellees to understand fundamental Islamic religious concepts and to relate them to real-life experiences. The students/counsellees will have the chance to examine the logic of an argument cautiously and critically before reaching a conclusion.

This approach aims to develop counsellee's learning capabilities in understanding and applying the religious knowledge gained during counselling sessions. In addition, counsellees can analyse and evaluate the different life circumstances he or she will face.

The da'i–mad'uw approach[3]

This approach involves a process that unfolds between equals – where the *mad'uw* or individual receives guidance from the *da'i* or preacher in order to become a better Muslim. In religious rehabilitation programmes, the *da'i* is the religious counsellor and the *mad'uw* is the counsellee. This approach aims to strengthen the relationship between counsellor and counsellee in the pursuit of facilitate positive development in rehabilitation.

This approach employs two techniques. First, the *da'i*/counsellor is required to motivate the *mad'uw*/counsellee to perform good deeds by explaining the rewards that will be forthcoming in this life and the hereafter. This process is known as *targheeb* and must be complemented with *tarheeb* or an attempt to warn against committing any sins by reminding of the consequences. This process allows the radicalised individuals to be exposed to a fair amount of Islamic scripture that prohibits unethical behaviours such as indiscriminate killing. At the same time, they are able to grasp the essence of Islam, which is based on compassion and mercy.

The second technique involves the three-step process of 'learn, unlearn and relearn'. In 'learning', the *dai'i* aids the *mad'uw* in guided learning on Islamic matters that the counsellee has no prior knowledge of. 'Unlearning' is an attempt to unsubscribe the *mad'uw* from radical narratives. The 're-learning' process encourages *mad'uw* to revisit and re-evaluate their understanding on Islamic matters, particularly on matters that contributed to radicalisation.

It can be observed that this approach is the way that Islam was propagated throughout history: the preacher or the learned one aspires to share his or her knowledge with others to elevate them to a better understanding of Islam. By implementing this approach, the counsellees acquire a new knowledge set as well as familiarity with an analytical process that helps them to replace dubious or deviated understanding with a sound and legitimate one.

The mufti–mustafti *approach*[4]

This approach is a manifestation of one-to-one counselling, which involves a religious counsellor taking up the role of a *mufti* and a detainee as a *mustafti*. A *mufti* is a rightful and legitimate authority on Islamic discourses and is responsible for issuing a *fatwa* or guidance to those who seek clarification about religious matters, in this case, to the *mustafti* or the one who seeks religious advice.

This approach enables a system of ideas being generated in which the *fatwa* is produced for the *mustafti*/counsellee to take heed. There are four essential stages in the formulation of a *fatwa*. The first stage involves the *mufti*/counsellor carrying out *taswir* or 'accurate conceptualisation' regarding understanding of an issue corresponding to the circumstances affecting the *mustafti*/counsellee and other realities on the ground. For example, when asked by the *mustafti*/counsellee about the permissibility of establishing an Islamic state through violent means, the *mufti* would need to address the *mustafti*s way of reasoning therefore prompting the counsellee to articulate the possible means by which such a state would be achieved.

The second stage requires the *mufti* to classify the issue under consideration according to the relevant categories under Islamic jurisprudence, a process known as *takyif* or 'classification'. For example, an issue may either be designated under 'acts of worships' or *jihad*. This process allows both parties to remain objective in the pursuit of seeking the truth.

The third stage calls for the *mufti* to perform *sharh* or 'explanation' in order to support the *fatwa*. At this stage, the explanation or evidences presented to *mustafti* are derived from the primary sources Islamic jurisprudence, i.e. the Quran, *Hadith* (prophetic traditions) and the consensus within the Islamic scholarly community.

The final stage is *isdar* or 'pronouncement'. At this point, the *mufti* would have established the ground that the *fatwa* does not violate the objectives of Islamic jurisprudence, does not contradict a definitive text in the Islamic legal tradition and is backed by unanimous consensus among Islamic scholars. This religious ruling or guidance is considered to be the exposition of rulings prescribed by God.

This approach aims to correct the mindset of a radicalised individual through series of steps of meticulous and customised guidance provided by the religious counsellor in the role of *mufti*. The intended goal is for the *mustafti* to understand how a religious ruling is made through arduous process and not as a simple reading of the Quran and *Hadith* and cherry-picking any verses or quotes to suit one's needs. This approach also carries the long-term effect of preventing radicalised individuals from being influenced by extremist narratives after being released from detention, due to their corrected pattern of thinking.

Conclusion

In the fight against terrorism, rehabilitation or deradicalisation can be seen as an innovative approach that goes beyond strategies that rely on harsh oppression and the detention of terrorists. Efforts to rehabilitate/deradicalise terrorists in prisons have provided a platform for convicted terrorists to express remorse, repent or recant their violent ideology. Religious scholars play a vital role in correcting the mindsets of detainees as they misinterpret religious concepts to serve their political end. Issues such as *jihad, takfir* (practice of excommunication) and *bai'ah* (pledge of allegiance) have been used by terrorist groups to justify their acts of aggression and violence.

The religious component in rehabilitation/deradicalisation programmes cannot be simply copied and pasted to suit the programme. While certain common principles can be shared among stakeholders, programmes must be tailored according to the demands of each country and be reflective of a continuous process of learning.

Religious rehabilitation should be part and parcel of a holistic approach in a deradicalisation programme. This is because unlike an ordinary detention process, the religious component of the programme targets the core of the problem, that is the religious ideologies misconstrued by terrorist groups. The religious component aims to eradicate the ideologies based on a misconstrued understanding of Islam and to replace them with the correct Islamic teachings. It is partly due to the success of the religious component, among others, that authorities had the confidence to release previously radicalised detainees back into society.

Notes

1 See www.rrg.sg and www.facebook.com/Religious-Rehabilitation-Group-RRG-218225878199660/.
2 For a full description of this approach see Mahfuh Haji Halimi, Muhammad Saiful Alam Shah Bin Sudiman and Zulkifli Mohamed Sultan (2014) 'The teacher–student approach to religious rehabilitation', *Counter Terrorist Trends and Analysis*, 6(2), March.
3 For a full description of this approach see Muhammad Saiful Alam Shah Bin Sudiman (2015) 'The *da'i–mad'uw* approach to religious rehabilitation', *Counter Terrorist Trends and Analysis*, 7(3), April.
4 For a full description of this approach see Ahmad Saiful Rijal Bin Hassan (2015) 'The *mufti–mustafti* approach to religious rehabilitation', *Counter Terrorist Trends and Analysis*, 7(3), April.

Bibliography

Angell, Ami and Rohan Gunaratna (2011) *Terrorist Rehabilitation: The U.S. Experience in Iraq*. Boca Raton, FL: CRC Press: 230–233, 270.
Ashour, Omar (2007) 'Lions tamed? An inquiry into the causes of de-radicalization of armed Islamist movements: the case of the Egyptian Islamic Group', *Middle East Journal*, 61(4), Autumn: 596–625.
Beg, Shahzadi (2010) 'Yemen's Committee for Dialogue', *1st Strategic Workshop on Rehabilitation and De-radicalization of Militants and Extremists*. Report on a Workshop

Organised by the FATA Secretariat Capacity Building Project, International Centre for Political Violence and Terrorism Research, 18–19 May: 15–18.

Blaydes, Lisa and Lawrence Rubin (2008) 'Ideological reorientation and counterterrorism: confronting militant Islam in Egypt', *Terrorism and Political Violence*, 20(4): 461–479.

Boucek, Christopher (2008) 'Saudi Arabia's "soft" counterterrorism strategy: prevention, rehabilitation, and aftercare', *Carnegie Papers*, (97): 1–27.

Dharmawardhane, Iromi (2013) 'Sri Lanka's post-conflict strategy: restorative justice for rebels and rebuilding of conflict-affected communities', *Perspectives on Terrorism*, 7(6): 35.

Gunaratna, Rohan (2009) 'The battlefield of the mind: rehabilitating Muslim terrorists,' *UNISCI Discussion Papers*: 148–163.

Hassan, Mohd Feisal Mohd (2010) 'Rehabilitation Programme in Singapore', *1st Strategic Workshop on Rehabilitation and De-radicalization of Militants and Extremists*. Report on a Workshop Organised by the FATA Secretariat Capacity Building Project, International Centre for Political Violence and Terrorism Research, 18–19 May.

Heng, Linette (2013) 'She fights terror her way', *Asiaone*, 29 March. Available at: www.asiaone.com/print/News/Latest%2BNews/Singapore/Story/A1Story20130327-411744.html (accessed 21 November 2016).

Hettiarachchi, Malkanthi (2013) 'Sri Lanka's rehabilitation programme: a new frontier in counter terrorism and counter insurgency', *PRISM: Journal of the Center for Complex Operations*, 4(2): 105–119.

International Centre for Political Violence and Terrorism Research (2010) *Combating Terrorism in Yemen through the Committee for Religious Dialogue: A Report on ICPVTR Visit to Yemen, Yemen*, July 2010.

Rabasa, Angela, Stacie L. Pettyjohn, Jeremy J. Ghez and Christopher Boucek (2010) *Deradicalizing Islamist Extremists*. Santa Monica, CA: RAND Corporation.

Rubin, Lawrence (2011) 'Non-kinetic approaches to counter-terrorism, a case study of Egypt and the Islamic Group', in Rohan Gunaratna, Jolene Jerard and Lawrence Rubin (eds) *Terrorist Rehabilitation and Counter-radicalisation*. New York: Routledge: 30.

Singapore Ministry of Home Affairs (2003) *The Jemaah Islamiyah Arrests and the Threat of Terrorism: White Paper*. Singapore: Ministry of Home Affairs.

'Sterling work against lure of terror', *The Straits Times*, 28 August 2014. Available at: www.straitstimes.com/opinion/sterling-work-against-lure-of-terror (accessed 21 November 2016).

Stone, Douglas M. (2011) 'Thinking strategically about terrorist rehabilitation', in Rohan Gunaratna, Jolene Jerard and Lawrence Rubin (eds) *Terrorist Rehabilitation and Counter-radicalisation*. New York: Routledge: 103.

Zolkepli, Farik (2017) 'Facing down terror', *The Star*, 23 April. Available at: www.thestar.com.my/news/nation/2017/04/23/facing-down-terror-the-man-who-leads-a-bukit-aman-division-in-fighting-terrorism-has-many-tales-to-s/ (accessed 4 May 2017).

4 Economic rehabilitation of terrorists
What can be learned from disarmament, demobilisation and reintegration programmes?

D.B. Subedi

Introduction

Rehabilitation of terrorists and violent extremists has recently emerged as a new field of policy and practice in the counterterrorism discourse as well as the discourse of countering violent extremism (CVE). Terrorist rehabilitation refers to a long-term process of transforming a terrorist's radical religious and ideological worldview and attendant attitudinal and behavioural patterns that drive terrorism and violence (Gunaratna 2011). The theory and practice of terrorist rehabilitation are premised on the proposition that punishing terrorists and extremists and alienating them from the rest of the society, for instance with imprisonment, cannot successfully deradicalise and disengage them from the terrorist networks and ideologies they held. Rather evidence suggests that imprisonment of terrorists has become a facilitator of radicalisation or re-radicalisation by fellow terrorist inmates (Mulcahy, Merrington and Bell 2013). A rehabilitation programme happening outside of a prison is, therefore, incredibly necessary. It is this proposition that has given impetus to the idea of community-based rehabilitation.

A number of dilemmas surrounds the rehabilitation of terrorists and violent extremists. The first is the dilemma of participation; that is the debate and contention around who should be involved in the rehabilitation programme: the terrorists and extremists, their families and community members in addition to the government and security personnel. Recognising that rehabilitation is a multi-dimensional process, recently it has been argued that the role of family and community in terrorist rehabilitation cannot and should not be overlooked (Gunaratna 2011).

Second, the dilemma concerns the programmatic focus of rehabilitation. In other words, in traditional rehabilitation programmes differences persist with regard to whether a rehabilitation programme should consist of social, economic, security and psychological dimensions. Traditional rehabilitation programmes focused a lot on the security dimension positing deradicalisation as a threat and challenge rather than seeing it as an opportunity to transform radicalised fighters into productive and well-adjusted civilians. As a result, most rehabilitation programmes in the past happened in prison with a limited engagement of community members (Gunaratna 2015). This dynamic is, however, changing with rehabilitation programmes involving religious rehabilitation, social rehabilitation, vocational rehabilitation and psychological rehabilitation (Gunaratna 2015).

Finally, a notable dilemma still persists with regard to what should be an anticipated outcome of a rehabilitation programme or, in other words, what is it intended to achieve – deradicalisation, disengagement, identity transformation of a terrorist, community acceptance of terrorists and, by default, better security outcomes for all of them. The debates and contention around this issue are ongoing although an ideal-type rehabilitation programme may aim, albeit ambitiously, to achieve as many of these outcomes as possible while the actual outcomes may depend on the infrastructures and social and economic conditions intrinsic to a rehabilitation programme.

Contrary to a traditional terrorist rehabilitation programme that mostly involves religious and ideological de-indoctrination and teaching and prison-based correctional methods, a new approach, which is recently gaining traction, recognises the role of both state and non-state actors including non-government organisations as well as the family of the terrorists themselves (Koehler 2017). This approach, which favours multi-actor, multi-dimensional and multi-layered processes of rehabilitation happening both in prisons and community where relevant, characterises what might be called the 'second generation' of terrorist rehabilitation programmes. In the words of Gunaratna (2015: 20), this kind of programme embraces a 'smart approach' to fighting terrorism and violent extremism.

This chapter expands the idea of the smart approach to terrorist rehabilitation by focusing on the economic dimension of rehabilitation or 'economic rehabilitation' – the dimension that involves economic activities by and for participants of rehabilitation and the way they facilitate the participants' involvement in economic life non-violently (Subedi 2014a). Recognising that economic rehabilitation complements and is complemented by social and psychosocial rehabilitation, this chapter also examines the links between economic and non-economic factors and conditions and the way they either facilitate or constrain rehabilitation. In doing so, social capital – defined here as social networks, trust and reciprocal relationships between individuals and groups (Putnam 1995) – as a theoretical approach is employed to further the idea of economic rehabilitation.

The theoretical approach presented in this chapter draws on the rich experience and diverse insights from ex-combatant-focused rehabilitation programmes in the context of disarmament, demobilisation and reintegration (DDR) in conflict and in post-conflict contexts. In countries emerging from civil wars and armed conflicts, DDR programmes aim at separating combatants and fighters from the weapons they possess, detaching them from their armed mobilisers and facilitating ex-combatants' re-entry into society as civilians (Muggah 2010; Özerdem 2009; Subedi 2014b). While it is acknowledged here that terrorist rehabilitation and DDR may come from different political, ideological and security contexts, there are also similarities. For instance, both DDR and terrorist rehabilitation involve interventions aimed at disengaging ex-combatants or terrorists respectively from their violent mobilisers and supporting them to adopt non-violent worldviews and life gradually. The idea of the transformation of an individual who subscribes to radical, extremist and violent worldviews into a civilian member of mainstream society connects the philosophical underpinning of rehabilitation programmes focused on both ex-combatants and terrorists. Furthermore, DDR and terrorist rehabilitation have also tended to merge in places where armed conflict overlaps with violent extremism such as in Libya, Iraq, Afghanistan and Somalia, among other countries.

The chapter begins by discussing similarities and differences between ex-combatant-focused rehabilitation and terrorist rehabilitation programmes and makes a case to claim that the insights and experiences drawn from ex-combatant-focused rehabilitation programmes could be useful to improve the practice of terrorist rehabilitation programmes. A discussion about economic rehabilitation and its different facets follows, with particular focus on the social-capital approach to economic rehabilitation. The last section highlights the key conclusions of the chapter.

Rehabilitation of ex-combatants and terrorists: similarities and differences

Since the United Nations first deployed a DDR mission in Central America in 1989, DDR has established itself as an important tool for addressing armed conflict, preventing violence and building peace in troubled areas affected by armed conflicts and civil wars. While the focus of disarmament in a DDR programme is on the collection, documentation, control and disposal of small arms, ammunition, explosives and light and heavy weapons used by combatants, demobilisation refers to the formal and controlled discharge of active combatants from armed forces or other armed groups (United Nations 2006). Reintegration or rehabilitation of ex-combatants, however, is a long-term and complex process through which ex-combatants acquire civilian status by gaining sustainable employment and income and also by rebuilding relationships with families and communities (United Nations 2006). Reintegration and rehabilitation are decisive elements of DDR because it entails both social and economic processes and a passage for ex-combatants to transform from an actor of violence to a part of the citizenry.

In the initial years of DDR programmes in the 1980s, the first generation of reintegration programmes perceived ex-combatants as security threats from micro (community) to macro (national and regional) levels; therefore much of the emphasis of reintegration then was on using reintegration and rehabilitation as an instrument of security promotion rather than seeing it as a means of transforming ex-combatants' identities and the social and economic conditions necessary to return to civilian life (Muggah 2010). As such, the first generation of reintegration programmes was highly security centric with limited roles for non-state actors such as ex-combatants' families and kin, and social networks. The security-centric approach to rehabilitation has, however, changed over the time in the 'second generation' of reintegration programmes. The subsequent rehabilitation and reintegration programmes expanded the focus of the programme from ex-combatants as the only target of rehabilitation to incorporating other state and non-state actors. Thus, much emphasis was placed on (1) changing and transforming identities of ex-combatants by engaging them in jobs and livelihood; (2) shifting the focus from security promotion to security, peace and development as the primary outcomes of rehabilitation; (3) providing psychosocial support to ex-combatants so that politically and ideologically radicalised and violent ex-combatants are gradually able to disengage from violent ideologies, attitudes and worldviews; and (4) involving families and communities so that ex-combatants are better accepted when they return to their communities (Özerdem 2002; Buxton 2008; Kilroy 2015). As such, identity transformation, social-capital formation, jobs and livelihood have emerged as major concepts that profoundly affect how ex-combatants can be deradicalised, de-mobilised and rehabilitated back into the society from where they emerged as an actor of violence.

With regard to programmatic focus, rehabilitation and reintegration programmes include two different but highly interconnected and interdependent economic and social dimensions. While the economic dimension of rehabilitation is crucial to generate jobs, skills and livelihoods for ex-combatants, social rehabilitation aims to rebuild the social, familial and personal networks of ex-combatants (Bowd and Özerdem 2013). Economic rehabilitation is dependent on or determined by social rehabilitation and vice versa because previous studies have shown that jobs and livelihood are important determinants of how economic independence reconstructs the social status and identity of ex-combatants, hitherto defined by violence (Subedi 2014a; Bowd 2002).

A goal of terrorist rehabilitation, on the other hand, is to strengthen the state's capability to deal with terrorists and violent extremists so that the rehabilitated terrorists will not pose security risks in future, hence working to reduce the recidivism rate among former terrorists. In this sense, an ideal type of terrorist rehabilitation programme is expected to 'reintegrate individuals into society through a de-radicalisation process that includes (religious) re-education, psychological counselling, social engagement and vocational training (when necessary)' (Gunaratna and Rubin 2011).

Terrorist rehabilitation is a multi-faceted and multi-dimensional process with emphasis on the religious, psychological, social and vocational dimensions of rehabilitation (Gunaratna and Rubin 2011). While the emerging multi-dimensional approach to rehabilitation is innovative and holds the potential to disengage and deradicalise terrorists and ultimately facilitate their rehabilitation into society, implanting such multi-dimensional rehabilitation programmes requires a balance between hard-security approaches and soft-security approaches to rehabilitation. A hard-security approach generally involves the use of force including surveillance, policing and the implementation of anti-terror laws as part of counterterrorism strategies, while, by contrast, a soft-security approach is based on understanding of social, cultural and political drivers of violence and finding ways to address their causes by involving both state and non-state actors (Subedi and

Jenkins 2016). In practice, friction continues on the ground between those who specialise in hard-security approaches to counterterrorism and those who favour soft-security approaches. As a result, there is always a risk and danger present for the rehabilitation programmes to be overtaken by a hard-security counterterrorism approach where the role of non-state actors such as civil society organisations, community, families of terrorists and religious leaders might be undermined. Notwithstanding the controversy with regard to the approach taken, when it comes to rehabilitating terrorists, it is argued that balancing between hard and soft approaches would change terrorist rehabilitation from being a challenge to an opportunity for addressing causes of radicalisation and drivers of re-radicalisation and recidivism (Gunaratna and Rubin 2011).

Differences

Ex-combatant-focused rehabilitation and terrorist rehabilitation programmes have notable differences. Most importantly, such differences are visible particularly with regard the context, namely where these programmes take place. Rehabilitation of ex-combatants takes place in conflict and post-conflict situations where political, criminal and opportunistic violence is an outcome of an armed conflict (Özerdem 2009). By contrast, terrorist rehabilitation takes place in situations where terrorists and violent extremists are in the process of exiting opportunistic networks of terrorists and highly radicalised groups, either voluntarily or through a facilitated process such as deradicalisation and disengagement in prisons. Not all terrorist rehabilitation happens in post-conflict contexts, although there are post-conflict countries where DDR programmes are geared towards aligning with the rehabilitation of extremists and terrorists, as is the case in Somalia, Libya, Afghanistan, Sri Lanka and Iraq.

However, rehabilitation of ex-combatants can take place in the highly political environment of transition from war to peace coupled with substantial financial assistance from donors such as the case of the rehabilitation of the National Armed Forces for the Liberation of East Timor combatants in Timor Leste and the rehabilitation of the Maoist People's Liberation Army combatants in Nepal. By contrast, terrorist rehabilitation programmes are relatively free from politicisation as is the case of Saudi Arabia, Iraq, Yemen, Singapore and Malaysia. The contextual differences also refer to the different capacities of the states in question. Apart from countries in the Global South where violent extremism, terrorism and armed conflicts are deeply interconnected, a majority of contemporary terrorist rehabilitation programmes has taken place in politically stable and economically strong states such as Indonesia, Malaysia, Singapore, Denmark, Australia and Saudi Arabia. Therefore, terrorist rehabilitation programmes in these countries do not experience resource constraints, which are characteristic of most post-conflict and fragile countries where rehabilitation programmes are highly donor dependent.

Unlike ex-combatant-focused rehabilitation programmes, which mainly operate in communities, terrorist rehabilitation programmes, especially rehabilitation of Islamist radical terrorists, typically begin in prisons and isolation with religious deradicalisation as a first intervention to make a terrorist mentally free from radical religious and ideological worldviews. Prison-based religious and psychological and religious deradicalisation are often followed by a guided community-based rehabilitation phase in which new non-state actors such as community leaders, families and the private sector are invited to become involved (Awan 2013; Entenmann et al. 2016).

Similarities

Despite some differences, similarities exist between the two types of rehabilitation programmes. One such similarity lies in the long-term goal of rehabilitation programmes. A basic philosophical similarity that underpins ex-combatant-focused rehabilitation and terrorist rehabilitation is that both types of actors of violence are the product of coercive or voluntary modes of radicalisation (be it religious, ideological or political) or an extreme motivation to support and drive violence for the quest of justice; these phenomena are socially constructed and can, therefore, be transformed through external intervention, support and facilitation. This philosophical proposition implies that terrorism and armed conflict can be addressed and that rehabilitation is an opportunity not a threat.

While terrorist rehabilitation programmes aim to prevent ex-terrorists being re-engaged, re-radicalised and remobilised by their terrorist networks (Gunaratna and Rubin 2011), ex-combatant-focused rehabilitation programmes also aim to prevent remobilisation of ex-combatants in violence by extremists and radical elements as well as by former mobilisers of former combatants (Subedi 2014c). With the goal of the prevention of recidivism and remobilisation, both types of rehabilitation programme have shared objectives: security promotion and identity transformation of the participants of rehabilitation. In other words, violence prevention and social integration through external facilitation and support are fundamental to the rehabilitation programmes either focused on ex-combatants or violent extremists and terrorists. Focus on this particular form of similarity is requisite to understand fully how the long experience in the field of DDR can generate new insights into expanding the smart approach to terrorist rehabilitation.

Understanding economic rehabilitation

In a DDR programme, a major concern for rehabilitation and reintegration of ex-combatants is on reconnecting them back to jobs and livelihoods, and this priority is premised on the proposition that a healthy civilian identity can be encouraged by economic activities promoted through vocational training and constructive works that contribute to individual and community well-being (International Labour Organization 1997). Thus, economic rehabilitation, by default, involves a range of activities by and for ex-combatants. These include creating jobs for ex-combatants either in the public or the private sector, enhancing their vocational and entrepreneurial skills and capacities, livelihood skills in such areas as farming, micro-enterprises and business, and the education needed for sustaining employment and income (Vencovsky 2006; International Labour Organization 2009). Economic rehabilitation also involves such skills, capacities and abilities to interact with people in economic spaces or, in other words, markets, in a non-violent way, and acquiring the skills and capacities to put vocational skills into practice in a sustained way without being influenced by any extremists or radical worldviews (Subedi 2014a). In this sense, the scope of economic rehabilitation is wider than that of vocational rehabilitation. According to Gunaratna (2011: 72), while vocational rehabilitation is

> designed to provide necessary skills for a job, vocational rehabilitation imparts skills useful to detainees and inmates upon release; this ranges from teaching them metal and woodwork, carpentry and masonry, dairy farming and agriculture, computer and language skills, and self-study and distance education.

Given that economic rehabilitation aims to promote skills and capabilities and opportunities, personal qualities and life skills (e.g. communication, interpersonal relations) for employability, vocational rehabilitation could actually be an element of economic rehabilitation.

The significance of economic rehabilitation goes beyond a mere livelihood concern to highlighting how one's economic freedom helps to create a dignified civilian identity and well-being. Thus, in a minimalist sense, economic rehabilitation of ideologically radicalised ex-combatants refers to creating jobs or sustainable livelihoods that will enable them to contribute to local development in the long run (Bragg 2006; SIDDR 2006; United Nations 2010). Yet, in the maximalist sense, economic rehabilitation is central to the processes of one's identity (re)construction, an identity that is non-violent, non-radical and is a part of mainstream society.

If carried out effectively and successfully, economic rehabilitation might also help to prevent recidivism and remobilisation of ex-combatants or terrorists. The relationship between poverty and terrorism is not so simple; indeed, this has become a subject of ongoing debate and controversy in counterterrorism and CVE studies. Some argue that, on the one hand, not all poor people become combatants and that not all poor people support extremist ideas (Brett and Specht 2004). On the other hand, poor, vulnerable, socially and economically marginalised youth have become the targets of terrorist recruitment efforts in such countries as Mali, Afghanistan, Somalia and Iraq among others. It is also argued that reducing poverty will only have a modest positive impact on counterterrorism while supporting poverty reduction and improving human security could be a relevant strategy to counterterrorism in places where armed conflict and violent extremism overlap such as in sub-Saharan Africa (Shinn 2016). That means while it would be simplistic to argue that reducing poverty reduces terrorism, it can, nonetheless, be contended that economic empowerment through jobs, employment or self-employment, sustainable income and sustained livelihood would minimise mobilisation of young people by terrorists and extremists who tend to target poor, economically vulnerable and marginalised youth in the Global South.

Thus, the idea of economic rehabilitation is important and in fact extremely necessary to help someone who is willing to exit a violent network and willing to be seen as an economically independent and socially dignified member of society. Since the ultimate goal of economic rehabilitation is to reconnect an ex-combatant to society, economic rehabilitation cannot operate in isolation from social interactions and social processes. In other words, economic rehabilitation and social rehabilitation are interdependent and share mutually reinforcing characteristics (Özerdem 2012).

Economic rehabilitation: what we can learn from ex-combatant-focused programmes?

Economic rehabilitation of ex-combatants depends on several non-economic factors and conditions such as political support from community members. However, the literature suggests that how and the extent to which ex-combatants can succeed in economic rehabilitation depends on their ability to gain social capital during and after the rehabilitation programme. This section discusses economic rehabilitation from a social-capital approach, with particular emphasis on the influence of social variables such as social networks, social relations, interaction and communication, and community participation and how they influence one's ability to engage in economic activities actively.

Social capital and economic rehabilitation

Social capital refers to non-material resources that are essential for individuals and groups to improve their social, political and economic opportunities (Adler and Kwon 2002). Social and personal networks, trust and interaction between individuals or groups enhance their social capital. One's economic participation and livelihood strategy is thought to depend on one's social capital because social relationships such as kinship, friendship, patron–client relations, relationships of trust, reciprocal arrangements, membership of formal groups and membership of organisations that provide loans, grants and other forms of insurance on which people can draw, work to expand livelihood options (Department for International Development 1997).

Depending on what function social capital plays in connecting people and groups, social capital is divided into two main categories: bonding social capital and bridging social capital (Putnam 2000). Bonding social capital enhances networks, relationships and connections between and among in-group members, whereas bridging social capital is an inter-group connector, which links groups and means group membership is extended to out-group members (Putnam 2000).

Social capital has both positive and negative functions. On the positive side, social capital is a productive resource, which connects people within groups.

Therefore, it is an in-group connector. Putnam calls this 'bridging' social capital (Putnam 2000). By contrast, another type of social capital is exclusionary and violence-prone. The study of criminal gangs in Russia revealed the dark side of the bonding social capital, which was instrumental in bringing actors of violence together and facilitating crimes collectively (Gilbert 2009). Bonding capital can exclude 'others' and non-members of a group from gaining access to resources, and this can alienate and divide people who are excluded from group membership (Gilbert 2009; Micolta 2009). While bridging social capital is essential for promoting social harmony, by contrast, bonding social capital creates social enclaves and alienates certain groups from social and political processes.

Ex-combatants form a physical as well as symbolic community with other ex-combatants, sharing a collective identity associated with armed conflict and violence. The shared identity is also a source of bonding social capital. It is, however, the bridging social capital – the ability and efficiency to reconnect with wider society – that is crucially important for ex-combatants' economic as well as social rehabilitation. For this reason, a social-capital approach to rehabilitation warrants efforts to examine the roles that families and communities play in the rehabilitation process.

Family and community

The literature demonstrates that family is a primary constituency in economic and social rehabilitation. In El Salvador, for example, a vast majority of reintegrated combatants stated that being reunified with their family was the most significant factor in transitioning to civilian life (Verhey 2001). Previous studies have shown that ex-combatants who are able to receive support from family, and kinship and social network find it easier to excel in jobs, micro-businesses, and earning livelihoods.

In Nepal, most of the Maoist ex-combatants were heavily radicalised with violent Maoist political ideology at the time of their recruitment and during the Maoist armed conflict (1996–2006) (Subedi 2013a; Eck 2010). When these ideologically radicalised ex-combatants returned from the war in 2012, they were provided with a cash package, categorised into four levels. Those falling in the lowest rank received 500,000 Nepalese rupees (NRs)[1] while the three remaining higher categories received NRs 600,000, NRs 700,000, and NRs 800,000, respectively, in ascending order (Subedi 2014b). The idea of rehabilitation consisted of an accompanied and facilitated rehabilitation package worth a minimum of NRs 600,000 to a maximum of NRs 900,000, including a provision for educational support and vocational training opportunities (Subedi 2014b). It was found that ex-combatants who were able to reconnect or forge social capital – that is building networks and connections with families, friends and kinship networks – found it easy to earn livelihoods through micro-enterprises, small businesses or jobs in the private sector. Family support in accessing credits for micro-businesses and self-employment was highly useful in this case, while the moral and emotional support ex-combatants receive in their transition to civilian life is perhaps the most important asset that family can provide. Thus, at the time of rehabilitation, family support functions as a safety net.

There are, however, some issues that must be considered. First, there is always difficulty in tracing the family link for someone who had joined an armed militia, insurgency or terrorist network for a significant part of their life, particularly if this began during childhood. In some cases, those who were separated from family at an early age can be reluctant to return to their families (Dolan and Schafer 1997). The extra economic burden caused by returnees to the family can also make some families unwilling to welcome the member who may have been away for a decade or more. Families may not always accept ex-combatants back because of a degree of stigma associated with how society at large perceives ex-combatants. In other words, when ex-combatants have a highly atrocious and incredibly violent background, for example, by joining an opportunistic and criminal network, the family might be reluctant to welcome ex-combatants home. In this situation, regular psychosocial counselling to families is as important as preparing an ex-combatant to return home.

From an economic rehabilitation point of view, some form of financial assistance, or what is known as 'insertion support', provided not only to ex-combatants but also to their families will reduce the economic burden of a household and it might also indirectly motivate families to accept ex-combatants (Özerdem and Podder 2008). The idea of insertion support as an economic 'safety net' for ex-combatants and their families would be necessary to cover additional expenses such as buying utensils, clothing and food, which are generally incurred at the time of receiving the ex-combatant back into the family. Apart from the economic value of insertion support, it can also function as a facilitator of social ties between returnee ex-combatants and their families.

The extent to which ex-combatants are accepted into or are willing to join a family can also be determined by how ex-combatants are accepted in the community. For instance, in Ethiopia, the more the ex-combatants participated in community activities, the better was the acceptance of the spouse and family (Özerdem and Podder 2008). This means that the role of family in economic rehabilitation is partly contingent upon the role of community.

Defining a community can be tricky, as the notion of community embraces both geographical/territorial and non-territorial/spatial or symbolic dimensions.[2] In peace, conflict and security studies, a community, therefore, must be defined in physical terms where people of similar backgrounds, identity and common social cause live and come together to pursue collective agendas. However, the community also must be defined in symbolic terms because people who do not necessarily live in a fixed territory can be connected to a common cause virtually. A community for a terrorist operates as a symbolic community rather than only a physical community. However, from a rehabilitation point of view, a community is often a graphically bounded physical and social setting, which facilitates social actions and interactions, and includes formal and informal social organisations and institutions.

Armed conflict disintegrates social structures, dividing people into an 'us' versus 'them' polarisation (Özerdem 2012: 63). Such polarisation has negative implications for ex-combatants' acceptance into the community, as was the case in Liberia and Sierra Leone (Özerdem 2012: 63). Verkoren (2005) provides an account of how a degree of mistrust and hostility between Khmer Rouge ex-combatants and people in the community had a negative impact on the acceptance of ex-combatants in the Khmer society in Cambodia.

Similarly, how the community perceives, celebrates or demonises an ex-combatant's identity has further implications. According to Özerdem, if ex-combatants return home as 'heroes' of war then social acceptance can be much easier than in a post-conflict environment where they are viewed as troublemakers (Özerdem 2012). It is obvious that the troublemakers are not easily accepted, but are, in fact, rejected by communities. This raises an important question about whether rehabilitation programmes can facilitate community acceptance. From experience in ex-combatant-focused rehabilitation programmes, it is learned that if ex-combatants are provided with material and physical support while other vulnerable youths are overlooked, it raises enormous tensions between ex-combatants and local communities. Therefore, to avert potential tension between the communities and ex-combatants, rehabilitation programmes must also include community-focused elements such as local development, community dialogue, social-cohesion support and so on.

From an economic rehabilitation point of view, if local communities do not accept ex-combatants, the chances of their engagement in economic activities such as jobs, or self-entrepreneurship after training and vocation education will not work effectively. There is a potential impact of identity on an ex-combatant's economic performance. Stereotyping of the identity of an ex-combatant is harmful to his/her economic performance and prosperity. In Nepal, for instance, the negative impact of identifying ex-combatants has led to ex-combatant marginalisation in the job market and disregard by local community members and businesses (Subedi 2014a).

The private sector, social capital and economic rehabilitation

Economic rehabilitation is almost unimaginable without the active and meaningful participation of the private sector mainly because the private sector is the largest job creator and is an incredibly important economic actor in the local and international economic systems. In the literature, the rationale for engaging the private sector in a rehabilitation programme is mainly justified with the view that the private sector has the potential to offer jobs to ex-combatants and absorb this labour force into the market (International Alert 2006).

Although the business of the private sector is to make a profit and some actors of the private sector benefit from the shadow economy that survives in conflict and insecurity (Subedi 2013b), the private sector, in general, has tremendous interest in peace and security and therefore it can be an important actor in peacebuilding and counterterrorism.

First and foremost, terrorism, armed conflict and violence cause losses in businesses and disrupt the business environment, which is detrimental to the growth of the private sector as well as to economic growth. Therefore, the interest of the private sector in peace and security emerges from its interests to protect business and improve the economic climate. It was for this reason that the Business for Peace Alliance in South Africa played a critical role in bringing conflicting parties to the negotiation table during the Apartheid conflict (International Alert 2006). In other conflict-affected countries, such as in Nepal, Northern Ireland and Columbia, the role of the private sector in conflict transformation was highly regarded while the private sector also expressed a commitment to offer jobs to ex-combatants (International Alert 2006).

In a rehabilitation programme, the private sector can perform several roles. In Nepal, for example, the private sector was involved in providing vocational and skill-based training to minors and unverified Maoist ex-combatants between 2010 and 2011. In Sri Lanka, for instance, the Sri Lankan blue-chip companies provided vocational training to build skills of the Liberation Tigers of Tamil Eelam cadres (Hettiarachchi 2014). The role of the private sector is valued as a vocational training provider where terrorism and armed violence weaken government capacity to deliver public services and programmes around human-capital formation.

The private sector, however, should not only be seen as a passive participant in a rehabilitation programme. Rather, it must be involved in the designing and training of workers in vocational programmes to increase the private sector's ownership in a rehabilitation programme. If an intended outcome of a vocational training and job internship is to support the participation of a rehabilitation programme to access jobs in the private sector, then it is highly important to ensure that vocational packages or self-entrepreneurship training packages meet the needs and demands of the market and other private-sector stakeholders (International Labour Organization 2009). Any mismatch between the market's need and the nature of vocational training will result in the failure of the rehabilitation programme.

Human capital and economic rehabilitation

The involvement of the private sector in a rehabilitation programme, however, cannot be taken for granted, partly because the private sector is hesitant to recruit people with violent backgrounds. Also, it has been found that participants of a rehabilitation programme who have been radicalised either religiously or politically and have been involved in armed conflicts, insurgencies or terrorism for a long time often lack the life skills and capacities to interact within the private sector. These life skills include, for example, inter-personal non-violent communication (both horizontal communication with peers and vertical communication with supervisors or managers), and the capacity to work with diverse teams

(Subedi 2014a). An economic rehabilitation programme, therefore, remains incomplete if it only focuses on enhancing vocation skills but ignores the life skills needed to succeed in jobs or businesses.

Education and psychosocial counselling play an important role in imparting life skills, which refer to education, knowledge and health, and these are the elements of human capital (Department for International Development 1997).

The private sector engagement: context matters

Every rehabilitation programme is unique; its economic, social and psychosocial dimensions and the elements they entail cannot be generalised, partly because the nature of a rehabilitation programme depends on the nature of the participants and the context in which the programme takes place. If a rehabilitation programme is implemented in a context where armed conflict overlaps with violent extremism, as is the case in Somalia, Afghanistan and Libya, the private sector might have a more limited role to play. In such contexts, the private sector itself is one of the frontline victims of armed conflict – a dwindling economic environment in which there is little that we can expect from the private sector in rehabilitating ex-combatants or extremists. A private-sector development programme in parallel with a rehabilitation programme is recommended so that the private sector is able to absorb human capital and labour forces of which the participants of a rehabilitation programme are a part. The reduction of barriers to doing business and access to credit, technology and technical support are some of the recommendations made to motivate the private sector to contribute to the rehabilitation of ex-combatants (SIDDR 2006).

On the contrary, if a rehabilitation programme, especially a terrorist rehabilitation programme, is implemented in economically stable and fast-growing countries such as Malaysia, Singapore, Indonesia and Saudi Arabia, the private sectors in those locales are mature and strong, so that they can play a bigger role. Such roles might include not only providing jobs to the participants of rehabilitation but also helping to implement violence-prevention programmes as part of the private sector's corporate social responsibility programme.

Conclusions: towards a social-capital approach to terrorist rehabilitation

This chapter has shown that rehabilitation of ex-combatants has evolved as a specialised field of practice in DDR programmes in conflict and post-conflict settings. More than three decades of DDR experiences have resulted in rehabilitating ex-combatants socially and economically. Building on a critical review of the DDR literature and practice, this chapter maintains that terrorist rehabilitation as part of counterterrorism and CVE discourse, which is still in its infancy, can learn valuable insights and lessons from DDR practices.

This is not to overstate that DDR and terrorist rehabilitation are similar phenomena. Indeed, there are contextual and ideological differences as highlighted in this chapter. However, there are some similarities worth considering when transferring lessons from DDR to CVE. A notable similarity of both DDR and CVE is the common objective of deradicalisation (either religious, political or psychological), and security promotion and peace. Both programmes deal with non-state security actors and the context. This results in the dynamics of armed conflict, terrorism and violence, which are socially, politically and psychologically constructed; this can be addressed, prevented, altered or transformed.

Prevention of violence and transformation of radical ideology is, therefore, a key underlying guiding principle that is central to rehabilitation programmes, whether focused on ex-combatants or terrorists. Transformation as an underlying principle implies that rehabilitation programmes must take a multi-dimensional transformative approach, which is hardly possible with a hard-security approach alone. Rather, transformation envisioned as an outcome of a rehabilitation programme should not only happen in one's mental and psychological domain but also in social, economic and societal or relational domains. This multi-faceted domain of change is what makes a rehabilitation programme a critical site of engagement for myriad actors including state actors and non-state actors. It is this critical premise of theory and praxis that draws parallels between DDR, counterterrorism and CVE programmes.

The critical transformative perspective adopted in this chapter in analysing ex-combatant-focused rehabilitation in a DDR context further suggests that rehabilitation has an important economic dimension, which shapes and is shaped by the social dimensions of rehabilitation. Thus, another lesson that can be drawn from DDR programmes is that economic rehabilitation of a terrorist must be conceived at an early programming stage taking into account the economic, social and psychological needs of participants so that the rehabilitation programme becomes collaborative not just an intervention imposed from above.

The interconnectedness of economic and social dimensions also means that the concept of economic rehabilitation is and should be fairly broad by contrast to a rather narrow focus on vocational rehabilitation. Vocational rehabilitation carries a minimalist approach because the emphasis is given to enhancing the skills and capacities needed to enter into the job market. By contrast, the insights from a DDR programme, as discussed in this chapter, reveal that economic rehabilitation should also include such elements as life skills, capacities and abilities so that participants of rehabilitation programmes can transfer vocational skill into practice and, in the long run, sustain jobs, employment or self-employment. In other words, economic rehabilitation is not only about imparting skills but also providing support to take advantage of those skills when participants enter into a highly competitive job market. Depending on the context, this might also require combining psychological and religious rehabilitation with economic rehabilitation. This must be done in a non-linear fashion because rehabilitation support that is inflexible and sequenced without taking account of local market needs, social contexts and individual capacity of participants is bound to fail.

The DDR literature also suggests that success of economic rehabilitation depends on individual context. Not all former terrorists are equally able to reconnect with society as a whole, including their families, peers and kinship and social networks. There has been much emphasis in ex-combatant-focused rehabilitation on the role of social capital as a facilitator of economic and social rehabilitation. As this chapter has discussed at length, social capital that emerges from family and community support functions as a safety net during an ex-combatant's transition to civilian life. It also removes the stigma attached to identity and provides ex-combatants with the moral, emotional, financial and other necessary support needed to succeed in employment or self-employment.

In terrorist rehabilitation programmes across South and Southeast Asia and the Middle East, the role of families and communities is essential in transforming the radicalised worldview, outlook, behaviour and attitudes to eventually prevent recidivism. In Saudi Arabia, Malaysia, Somalia and Yemen, for instance, the role of family or tribal elders and religious leaders was integral in changing ideological, political and radical attitudes, behaviour and worldviews (Botha and Abdile 2014; Fink 2015). However, the extent to which family and community, as well as the private sector, have played any role in helping rehabilitate participants in the economic rehabilitation process is unknown.

The fact that social capital also reduces the social stigma associated with the identity of an ex-combatant helps us to argue further that the social-capital approach to economic rehabilitation is fundamental to preventing recidivism, transforming the identity of ex-terrorists and helping them achieve economic independence to enable them to reject radical ideologies and a radical worldview. A key conclusion that must be noted here is that in addition to enhancing skills through vocational training, it is necessary to gauge how those skills are transferred into earning potential, which should be an emphasis in economic rehabilitation. This will require strengthening social-capital formation as a process as well as the outcome of terrorist rehabilitation so that a smart approach to rehabilitation will bring transformative change in the lives of ex-combatants and their families as well as to the community.

Notes

1 One US dollar is roughly equivalent to 100 Nepali rupees.
2 For more about the concepts of community, see Peter Block (2009) *Community: The Structure of Belonging*. San Francisco: Berrett-Koehler Publishers; Anthony P. Cohen (1985) *The Symbolic Construction of Community*. London and New York: Tavistock Publications.

Bibliography

Adler, Paul S. and Seok-Woo Kwon (2002) 'Social capital: prospects for a new concept', *Academy of Management Review*, 27(1): 17–40.

Awan, Imran (2013) 'Muslim prisoners, radicalization and rehabilitation in British prisons', *Journal of Muslim Minority Affairs*, 33: 371–384.

Botha, Anneli and Mahdi Abdile (2014) 'Radicalisation and al-Shabaab recruitment in Somalia', *Institute for Security Studies*, ISS Paper 266. Pretoria: Institute for Security Studies and Finn Church Aid. Available at: https://issafrica.s3.amazonaws.com/site/uploads/Paper266.pdf (accessed 2 May 2017).

Bowd, Richard (2002) 'The (non)transformation of identity of ex-Kosovo Liberation Army (KLA) combatants through the Disarmament, Demobilisation and Reintegration (DDR) programme.' Paper presented at the ECPR Graduate Conference. University of Essex. 7–9 September.

Bowd, Richard and Alpaslan Özerdem (2013) 'How to assess social reintegration of ex-combatants', *Journal of Intervention and Statebuilding*, 7(4): 453–475.

Bragg, Caroline (2006) 'Challenges to policy and practice in the disarmament, demobilisation, reintegration and rehabilitation of youth combatants in Liberia', *Sussex Center for Migration Studies*, Working Paper No. 29. Available at: https://www.sussex.ac.uk/webteam/gateway/file.php?name=mwp29.pdf&site=252 (accessed 14 December 2016).

Brett, Rachel and Irma Specht (2004) *Young Soldiers: Why They Choose to Fight*. Boulder, CO and London: Lynne Rienner Publishers.

Buxton, Julia (2008) 'Reintegration and long-term development: linkages and challenges', Thematic Working Paper 5, *Center for International Cooperation and Security*, University of Bradford. Available at: https://bradscholars.brad.ac.uk/handle/10454/7312 (accessed 8 March 2017).

Department for International Development (1997) *Sustainable Livelihoods Guidance Sheets*. London: Department for International Development. Available at: www.livelihoodscentre.org/documents/20720/100145/Sustainable+livelihoods+guidance+sheets/8f35b59f-8207-43fc-8b99-df75d3000e86 (accessed 12 May 2017).

Dolan, Chris and Jessica Schafer (1997) *The Reintegration of Ex-combatants in Mozambique: Manica and Zambezia Provinces*. Oxford: University of Oxford. Available at: http://pdf.usaid.gov/pdf_docs/PNACC248.pdf (accessed 13 May 2017).

Eck, Kristine (2010) 'Recruiting rebels: Indoctrination and political education in Nepal', in Mahendra Lawoti and Anup K. Pahari (eds), *The Maoist Insurgency in Nepal: Revolution in the Twenty-first Century*. New York: Routledge: 33–51.

Entenmann, Eva, Liesbeth van der Heide, Daan Weggemans and Jessica Dorsey (2016) *Rehabilitation for Foreign Fighters? Relevance, Challenges and Opportunities for the Criminal Justice Sector*. The Hague: The International Centre for Counter-Terrorism. Available at: www.icct.nl/wp-content/uploads/2016/01/ICCT-Entenmann-Heide-Weggemans-Dorsey-Rehabilitation-for-Foreign-Fighters-December2015.pdf (accessed 5 May 2017).

Fink, Naureen Chaudhari (2015) 'The blue flag in grey zones: exploring the relationship between countering violent extremism (CVE) and disarmament, demobilisation and reintegration (DDR) in UN field operations', in James Cockayne and Siobhan O'Neil (eds), *UN DDR in an Era of Violent Extremism: Is it Fit for Purpose?* Tokyo and New York: United Nations University: 62–79.

Gilbert, Leah (2009) 'Analysing the dark side of social capital: organised crime in Russia', in Michaelene Cox (ed.), *Social Capital and Peace-Building: Creating and Resolving Conflict with Trust and Social Networks*. London and New York: Routledge: 57–74.

Gunaratna, Rohan (2011) 'Terrorist rehabilitation: a global imperative', *Journal of Policing, Intelligence and Counter Terrorism*, 6(1): 65–82.

Gunaratna, Rohan (2015) 'Terrorist rehabilitation: genesis, genealogy and likely future', in Rohan Gunaratna and Mohamed Bin Ali (eds), *Terrorist Rehabilitation: A New Frontier in Counter-terrorism*. Singapore: Imperial College Press: 3–26.

Gunaratna, Rohan and Lawrance Rubin (2011) 'Introduction', in Rohan Gunaratna, Jolene Jerard and Lawrance Rubin (eds), *Terrorist Rehabiliation and Counter-radicalisation: New Approaches to Counter-terrorism*. Oxford and New York: Routledge: 1–10.

Hettiarachchi, Malkanthi (2014) 'Sri Lanka's Rehabilitation program: a new frontier in counter terrorism and counter insurgency', *PRISM*, 4(2): 105–121. Available at: http://cco.ndu.edu/Portals/96/Documents/prism/prism_4-2/prism105-122_Hettiarachchi.pdf (accessed 3 May 2017).

International Alert (2006) *Local Business, Local Peace: The Peacebuilding Potentials of the Domestic Private Sector*. London: International Alert.

International Labour Organization (1997) *ILO and Conflict-affected Peoples and Countries: Promoting Lasting Peace through Employment Promotion*. Geneva: International Labour Organization.

International Labour Organization (2009) *Socio-economic Reintegration of Ex-combatants: Guidelines*. Geneva: International Labour Organization/Crisis Response and Reconstruction Programme.

Kilroy, Walt (2015) *Reintegration of Ex-combatants after Conflicts: Participatory Approaches in Sierra Leone and Liberia*. London: Palgrave MacMillan.

Koehler, Daniel (2017) *Understanding Deradicalization: Methods, Tools and Programs for Countering Violent Extremism*. London: Routledge.

Micolta, P.H. (2009) 'Illicit interest groups, social capital and conflict: a study of the FARC', in Michaelene Cox (ed.), *Social Capital and Peace-building: Creating and Resolving Conflict with Trust and Social Networks*. London and New York: Routledge: 75–91.

Muggah, Robert (2010) 'Innovations in disarmament, demobilization and reintegration policy and research: Reflections on the last decade'. *NUPI Working Paper 774*. Norwegian Institue of International Affairs. Available at: https://brage.bibsys.no/xmlui/bitstream/handle/11250/277971/WP-774-Muggah.pdf?sequence=3&isAllowed=y (accessed 9 March 2017).

Mulcahy, Elizabeth, Shannon Merrington and Peter Bell (2013) 'The radicalisation of prison inmates: exploring recruitment, religion and prisoner vulnerability', *Journal of Human Security*, 9(1): 4–14. Available at: https://research-repository.griffith.edu.au/bitstream/handle/10072/64669/98691_1.pdf?sequence=1 (accessed 11 March 2017).

Özerdem, Alpaslan (2002) 'Disarmament, demobilization and reintegration of former combatants in Afganistan: lessons learned from a cross-cultural perspective', *Third World Quarterly*, 23(5): 961–975.

Özerdem, Alpaslan (2009) *Post-war Recovery: Disarmament, Demobilization and Reintegration*. London and New York: I.B. Tauris.

Özerdem, Alpaslan (2012) 'A re-conceptualisation of ex-combatant reintegration: "social reintegration" approach', *Conflict, Security & Development*, 12(1): 51–73.

Özerdem, Alpaslan and Sukanya Podder (2008) 'Reinsertion assistance and the reintegration of ex-combatants in war to peace transitions', Thematic Working Paper 4. Bradford: Center for International Cooperation and Security, Bradford University. Available at: https://bradscholars.brad.ac.uk/bitstream/handle/10454/7311/DDR%20Working%20Paper%204.pdf?sequence=2&isAllowed=y (accessed 12 May 2017).

Putnam, Robert D. (1995) 'Turning in, turning out: the strange disappearance of social capital in America', *Political Science & Politics*, 28(4): 664–683.

Putnam, Robert D. (2000) *Bowling Alone: The Collapse and Revival of American Community*. New York: Simon & Schuster Inc.

Shinn, David (2016) 'Poverty and terrorism in Africa: the debate continues', *Georgetown Journal of International Affairs*, 17(2): 16–22.

SIDDR (2006) *Stockholm Initiative on Disarmament Demobilisation Reintegration (SIDDR): Final Report*. Stockholm: Ministry of Foreign Affairs, Sweden. Available at: https://

reliefweb.int/sites/reliefweb.int/files/resources/ED1EF744FE93A788C125742800 3110CB-gvtSweden_feb2006.pdf (accessed 2 June 2018).

Subedi, D.B. (2013a) 'From civilian to combatant: armed recruitment and participation in the Maoists' conflict in Nepal', *Contemporary South Asia*, 2(4): 429–443.

Subedi, D.B. (2013b) '"Pro-peace entrepreneur" or "conflict profiteer"? Critical perspective on the private sector and peacebuilding in Nepal', *Peace and Change: A Journal of Peace Research*, 38(2): 181–206.

Subedi, D.B. (2014a) 'Conflict, combatants and cash: economic reintegration of and livelihoods of the Maoist ex-combatants in Nepal', *World Development*, 59: 238–250.

Subedi, D.B. (2014b) 'Dealing with ex-combatants in a negotiated peace process: impacts of transitional politics on the DDR programme in Nepal', *Journal of Asian and African Studies*, 49(6): 672–689.

Subedi, D.B. (2014c) 'Ex-combatants, security and post-conflict violence: unpacking the experience from Nepal', *Millennial Asia: An International Journal of Asian Studies*, 5(1): 41–65.

Subedi, D.B. and Bert Jenkins (2016) 'Preventing and countering violent extremism: engaging peacebuilding and development actors', *Counter Terrorist Trends and Analysis*, 8(10): 13–19.

United Nations (2006) 'Disarmament, demobilization and reintegration: report of the Secretary-General', *United Nations General Assembly*, A/60/705: 8.

United Nations (2010) *Second Generation Disarmament, Demobilization and Reintegration (DDR) Practices in Peace Operations*. New York: UNDPKO, Office of Law and Security Institutions, DDR Section. Available at: www.un.org/en/peacekeeping/documents/2GDDR_ENG_WITH_COVER.pdf (accessed 13 May 2017).

Vencovsky, Daniel (2006) 'Economic Reintegration of Ex-combatants', in Erin McCandless and Tony Karbo (eds), *Peace, Conflict and Development in Africa: A Reader*. Geneva: University for Peace: 264–268.

Verhey, Beth (2001) *Child Soldiers: Preventing, Demobilizing and Reintegrating*. Africa Region Working Paper Series, 23. Washington, DC: The World Bank. Available at: http://documents.worldbank.org/curated/en/284531468770734839/Child-soldiers-preventing-demobilizing-and-reintegrating (accessed 12 May 2017).

Verkoren, Willemijn (2005) 'Bringing it all together: a case study of Cambodia', in Gerd Junne and Willemijn Verkoren (eds), *Postconflict Development: Meeting New Challenges*. London: Lynne Rienner: 289–294.

5 Entrepreneurial rehabilitation
The promise of social entrepreneurship in disengaging religious terrorists

Yanto Chandra

Introduction

The ubiquity of religiously inspired terrorist attacks in recent years, from New York's 9/11 attack (2001), the Bali bombing (2002), Paris' Charlie Hebdo attack (2015) and the Manchester attack (2017), has continuously reminded the world of the persistence of religious terrorism. Religious terrorism is a type of terrorism that legitimizes violence based on religious precepts and is thus considered far more *lethal* than its secular counterpart (Victoroff 2005; Hoffman 1995). Religious terrorism is an old phenonenon that predates modernity, from the radical Sikh and Hindu Thugs movements in India, the radical Buddhist monks who incited bigotry and violence against Muslims, to the contemporary Al-Qaeda and the Islamic State of Iraq and Syria (ISIS) (Hoffman 1995; Oppenheim 2017; Schmid 2004; Stern and Berger 2015). Experts argued that government-led military style interventions have failed (Thrall and Goepner 2017) and only led to counter attacks by terrorists and helped terrorists search for new and better tactics (Cockburn 2017). The 'War on Terror' approach seems to offer no *sustainable* solutions to stop religious terrorism and the terrorist movement (Thrall and Goepner 2017; Lum et al. 2006). As evidence shows, the weakened Al-Qaeda (Miller and Whitlock 2014) does not end religious terrorism but rather gave impetus for the rise of ISIS, which is known to be far more radical than Al-Qaeda and which has gained support from 31 terrorist/radical groups worldwide (Rabouin 2015), including Nigeria-based Boko Haram, Phillipines-based Abu Sayyaf Group and Indonesia-based Mujahidin Indonesia Timur. Where does that leave us? These terrorist movements raise two fundamental questions: *How do we reduce the threat of future terrorist acts* and *what are the steps to be taken to promote peace?*

The study of religious terrorism, particularly in the context of Muslim extremists, can be advanced by studying Indonesia as a 'strategic research site' (Merton 1987), as it has a record of religious terrorism dating back to the 1940s (e.g. the Darul Islam revolt in 1947; Ramakrishna 2005) and a resurgence of terror attacks claiming religious justifications (Nugroho 2016; Putra and Sukabdi 2013). In Indonesia alone, the National Police has arrested over 800 suspected (religiously inspired) terrorists since the 2002 Bali bombing incident (Jakarta Post 2013;

Gunaratna 2012). Around 250 terrorists were released in 2014 (Collins 2013), and more will be released in the near future. Unfortunately, the government is not ready to help them. Some might ask if the terrorists deserve any help at all given the atrocities they commited. Do they or do they not deserve help? In this study,[1] I do not aim to offer a philosophical or moral debate on the ethics of helping religious terrorists return to normalcy but rather offer a strategic and intervention-based perspective to explore deeper into the how and why religious-based terrorists and extremists in Indonesia can be assisted to return to a normal, mainstream lifestyle.

Besides a lack of coordination among state institutions on what to do with the terrorists after their capture and subsequent release into society, there is also a stigma attached to ex-terrorists and terrorists recently released from prison. For instance, terrorist convicts and their families in Indonesia often face social discrimination (Nur Asiyah et al. 2014) and discrimination in the job market, both in the private and public sector. This stigmatization discourages the terrorists to return to a normal, mainstream lifestyle. This eventually leaves terrorists with no option but to return to their radical groups and perpetuate the cycle of violence.

Second, the Indonesian judiciary system adopts a conditional release system, which allows prisoners to be released after serving two-thirds of their sentence (or *voorwaardelijke invrijheidstelling*, as stated in article 15a (3) juncto article 14d (1) of the Indonesian Code of Criminal Procedure, juncto article 30 (1) part (c) of Indonesian Law No. 16, 2004 on the Attorney-General). This conditional release system requires a prisoner to report once per month at the District Attorney's office. Moreover, as a former Indonesian terrorist lamented, there is also a lack of coaching and guidance for just-released terrorists. Combined with the periodic reporting process, the circumstances prevent terrorists from finding new careers and lifestyles beyond terrorism.

Third, research shows that prisons are generally an effective place of recruitment and training ground for terrorists (Jones 2014). According to the International Crisis Group, in Indonesia terrorist recruitments occurred in various prisons from those in East Java, Jakarta to Semarang and Bali and Makasar (Karmini 2011; International Crisis Group 2007). Terrorists had also successfully radicalized prison officers into terrorists such as in the case of Beni Irawan, a Kerobokan prison officer who became an associate of Imam Samudra (International Crisis Group 2007). Additionally, due to the difficulty in monitoring, terrorists used prisons to send money from jail to jail, and, at least once, coordinated an attack outside of the prison (Sheridan 2011). Thus mixing terrorists and 'bad apples' in prisons may only perpetuate more radicalization and ease of coordination for future terrorist attacks. Alternative solutions beyond incarceration, legal enforcement and military action have not been well explored in dealing with religious terrorists.

To put things in perspective, the rise of religious terrorism and extremism in Indonesia is by no means accidental as it has a long history dating back to the movements in the 1940s that aimed to convert Indonesia into an Islamic caliphate (Elson and Formichi 2011). This is further enhanced by the locals' perception and subsequent response to the former President Soeharto's New Order government pressure on Islam in the 1970s (Carnegie 2015; Hefner 2011), 'soft' post-Soeharto governments that leave behind records of alarming rates of religious conflicts and terrorism activities (Heiduk 2012; McCoy 2013) and the proliferation of many radical vigilante forces (Van Bruinessen 2013). Other contributing factors include the return of local scholars from years of training in the Middle East who spread newly adopted radical thoughts (Lim 2011) and local politicians' use of divisive rhetoric along religion–ethnicity–social–economic status differences as a weapon to win votes. According to scholars, *madrasahs* (Islamic schools) have turned into a vast network *jihad* factories spreading radical teachings (Afrianty 2012; Bachelard 2012) and anti-multicultural values such as self-righteousness, prejudice and stereotypes of other groups (Baidhawy 2010).

Despite the big questions in taming religious terrorism – philosophical, moral, institutional, legal, sociological and historical perspectives – there is a quiet movement that emerges from within the society, initiated by those who had traversed the paths of terrorism but 'have found a new way out'. This offers a new hope and potential remedy for the problems, as discussed in the next section.

A civil society-led entrepreneurial rehabilitation

My focus on novel solutions to religious terrorism led to the discovery of Alpha,[2] a reformed extremist and former student at a *madrasah* in Java. Alpha was inspired by the work of a non-governmental organization in Northern Ireland that helps former combatants in Ireland to return to normalcy – a new idea that he learned during his study at a leading European university. Alpha has for the past nine years experimented with various models of counterterrorism work and refined a promising model that can prevent terrorism in a more inclusive and sustainable manner. Alpha acknowledges the philosophical, institutional, legal, sociological and historical challenges of addressing religious terrorism. He reflected on his own journey of transformation from a radical person to a moderate and intellectual Muslim and an entrepreneur of a consulting company, and recognized opportunities to transform other terrorists' lives.

Based on interviews with Alpha, the terrorists' 'first twelve months' after jail release is critical in determining whether one will re-engage as a terrorist or reintegrate into society. As terrorists are often faced with a difficult post-prison transition period, such as difficulties in finding jobs and facing stigmatization from the society, they can easily turn back to their old groups for care and support. This is why Alpha focuses on this critical period as a window of opportunity to help terrorists return to normalcy and adopt an alternative career to terrorism. Alpha's model focuses on *empowering* and *rehabilitating* terrorists by giving them opportunities to build careers as managers and shareholders of culinary businesses that sell various products, from satays[3] to fried rice, and baked goods. Alpha developed a mission-driven organization known as a social enterprise – organizations that use business principles to achieve social goals (Chandra

2016a, 2017; Doherty et al. 2014) – to facilitate the rehabilitation of terrorists. His organization, Good Food,[4] a culinary arts social enterprise, is a restaurant like any other except that it has a strong social mission (Short et al. 2009) and seeks to use business as an instrument for social change (Montesano Montessori 2016; Steyaert and Hjorth 2008). That is, the profits earned from the business are ploughed back into the enterprise to help scale up its social impact, offering empowerment to more former terrorists, and enticing soon-to-be-released terrorists with new opportunities.

Good Food sells satays, a culinary product that embraces the Javanese identity. This social enterprise has 'graduated' ten former terrorists as well as many local school dropouts and currently employs some former terrorists. Over the years, Good Food has emerged as a *transit point* for many former terrorists before they return to a mainstream lifestyle. Being employed here gives ex-terrorists an opportunity to take a year or several months for reflection, gaining a new identity and exploring new options before rejoining society and adopting a new lifestyle. The former terrorists who eventually left Good Food had returned to their previous professions. Most of them embraced entrepreneurship (which they learned in Good Food) by becoming small business owners selling laptops, managing a glass installation service, giving private mathematics tutorials and running cafés in conflict-torn cities, to name but a few. Entrepreneurship is the preferred choice of vocation as it liberates the former terrorists from discrimination by employers in the public and private sectors and removes the economic and social constraints (Tobias et al. 2013) commonly faced by former terrorists.

One of Good Food's beneficiaries is Beta, who joined fellow terrorists in Mindanao and who was later sentenced to ten years in the prison for the possession of explosives in Indonesia. Based on my interviews with Beta (in 2013), Beta grew up in a middle-class family in East Java. His parents are the richest in the village and own a large house, a paddy field, a mosque among other things. According to Alpha, Beta was the top class performer in the elementary and secondary schools. Beta was inspired by the Islamic movement since childhood and read various literatures on this topic. His encounter with radical Islamic teachings in radical schools led him to a journey to Mindanao and three years of training and combat alongside the terrorists in the southern part of the Philippines. In hindsight, Beta said that he initially did not intend to 'wage *jihad* war' but was rather driven by a *curiosity* about what happens to fellow Muslims in conflict-torn regions and a desire to be a *volunteer* to help fellow Muslims.

While working as a journalist between 2003 and 2004, Alpha interviewed hundreds of terrorists locked in a Central Java prison and there met Beta, who was in prison serving his ten-year sentence. After his conditional release, Beta approached Alpha through the local mosque network to explore economic advancement in life. He could not find a proper job after his jail time in Central Java. In 2009, after a nine-month stint in a *warung* (Indonesian-style eatery) – where he faced constraints caused by the frequent reporting to officers in the District Attorney's office and felt dissatisfied with the working conditions at the *warung* – Beta brought along three underprivileged co-workers and joined Alpha's plan to start Good Food. For Beta and the three friends, Good Food is a place to learn, earn an income and find a new identity, but for Alpha it is a platform to give back to society. Alpha used the income from a consulting company that he set up in Jakarta and his personal savings to start up Good Food. The ownership model gives Beta and three friends a share of 12.5 per cent each, while Alpha held the remaining 50 per cent (which he reinvested into the business for expansion). From one shop in Central Java, Good Food has expanded to other cities and has entered into new ventures such as setting up a canteen, a fried noodle shop and a doughnut bakery – where *food is the core business*. As of 2014, Alpha and the team are working to open the next Good Food in a conflict-torn city. Beta has turned over a new leaf and became a general manager and a shareholder of Good Food and a poster boy for the success of Good Food's intervention.

Alpha leveraged his prior experience as a marketing manager at a large hospitality business in Java, and Beta's and his three co-workers' experience in a *warung* to start Good Food. This was a rational choice as it allows them to combine a rich collective experience in culinary businesses and thus reduces the probability of failure. This 'prior experience' later appears to be a key success factor as it helps the social enterprise to remain innovative and market-oriented in the highly competitive local culinary markets.

Good Food positions itself as a provider of 'low-cost' but 'high-class taste' satays. This positioning fits well with the aspiration of a large and fast-growing middle class in Indonesia who (like their middle-class counterparts in China and India) crave a fusion of local cuisines with modern touch, also know as the 'fusion movement'. To develop the high-end satay house, Alpha leveraged his friendship with professional chefs from a five-star hotel and a European chef to train the former terrorists how to cook. Alpha also invited Beta and the team to patronize high-end restaurants and satay houses as a form of market research to understand different style of satays, and how satay businesses operate. Thus, Good Food turns local cuisine into high-quality cuisine while still at an affordable price for local customers.

Alpha, Beta and the team designed the menu concept and the theme of the satay house. The theme is one that combines Javanese identity with a modern style of presenting the food. The reason behind the fusion theme is to bring back a retro (old style) feel to the restaurant, a strategy that has been successfully used by local entrepreneurs in marketing various products including bottled tea, soy sauce, *jamu* (herbal supplements) and various local cuisines in high-end shopping malls. The hybrid of the Javanese and modern cuisine is also *a symbol of welcoming diversity and embracing differences*. This has been designed as part of the social enterprise's identity since day one. The key distinctiveness of the menu is the infusion of strong spices that suits the local customers' love for spicy food. Among the most popular items on the menu is the 'penis satay', a dish popular among male customers for its sexual-performance-enhancing qualities. It adds an interesting point of *conversation* between customers and the ex-terrorist staff; such conversation helps the former terrorists to 'open up' and broaden their social circles. They also serve various other types of satay and complement them with local vegetables.

Social enterprise's intervention strategies to disengage terrorists

Why does Good Food's social entrepreneurship-based intervention model work effectively in disengaging terrorists? My analyses point to a number of psychological, organizational and sociological explanations. First, *in the culinary business, one is conditioned to meeting different people and serving customers indiscriminately*. When asked why a culinary business was chosen as a social intervention strategy, Alpha, the founder, explained that in the culinary business every customer who walks in must be served regardless of his or her ethnicity, religion or race. Thus, this helps the ex-terrorists to learn about different people and broaden their life perspectives. This is nicely summarized by Alpha in his interview with the author: 'Although he is Alpha (a Muslim), but if the client is John (a Christian), he must serve John.'

Alpha also invited his Western and Australian chef friends from Europe, who are Christians, and local Chinese-Indonesian entrepreneurs, who are Buddhists, to train the ex-terrorists in cooking and entrepreneurship. Through a chance encounter, while Alpha was giving a seminar about the social function of food, a Swiss journalist wrote about Good Food and later a Swiss church activist created Good Food's menu and donated all the revenues earned from the church to help Alpha expand his social enterprise activities. This is well illustrated in Alpha's conversation with the author: 'Indirectly Good Food and Beta obtained funds from the church . . . so this opened up various things that were not imaginable before.' These efforts reduce the *religious, ethnicity and racial distance* between the ex-terrorists and others. These slowly change how the ex-terrorists identify themselves with different people and shape their perceptions and beliefs that others who are different are not necessarily evil as preached by their radical peers or teachers.

Second, *serving conditions a person to humble oneself before the person being served*. Cooking and serving others indiscriminately in the satay house gradually shape Beta's and other ex-terrorists' attitudes to life by learning to *respect others* and *themselves*. This intervention aimed at the motives behind why people become religious terrorists. As clearly summarized by Alpha in his interviews with the author: 'Why these people become terrorists . . . it's because they think they are the most righteous, like a committee promised to enter the Heaven, who represent the voice of God.' Therefore, Good Food works by rewarding (reinforcing) certain types of behaviour (e.g. connecting with others who are religiously, ethnically, racially different) and eliminating certain types of superior attitude (e.g. the 'I'm the most righteous' attitude) through the 'serving/ humbling exercise'. This humbling exercise demonstrates the application of *operant conditioning* (Jablonksy and DeVries 1972; Babb and Kopp 1978) in the psychology literature that is performed naturally in the satay house. The duty of serving others and humbling oneself before others help the former terrorists *respect others with a different background* and make them realize that different others are not necessarily evil. As simple as these may seem, they have been effective instruments in shaping how the ex-terrorists relate to others.

Third, *former terrorists will gain more trust from fellow terrorists and can leverage their past to persuade fellow terrorists to adopt alternative lifestyle better than government-led or cleric-led intervention.* Alpha's background as a former disciple of a radical cleric at a well-known *madrasah* in Java, a radical associated with an Islamist movement, and his new identity as a reformed radical – thanks to his work in the *secular* world as a manager in a large hospitality business, a journalist, as well as higher education in Europe, and friendships with many non-Javanese, non-Muslim friends – positioned him well to bridge the world of Islam and the West. Alpha's unique background as a 'former' disciple allows him to develop deep empathy and understanding of the radical groups and what can be done to help. Alpha calls himself 'a social broker' of peace. In his eyes, the conventional approach of relying on state officials to engage in dialogue with the terrorist groups has failed since there is more suspicion towards people who hunt terrorists. Clerics could not disengage terrorists either because they have never lived the paths traversed by terrorists. As Alpha illustrated:

> What the government did was, for example, to gather the ex-terrorists and send religious teachers to have a dialogue with them . . . that means focusing on their ideology first. When asked, the religious teachers always lost the debate with them . . . [in] just one question, 'have you joined *Jihad*, Sir?' Certainly these *Ustadz* (religious clerics) have never taken up weapons or wanted to participate in jihad in Afghanistan or Ambon. The religious life of the religious teachers in Indonesia is flawed, they lived in a life of luxury. So the religious people create the world using their own ways. Now, *Ustadz* is a profession, the religious heads become a profession.

In other words, there is a legitimacy question in using state officials and clerics to perform social intervention here since clerics are deemed 'not qualified to preach' and 'not morally pure' enough in the eyes of the terrorists.

Fourth, *a strong market orientation helps sustain the business side of the social enterprise, which in turn sustains its social intervention efforts.* Good Food's low-cost but with high-quality products and friendly service, attracts customers and fosters customer loyalty. Good Food does not rely on a charity model nor is it based on 'compassionate buying' (buying out of pity) but rather it relies on a competitive market offering that fills peoples' real needs and wants. The fact that Good Food's sales have grown fast over the years and that the operation has expanded to other cities reflect consumers' acceptance of its products and services and that its overall management has done something right in its business practices amid the hyper-competitive culinary market. According to Alpha, Good Food does not need to be associated with 'terrorism' issues as it can be packaged as a general business proposition to any investor in or outside the country who wishes to pursue a social mission while still generating decent profits. In fact, customers do not know much about Good Food's social mission. As Alpha stated nicely: 'we do not brand [the satay house] as a *Jihadi* club'. This clever positioning and market orientation help Good Food grow its businesses.

Fifth, *the founder leveraged his prior knowledge and social capital creatively to enhance the success of the social enterprise and its social intervention mechanism*. Alpha convinced his friends, a chef at five-star hotel in Java, and European and Australian chefs, to train the 'boys' to produce high-quality satays and other products as well as the art of running a satay house. Rather than starting from scratch, Alpha relied on existing and proven resources, and made do with what is at hand. This process is known as *social bricolage* in the organization science literature (Baker and Nelson 2005; Di Domenico et al. 2010; Chandra 2016b). Alpha also purposefully placed Good Food in a city close enough to where he lives so he could monitor the early process of co-creation and innovations in the venture. When he opened the second branch in another city in Java, he dispatched one of the most talented founding members to lead and share the best practices there. All along, they refined their knowledge and best practices in running and expanding the social enterprise. This helps reduce the uncertainty commonly found in the early stages of a start-up. Alpha also plays the role of motivational speaker and life coach and always 'nudges' Beta and other ex-terrorist staff to improve their skills: from learning how to drive, attending motivational speaker workshops to entrepreneurship training and much more.

Sixth, *Beta, a reformed terrorist, naturally follows Alpha's steps by motivating fellow terrorists in jail to pursue an alternative career to terrorism and a new lifestyle*. Beta regularly visited other terrorists in prison to show them that he has achieved success in business and has a new social life, as a general manager and shareholder of Good Food. He was showing that if he could do well and rejoin a mainstream lifestyle, his soon-to-be-released terrorist friends could do well too. As well-summarized in his interviews with the author, Beta used his own rhetoric to persuade fellow terrorists: 'You just tried our [satays]. Aren't they delicious? Now, what if this can make money?' With his tainted past and reformed identity, Beta has the *legitimacy* and *trust* to positively influence fellow terrorists. From *negative change makers*, Beta and Alpha had transformed into *positive change makers* by influencing other terrorists to pursue similar paths to normalcy. Beta has become a role model for 30 small-scale enterprises; he was elected by the Cooperative Services in a city in Java to supervise culinary enterprises in the area, train local entrepreneurs and give guest lectures at local universities. These are things previously unimaginable for someone like Beta. The reformed Beta sees his prior life as 'an old world with many deficiencies and weaknesses'. Alpha donated all of the income he received from the social enterprise and part of his other income-generating activities to Beta to *help 'pay for' the meals for fellow terrorists in prison* and *those who dine in but have no resources to pay*. Not only was this strategy financially beneficial for the social enterprise and the terrorists, but it also *reduces the suspicion among radical groups* that Alpha is an agent of the West and receives money from the West. This is a key strategy in *winning the hearts* of the terrorists and helping them *see a new alternative* to terrorism rather than starting out with *ideological intervention and counselling*, an approach that is commonly used in the terrorist rehabilitation programmes in Indonesia, Singapore, Yemen and Saudi Arabia (Gunaratna et al. 2011).

Conclusion

Recent research on counterterrorism (Putra and Sukabdi 2013; Milla et al. 2013; Sukabdi 2015) suggests that economic deprivation and the Indonesian government taking sides of non-Muslims on both economic and political fronts are key factors that drive religious terrorism activities. This suggests that *economic matters* are a key driver behind the rise of, as well as a plausible solution to, religious terrorism. This is echoed by Omega, a counterterrorism psychologist in Indonesia, who states that the success of Good Food may be attributed to its 'economic approach' to solving terrorism problems. While other alternative methods for counterterrorism exist, such as the cognitive behavioural therapy (Bryant et al. 2011), Good Food's economic approach to counterterrorism reminds us of the efficacy of 'soft power' (Nye 2004, 2008), particularly social entrepreneurship as a vehicle of *transformation* and *liberation* (Rindova et al. 2009; Tobias et al. 2013; Venkataraman 2004) of terrorists. This study shows that social entrepreneurship can be fruitfully used to remove economic and social constraints to improve the wellbeing of society. A few concluding thoughts are proposed below.

First, *entrepreneurship can condition (reinforce and reward) how people think, behave and relate to different others for good purposes* (Jablonksy and DeVries 1972; Babb and Kopp 1978). When a certain behaviours, such as respect for different people and humbling oneself before others, are rewarded and cultivated (e.g. 'cooking for and serving others'), as is evident in Good Food, it helps gradually shape the ex-terrorists' mindset and behaviour towards others (Horgan 2005). This reduces *religious, ethnic and the racial distance* between the terrorists and different people and thus reduces radically negative bias towards others. Good Food's concept of *economic empowerment* (Kabeer 1999; Chandra and Shang 2017) differs from the small-scale enterprises that have been established by local radical organizations. For example, networks of small-scale businesses (e.g. publishing houses, bookstores, event organizers and traditional herbal treatments) focus on trading and building bonds among the *inner circles of radicals*, while Good Food focuses on *broadening the social circles of its beneficiaries* (i.e. ex-terrorists and school dropouts). Moreover, Good Food focuses on the psychological effect of humbling by serving others, and empowering ex-terrorists with the skills and resources to be independent entrepreneurs and offering a strong motivation to excel in life.

Second, *secular and material success can help disengage terrorists from the vicious cycle of terrorism as they in turn naturally engage other terrorists to pursue an alternative lifestyle and career*. Once Beta and other former terrorists and school dropouts experienced the fruits of their economic success, the initial opportunities begot more and more opportunities (Holcombe 2003; Chandra 2017) both economically and socially and therefore diverted ex-terrorists further away from terrorism. The fact that Beta has enjoyed higher *social status* and developed a new *identity* – by acting as a 'philanthropist' who provides financial and logistical support for the children and families of the detained terrorists and enticing inmates with business and work opportunities etc. – demonstrates how *secular and material success* can be effective in preventing terrorism and sustaining counterterrorism efforts. Beta has also become the financial backbone of his family, and this sense of *social responsibility* discourages him from re-engaging with the old groups.

In reflecting on his past, Beta's rhetoric has focused on his 'opportunity costs' of having being detained for too long, which prevented him from providing material needs for his parents, wife and parents-in-law. Today, with his status as a co-owner of Good Food, elected head of small enterprise association in a city in Java and, since 2014, a new owner of a car-rental agency, Beta will face a huge opportunity cost if he were to return to his old world. While *capitalist ideology* has been accused as the cause of excessive greed and the unethical pursuit of wealth creation (Pirson 2012; Porter and Kramer 2011), *extremist ideology* drives youths into excessive violence and wealth destruction (Czinkota et al. 2010; Ramiah and Graham 2013). However, economic success and social mission through social entrepreneurship seem to have a positive effect on the ex-terrorists' behaviour. As this study demonstrates, social entrepreneurship and 'being one's own boss' offer a better alternative than being a recidivist.

Alpha's social enterprise idea has inspired others to engage in 'entrepreneurship with a social mission' to help former terrorists return to normalcy. For instance, a good friend of Alpha learned about his Good Food approach and started *catfish farming* by turning former Afghanistan-trained 'boys' into co-owners of the aquaculture business. Catfish is a popular dish in Indonesia and offers immense culinary business opportunities. In the catfish farming, ex-terrorists are trained to grow catfish using the top part of used oil drums and grow vegetables using the bottom of the drums; this creates closed-loop resources that are beneficial for both the fish and vegetables. From *negative change makers* who force others to adopt one's world view (i.e. religious terrorism), Alpha and Beta have transformed into *positive change makers* who persuade others with a similar background to nurture and grow in a positive way within mainstream society.

Implications for public policy

Terrorism has long been regarded as the state's responsibility. Not many people worldwide, including those in Indonesia, have thought that counterterrorism could be part of civil society's responsibility. As Alpha nicely stated in the interviews:

> There is no need to have the big and scary police officers or using repressive approach. But give the society a firewall, a form of understanding that they need to maintain their own peace, for without it they couldn't live well. And all these activities must [be] self-sustained, otherwise there is no point of doing all this.

The rise of Good Food as a social enterprise that disengages terrorists highlights the power of the civil society and social innovators in helping bridge some of the social problems that the state has failed to address or could not solve efficiently, and also the commercial sector's lack of interest in solving societal problems. Peace is a *public good* and is thus the business of the state. However, the state does not have to be the sole provider of peace. There are areas where social entrepreneurship could act and fill the gaps that the public sector, commercial sector and non-profit organization sectors could not do well, such as counterterrorism. This study shows that social entrepreneurship is a promising platform to pursue peace and counterterrorism work innovatively and cost-effectively.

The role of business in facilitating peace is not new. The 'peace-through-commerce' concept (Fort and Schipani 2004; Wenger and Möckli 2003; Tobias et al. 2013) suggests that businesses can design policies that create peace by preventing conflicts (e.g. De Beer's no-blood-diamond procurement policy aims at preventing conflicts in diamond-producing regions in Africa). However, terrorism is a different type of problem from economically driven conflicts such as the diamond or coffee conflicts. Commercial enterprises are afraid of the retaliation of terrorists and thus are less likely to take part in counterterrorism work. The state and clerics lack the legitimacy and trust needed to work with terrorists. However, former terrorists turned social entrepreneurs have the legitimacy and trust to *empower* ex-terrorists to embrace *secular and material values* and redevelop former terrorists' *identity* in a way that benefits the broadest segments of the society.

Last but not least, this study demonstrates that former terrorists like Alpha and Beta are a perfect candidate to address terrorism peacefully. My data reveal that only '*the formers*' like Alpha and Beta understood the mindsets of terrorists and had the *legitimacy* to persuade fellow terrorists to pursue an alternative lifestyle. Only 'the formers' can build *trusted relationships* in persuading and helping terrorists to return to normalcy and adopt alternative careers to terrorism. The state and clerics who are part of government-led intervention programmes are often regarded as enemies and not trusted by terrorist groups. This renders any intervention by the state and clerics unsuccessful. This study shows the promise of former terrorists as a new force in counterterrorism work – not through coercive power, alienation or incarceration – but engaging terrorists in social entrepreneurship as a peaceful, non-violent approach to influence and cultivate positive behaviour.

I hope that this study will inspire further investigation into the why, how and what behind the efficacy of social entrepreneurship in solving the religious terrorism problem. I suspect that there may be a limitation on how and when social entrepreneurship can work effectively in taming terrorism. We do not yet know if alternative mechanisms of empowering terrorists exist and what outcomes have been produced. This requires further investigation into the different models of civil-society-based counterterrorism work. We also do not know if Alpha and Beta are just accidental or outlier cases, and whether and how social entrepreneurship can transform terrorist leaders into positive change makers. I do not suggest that other measures of counterterrorism such as law enforcement and intelligence work must be stopped and replaced by social entrepreneurship but rather see them as an *integrated soft and hard approach* (Nye 2009) to creating a peaceful and inclusive world for every man and woman regardless of their religious, ethnic and racial background.

Notes

1 This study was based on primary data collected through interviews with Alpha and Beta, two former terrorists from Indonesia, and Omega, a counterterrorism psychologist, as well as secondary data collected from the media and online sources following the theory-building approach (Yin 2003; Eisenhardt and Graebner 2007).
2 I anonymized all names, places, products, organizations and other details and their source materials for security reasons.
3 The nature of the products sold by the social enterprise has been disguised to ensure complete anonymity of the social enterprise.
4 The name of this social enterprise was altered in order to protect the organization and its members.

Bibliography

Afrianty, D. (2012). 'Islamic education and youth extremism in Indonesia'. *Journal of Policing, Intelligence and Counter Terrorism*, 7(2): 134–146.

Babb, H.W. and Kopp, D.G. (1978). 'Applications of behavior modification in organizations: a review and critique'. *Academy of Management Review*, 3(2): 281–292.

Bachelard, M. (2012). 'Indonesia's jihad factories: uncovering nurseries of terrorism's next generation', *The Sydney Morning Herald*, 7 October 2012. Available at: www.smh.com.au/world/indonesias-jihad-factories-uncovering-nurseries-of-terrorisms-next-generation-20121006-275wh.html (accessed 5 May 2018).

Baidhawy, Z. (2010). 'The problem of multiculturalism: radicalism mainstreaming through religious preaching in Surakarta'. *Journal of Indonesian Islam*, 4(2): 268–286.

Baker, T. and Nelson, R. (2005). 'Creating something from nothing: resource construction through entrepreneurial bricolage'. *Administrative Science Quarterly*, 50(3): 329–366.

Bryant, R.A., Ekasawin, S., Chakrabhand, S., Suwanmitri, S., Duangchun, O. and Chantaluckwong, T. (2011). 'A randomized controlled effectiveness trial of cognitive behavior therapy for post-traumatic stress disorder in terrorist affected people in Thailand'. *World Psychiatry*, 10(3): 205–209.

Carnegie, P.J. (2015). 'Countering the (re-) production of militancy in Indonesia: between coercion and persuasion'. *Perspectives on Terrorism*, 9(5): 15–26.

Chandra, Y. (2016a). 'A rhetoric-orientation view of social entrepreneurship'. *Social Enterprise Journal*, 12(2), 161–200.

Chandra, Y. (2016b). 'The entrepreneurship process in high performing hybrid organizations: insights from Diamond Cab'. In Chandra, Y. and Wong, L (eds), *Social Entrepreneurship in the Greater China: Policy and Cases*. Abingdon: Routledge: 109–125.

Chandra, Y. (2017). 'A time-based process model of international entrepreneurial opportunity evaluation'. *Journal of International Business Studies*, 48(4): 423–451.

Chandra, Y. and Shang, L. (2017). 'Social enterprise as a mechanism of youth empowerment'. *Hong Kong Journal of Social Work*, 51(1/2): 115–144 (special issue).

Cockburn, P. (2017). 'The government has known since 2003 that the failed "war on terror" could cause an attack like the one in Manchester', *The Independent*, 26 May 2017.

Available at: www.independent.co.uk/voices/corbyn-speech-manchester-attack-war-on-terror-did-cause-it-a7758066.html (accessed 15 May 2018).

Collins, B. (2013). 'More than 300 terrorists to be released from Indonesian jails in the next year'. *Business Insider*, 21 November 2013. Available at: www.businessinsider.com.au/more-than-300-terrorists-to-be-released-from-indonesian-jails-in-the-next-year-report-2013-11 (accessed 21 November 2014).

Czinkota, M.R., Knight, G., Liesch, P. W. and Steen, J. (2010). 'Terrorism and international business: A research agenda'. *Journal of International Business Studies*, 41(5): 826–843.

Di Domenico, M., Haugh, H. and Tracey, P. (2010). 'Social bricolage: theorizing social value creation in social enterprises'. *Entrepreneurship Theory & Practice*, 34(4): 681–703.

Doherty, B., Haugh, H. and Lyon, F. (2014). 'Social enterprises as hybrid organizations: a review and research agenda'. *International Journal of Management Reviews*, 16(4): 417–436.

Eisenhardt, K. and Graebner, M. (2007). 'Theory building from cases: opportunities and challenges'. *Academy of Management Journal*, 50(1): 25–32.

Elson, R.E. and Formichi, C. (2011). 'Why did Kartosuwiryo start shooting? An account of Dutch-Republican-Islamic forces interaction in West Java, 1945–49'. *Journal of Southeast Asian Studies*, 42(3): 458–486.

Fort, T. L. and Schipani, C. A. (2004). *The Role of Business in Fostering Peaceful Societies*. Cambridge: Cambridge University Press.

Gunaratna, R. (2012). 'After Bali: Southeast Asia under threat'. *RSIS Commentaries*. Singapore: S. Rajaratnam School of International Studies, Nanyang University of Technology.

Gunaratna, R., Jerard, J. and Rubin, L. (2011). *Terrorist Rehabilitation and Counter-radicalisation*. Abingdone: Routledge.

Hefner, R.W. (2011). *Civil Islam: Muslims and Democratization in Indonesia*. Princeton, NJ: Princeton University Press.

Heiduk, F. (2012). 'Between a rock and a hard place: radical Islam in post-Soeharto Indonesia'. *International Journal of Conflict and Violence*, 6(1): 26–40.

Hoffman, B. (1995). '"Holy terror": the implications of terrorism motivated by a religious imperative'. *Studies of Conflict and Terrorism*, 18: 271–284.

Holcombe, R.G. (2003). 'The origins of entrepreneurial opportunities'. *The Review of Austrian Economics*, 16(1), 25–43.

Horgan, J. (2005). *The Psychology of Terrorism*. Abingdon: Routledge.

International Crisis Group. (2007). 'Deradicalisation and Indonesian prisons'. *Asia Report 142*.

Jablonksy, S.F. and DeVries, D.L. (1972). 'Operant conditioning principles extrapolated to the theory of management'. *Organizational Behavior and Human Performance*, 7: 340–358.

Jakarta Post. (2013). '*Police play down US terror list*', September 21, 2013. Available at: www.thejakartapost.com/news/2013/09/21/police-play-down-us-terror-list.html (accessed 8 October 2014).

Jones, S. (2014). Author's interview with Sidney Jones, Indonesian counterterrorism expert, Hong Kong.

Kabeer, N. (1999). 'Resources, agency, achievements: reflections on the measurement of women's empowerment'. *Development and Change*, 30(3): 435–464.

Karmini, N. (2011). 'Terrorists recruit fellow prisoners in Indonesia to fight for Islamist cause'. *Washington Times*, 21 July 2011. Available at: www.washingtontimes.com/news/2011/jul/21/terrorists-recruit-fellow-prisoners-in-indonesia-t/?page=all (accessed 23 April 2015).

Lim, M. (2011). 'Radical Islamism in Indonesia and its Middle Eastern connections'. *Rubin Center Research for International Affairs*, 29 August 2011. Available at: www.rubincenter.org/2011/08/radical-islamism-in-indonesia-and-its-middle-eastern-connections/ (accessed 15 May 2018).

Lum, C., Kennedy, L.W. and Sherley, A. (2006). 'Are counter terrorism strategies effective? The results of the campbell systematic review on counter terrorism evaluation research'. *Journal of Experimental Criminology*, 2(4): 489–516.

McCoy, M.E. (2013). 'Purifying Islam in post-authoritarian Indonesia: corporatist methaphors and the rise of religious intolerance'. *Rhetoric & Public Affairs*, 16(2): 275–316.

Merton, R.K. (1987). 'Three fragments from a sociologist's notebooks: establishing the phenomenon, specified ignorance, and strategic research materials'. *Annual Review of Sociology*, 13(1): 1–29.

Milla, M.N., Faturochman and Ancok, D. (2013). 'The impact of leader-follower interactions on the radicalization of terrorists: a case study of the Bali bombers'. *Asian Journal of Social Psychology*, 16(2): 92–100.

Miller, G. and Whitlock, C. (2014). 'U.S. weakens al-Qaeda groups around the world but hasn't wiped any out;. *Washington Post*, 11 September 2014. Available at: www.washingtonpost.com/world/national-security/us-weakens-al-qaeda-groups-around-the-world-but-hasnt-wiped-any-out/2014/09/11/3c28d626-39bb-11e4-8601-97ba88884ffd_story.html (accessed 15 May 2018).

Montesano Montessori, N. (2016). 'A theoretical and methodological approach to social entrepreneurship as world-making and emancipation: social change as a projection in space and time'. *Entrepreneurship & Regional Development*, 28(7/8): 536–562.

Nugroho, W. (2016). 'Indonesia and the globalization of religious terrorism'. *The Jakarta Post*, 9 September 2016. Available at: www.thejakartapost.com/academia/2016/09/09/ri-and-the-globalization-of-religious-terrorism.html (accessed 15 May 2018).

Nur Asiyah, S., Fauziyah, N., Khotimah, S.K. and Balgies, S. (2014). 'The social discrimination against former terrorist convicts and their families: psychological perspectives'. *Journal of Indonesian Islam*, 8(1): 71–90.

Nye Jr, J.S. (2004). 'Soft power and American foreign policy'. *Political Science Quarterly*, 119(2): 255–270.

Nye Jr, J.S. (2008). 'Public diplomacy and soft power'. *The Annals of the American Academy of Political and Social Science*, 616(1): 94–109.

Nye Jr, J.S. (2009). 'Get smart: combining hard and soft power'. *Foreign Affairs*, 88(4): 160–163.

Oppenheim, M. (2017). '"It only takes one terrorist": the Buddhist monk who reviles Myanmar's Muslims'. *The Guardian*, 12 May 2017. Available at: www.theguardian.com/global-development/2017/may/12/only-takes-one-terrorist-buddhist-monk-reviles-myanmar-muslims-rohingya-refugees-ashin-wirathu (accessed 15 May 2018).

Pirson, M. (2012). 'Social entrepreneurs as the paragons of shared value creation? A critical perspective'. *Social Enterprise Journal*, 8(1): 31–48.

Porter, M. and Kramer, M.R. (2011). 'Creating shared value'. *Harvard Business Review*, 89(1/2): 62–77.

Putra, I.E. and Sukabdi, Z.A. (2013). 'Basic concepts and reasons behind the emergence of religious terror activities in Indonesia: an inside view'. *Asian Journal of Social Psychology*, 16(2): 83–91.

Rabouin, D. (2015). 'Boko Haram swears allegiance to ISIS: 31 groups now pledge support or allegiance to Islamic State group'. *International Business Times*, 8 April 2015.

Available at: www.ibtimes.com/boko-haram-swears-allegiance-isis-31-groups-now-pledge-support-or-allegiance-islamic-1839784 (accessed 15 May 2018).

Ramakrishna, K. (2005). 'Delegitimizing global Jihadi ideology in Southeast Asia'. *Contemporary Southeast Asia*, 27(3): 343–369.

Ramiah, V. and Graham, M. (2013). 'The impact of domestic and international terrorism on equity markets: evidence from Indonesia'. *International Journal of Accounting & Information Management*, 21(1): 91–107.

Rindova, V., Barry, D. and Ketchens, D.R. (2009). 'Entrepreneuring as emancipation'. *Academy of Management Review*, 34(3): 477–491.

Schmid, A.P. (2004). 'Frameworks for conceptualizing terrorism'. *Terrorism and Political Violence*, 16(2): 197–221.

Sheridan, G. (2011). 'Terrorist network thriving in Indonesian prison'. *The Australian*, 19 May 2011. Available at: www.theaustralian.com.au/national-affairs/terrorist-network-thriving-in-indonesian-prison/story-fn59niix-1226058530095 (accessed 15 May 2018).

Short, J.C., Moss, T.W. and Lumpkin, G.T. (2009). 'Research in social entrepreneurship: past contributions and future opportunities'. *Strategic Entrepreneurship Journal*, 3: 161–194.

Stern, J. and Berger, J.M. (2015). *ISIS: The State of Terror*. New York: Harper Collins.

Steyaert, C. and Hjorth, D. (eds) (2008). *Entrepreneurship as Social Change: A Third New Movements in Entrepreneurship* (Vol. 3). Cheltenham: Edward Elgar Publishing.

Sukabdi, Z. (2015). 'Terrorism in Indonesia: a review on rehabilitation and deradicalization'. *Journal of Terrorism Research*, 6(2): 36–56.

Thrall, A.T. and Goepner, E. (2017). 'Step back: lessons for U.S. foreign policy from the failed war on terror'. *Policy Analysis No. 814*. CATO Institute. Available at: www.cato.org/publications/policy-analysis/step-back-lessons-us-foreign-policy-failed-war-terror (accessed 15 May 2018).

Tobias, J.M., Mair, J. and Barbosa-Leiker, C. (2013). 'Toward a theory of transformative entrepreneuring: poverty reduction and conflict resolution in Rwanda's entrepreneurial coffee sector'. *Journal of Business Venturing*, 28: 728–742.

Van Bruinessen, M. (2013). *Contemporary Developments in Indonesian Islam: Explaining the 'Conservative Turn'*. Singapore: ISEAS Publishing.

Venkataraman, S. (2004). 'Regional transformation through technological entrepreneurship'. *Journal of Business Venturing*, 19: 153–167.

Victoroff, J. (2005). 'The mind of the terrorist: a review and critiques of psychological approaches'. *Journal of Conflict Resolution*, 49(1): 3–42.

Wenger, A. and Möckli, D. (2003). *Conflict Prevention: The Untapped Potential of the Business Sector*. Boulder, CO: Lynne Rienner Publishers.

Yin, R.K. (2003). *Case Study Research: Design and Methods* (Vol. 5). Thousand Oaks, CA: Sage.

6 Family and social rehabilitation as a mode of holistic rehabilitation programme

Muhammad Saiful Alam Shah Bin Sudiman and Nur Irfani Saripi

Introduction

While there has been a number of research projects and chapters on engagement and rehabilitation of terrorist detainees, much still has to be studied about their families who have to cope with the absence of the breadwinners and face society upon the offenders' death or incarceration. When detainees are released, their family members are the best support and monitoring functions to prevent recidivism. For offenders who are detained, returning to society may not be an easy feat. They may face challenges such as stigmatisation, getting gainfully employed and overcoming the trauma they might have encountered during their period of imprisonment.

This chapter will cover the importance of family and social rehabilitation, as well as provide insights into family and social rehabilitation and how it can be implemented. It will also highlight several countries' experiences in adopting social rehabilitation as a complementary mode in their terrorist rehabilitation approaches. It will also explore the multi-faceted challenges that nations have faced or may face in implementing social rehabilitation. Lastly, the chapter will suggest solutions to overcome these challenges.

A note on terminology

There are different terms to describe persons who have been arrested for involvement in terrorism. In Indonesia, after they are convicted and sentenced, they would be called 'terrorist prisoners' or 'terrorist inmates'. In countries like Singapore and Iraq, they are called 'detainees'. In Saudi Arabia, they are called 'beneficiaries'. In some cases, they are called 'radicals', 'extremists' or 'terrorists'. Sometimes they are dubiously labelled as 'individuals'.

For the purpose of uniformity in the writing of this chapter, persons who are arrested or detained for matters related to terrorism activities will herein be referred to as 'detainees' so long they are incarcerated. Detainees who have undergone rehabilitation programmes and released will be referred to as 'beneficiaries'. Those who espouse the ideology of al-Qaeda, Jemaah Islamiyah (JI) or the Islamic State of Iraq and Syria (ISIS) but have not committed any violent action and have necessarily been detained will be referred to as 'extremists'.

This chapter will only focus on rehabilitation in Saudi Arabia, Sri Lanka and Singapore. Unless stated otherwise, what is written henceforth is based on the study of these three countries only.

Overview of family and social rehabilitation

Rehabilitation is a term traditionally used for medical purposes. Rehabilitation essentially is a combination of two words '*re*' and '*habilis*'. In French, '*re*' means to return or repetition, while '*habilis*' is a Latin word that means competent. The word rehabilitation itself carries the meaning of returning to competence (Mathiesen 2006: 27). In the case of terrorism and extremism born from misunderstood religious concepts, the purpose of a terrorist rehabilitation programme is the cessation of believing in violent ideology and being involved with it, and ultimately returning former terrorists to moderation and inclusivity.

The term rehabilitation in relation to counterterrorism or specifically counter-ideology was used as early as 1985 (Hoffman 1985). For this form of rehabilitation, re-education and winning hearts and minds are at the core of its approach. Other complementary approaches may include, among others, psychological intervention, vocational training and social and family rehabilitation (Gunaratna 2009).

Another term used is deradicalisation, which can be defined as 'a change in people's attitudes and beliefs entailed in the terrorism justifying ideology' (Kruglanski et al. n.d.). In this chapter, we use the term rehabilitation, in which deradicalisation is an integral part of the process.

In doing this research, we found that there is a lack of conceptual clarity or a single definition of what is family and social rehabilitation. However, there is a consistency in the practice of this mode of rehabilitation. What *family and social rehabilitation* seems to entail is the inclusion of the family of detainees or extremists in a holistic rehabilitation programme. What this mode of rehabilitation does *not* mean is the generalisation that the family is also involved in terrorism activities or has the same ideological inclinations as the detainee. Family and social rehabilitation can be a preventive measure against these matters and even acts as an educational tool to address them should there be an ideological indoctrination to a certain degree, but family and social rehabilitation are not provided based on the assumption that a terrorist's family members are also terrorists or extremists.

While receiving rehabilitation, families should be clear that their attitude towards the rehabilitation does not equate to the detainees' quicker release. It does not and should not mean the detainees are released earlier because of the families' 'cooperation' as this would hamper the detainees' own rehabilitation process. However, in view that the families are well taken care of by the government and communities, this may have a positive impact on the offenders' overall rehabilitation progress.

Family and social rehabilitation is presented as a form of assistance to help families cope with life in the absence of husbands or other family members. The programme is a community-based approach where society gives support to the family[1], for example, assistance rendered by non-governmental organisations (NGOs) or social workers. Understandably, with the absence of a family member, in many cases the sole breadwinner, the remaining family members would face certain difficulties. The essence of social and family rehabilitation is in addressing the concerns of a family after their family member is either killed or captured (Gunaratna 2009). This mode of rehabilitation is arguably as important as rehabilitating the terrorists and extremists themselves as it shows that in the fight against terrorism, the families are not neglected: 'I can understand why, but many people didn't want to be associated with us, given we were the children of El Sayyid Nosair. So I was ostracized to a certain degree because of that' (Zak Ebrahim cited in Breakwell 2014).

Zak Ebrahim's father, El Sayyid Nosair, assassinated Meir Kahane, the rabbi who founded the Jewish Defense League, in 1990. In 1993, Nosair helped plot the World Trade Centre bombing from prison. Growing up, Zak Ebrahim made the choice to promote peace and tolerance after his father was arrested. He wrote the book '*The Terrorist's Son*' to share his journey to escape his father's legacy. However, he faced tremendous difficulty living in the 'ideological bubble'. From his father's arrest up until he was 19 years old, he had to move 20 times. He barely had friends and was constantly a subject of bullies in school. Social and family rehabilitation could have changed that to facilitate his growing-up journey being a more pleasant experience. Family and social rehabilitation, in this regard, is an effort to ensure that there are no more Zak Ebrahims.

Family and social rehabilitation is also evidence that the government and community embrace the families as part of the nation, neither discriminating against them nor stigmatising them. Social rehabilitation is an effort to see that a family does not fall between the fault lines of a counterterrorism strategy and, more importantly, their concerns are not addressed by the terrorist fraternity, thus propelling them further into the very environment that their former radical family members were once in.

There is no denying that putting a family member in detention may cause difficulties to their family. However, it is still necessary. There is a need to isolate radical extremists from society and even from their own families until they are fully rehabilitated. In detention, they are unable to directly indoctrinate their families with radical ideology. As Zak Ebrahim (cited in Breakwell 2014) puts it:

> The fact that my father went to prison for an unfathomable crime when I was seven just about ruined my life. But it also made my life possible. He could not fill me with hate from jail. And, more than that, he could not stop me from coming in contact with the sorts of people he demonized and discovering that they were human beings—people I could care about and who could care about me.

Conditions of social rehabilitation

The stakeholders have to be identified first to implement social rehabilitation. As families are the main beneficiaries, the skills of religious clerics, social workers, counsellors, psychologists, NGOs and civil society can be tapped into. Ideally, an aftercare programme with families should begin immediately after the detainee's incarceration. The sooner engagement starts, the lesser the risk of resentment developing in the families.

In rehabilitation, it is important for the rehab team not to be judgemental towards the families and to build a strong rapport with them. Effective counter-terrorism requires a nation to perceive each member of the society as potential partner in preserving national security. The main purposes of social rehabilitation are to help the families cope with the difficulties of having their family member detained, stop the regeneration of terrorists and assist in the reintegration of detainees after their release.

Components of social rehabilitation

We propose the following four areas to be included to achieve a holistic family and social rehabilitation. It is not limited to these four points and can be expanded further, but these are the fundamental ones that would be beneficial for social rehabilitation.

Religious guidance

Religious or spiritual guidance is the most important part of rehabilitation because it addresses extremism, which is rooted in ideology. Dismantling terrorist organisations by attacking their military training camps and killing their leadership is important, but insufficient. Those who espouse the ideology are not required to be a part of any group or organisation. Individually or as a group, they are able to pose a threat to national security (Sageman 2008: 31). As the crux of the problem is the ideology that they adhere to (Briggs 2012), this ideology will persist if not effectively addressed. Its expansion will generate new leadership and new operatives to replace the old ones.

Cases of whole families including young children being exposed to radical ideology are not something new. There are families who travel together to join the terrorist network ISIS such as a family from Indonesia and another from Singapore who brought with them three young children aged between 2 to 11 years old (Straits Times 2014). Without proper religious-educational intervention, these children are at risk of becoming the next generation of a terrorist network.

For those arrested and detained, they would receive religious guidance during the detention period like in Singapore and Saudi Arabia. Their families, especially the wives, will be provided with similar assistance by a volunteer female cleric. The wives are expected to impart the teaching to their children and lessen the resentment they may feel. Engaging the families by challenging radical and, to some extent, violent ideology and replacing them with peaceful narratives and a moderate understanding of Islam would minimise the sympathy and support for an extremist confused worldview.

Emotional and psychological support

When a terrorist is either killed or captured, the threat they pose to the security of a nation is mitigated; however, it also means that a family has lost its family member temporarily or forever if killed, and this causes significant emotional trauma. Psychological counselling would be essential to help families cope with the grief and it also helps to ease any resentment that they may feel. This engagement would give a voice of reason and a form of comfort to the families (Rahmat 2008).

Financial support

When the breadwinner of the family ceases to exist, naturally the family would face difficulties. Family and social rehabilitation should ensure that the family of a detainee does not fall into destitution during the period of detention. If the family is already in a poor state before the detention, family and social rehabilitation can help ease the burden. Rehabilitation should also ensure that the children still have the means to go to school and study. Financial support will assist the family to get by until they can stand on their own two feet. Some of the things that this mode of support should cover are house mortgage payments, electric bills, school fees and textbooks for children and food. The role of social workers is most important in this area.

Skills upgrading

To quote Nelson Mandela: 'Education is the most powerful weapon which you can use to change the world.' Most of the detainees in Singapore were sole breadwinners, while their wives are homemakers. Although financial assistance was provided, many families would prefer to be independent, or be less dependent on others' support. Skills and vocational upgrading help boost their confidence and facilitate them in terms of job opportunities. This can assist the family to progress towards becoming more self-reliant during the period of detainees' incarceration and before they are gainfully employed after release. Providing vocational training and skills upgrading can also help families to be more confident and reduce dependency upon others.

Social workers can further facilitate by advising the type of training suitable for the wives and by helping source employment. One example for this was narrated by Sharifah Sakinah Ali Alkaff from Yayasan Mendaki, an NGO in Singapore that helps families of detainees with educational assistance. Through Yayasan Mendaki, a detainee's wife, Madam A (not her real name) obtained a certificate in office skills, which helped her land a job as an administrative clerk.

Yayasan Mendaki also helped get a tuition-fee waiver and book vouchers for her school-going children (Alkaff 2009).

Case studies

There is no universally applicable counterterrorism policy or a one-size-fits-all approach in terrorist rehabilitation (Shanmugam 2009). Experience from countries that have adopted rehabilitation in their strategic counterterrorism efforts shows that while there are similarities in approach, there are also key differences to suit each country's context. The best way forward is for each national government to take into account the nature and severity of the threat and its context to design an appropriate and effective response (Wilkinson 2006: 203–206).

This section will examine the family and social rehabilitation component applied in rehabilitation programmes in three countries: Singapore, Saudi Arabia and Sri Lanka.

Singapore (Hassan 2007)

Singapore's rehabilitation approach is largely a community-based initiative supported by the government. Social rehabilitation in Singapore comes from the Religious Rehabilitation Group (RRG) that provides religious guidance and the Inter-Agency Aftercare Group (ACG) that provides social support.

RRG

Singapore's government understood that the religious dimension in the threat of terrorism in Singapore requires the expertise of religious scholars. This has led to the formation of the RRG. The RRG brings together religious scholars as volunteers who provide religious counselling for detainees, supervisees (those under Restriction Orders) and their wives. Aside from the regular family visits, there are female *ustazaats* (clerics) in the RRG who give counselling to the detainees' wives. The clerics also counsel Singaporean female Internal Security Act (ISA) detainees who are held for harbouring the intention to travel to conflict zones to join ISIS.

In an interview with an RRG female counsellor who counselled a JI detainee's wife, she said: 'They led very secluded lives and all of a sudden, their husbands were gone and they did not know for how long. They had no family support. It was very traumatising for them' (Abdul Hamid 2008: 154).

Counselling for the wives of detainees was initiated upon the realisation that it was important to counter extremist teachings by educating the wives on the rightful understanding of Islam, as they will be the first pillar of support for their husbands upon their release. As most of them are mothers, this is also to prevent them from educating their children with the extremist version of religious understanding propounded by their husbands. Furthermore, in the event of re-radicalisation of their husbands, they would be better equipped with peaceful

Islamic knowledge to help guide their husbands back to moderation or seek out a counsellor for guidance.

As members of the RRG are also active religious preachers, they are also the best ambassadors to spread the message of peace and love for the nation to the wider Muslim community through public speeches and forums.

ACG

Many of the JI detainees were sole breadwinners of their families, and their wives were homemakers. One of the measures taken in ensuring that the families' needs and welfare are taken care of while the head of the family is in detention was the establishment of the ACG. Local Muslim groups and organisations such as Taman Bacaan, Yayasan Mendaki, Association of Muslim Professionals (AMP) and the Young Muslim Women's Association come together with their own expertise in assisting families with emotional and financial support. The ACG also ensures that education of their children is not disrupted and they are able to lead their lives as normally as possible. For instance, Yayasan Mendaki provides free or subsidised tuition and educational programme fees for the children while AMP provides counselling for the wives and families.

Saudi Arabia (Boucek 2008; International Centre for Political Violence and Terrorism Research 2010b; Al-Hadlaq 2011)

Saudi Arabia boasts the largest terrorist rehabilitation centre and one of the most comprehensive rehabilitation programmes in the world. In Saudi Arabia, the family plays a crucial role in the rehabilitation and reintegration process. Saudis believe that if a family feels that everything is being done for them, they are more likely to be willing to participate in the programme. Under its Prevention, Rehabilitation and Aftercare strategy, Saudi Arabia has an office – the Psychological and Social Subcommittee – that deals especially with the social needs of detainees' families. It aims to identify and deliver assistance before it is even requested to deter families from becoming radicalised. Programmes to help unmarried detainees find spouses and get married are also conducted in addition to supporting the families of incarcerated breadwinners. The subcommittee is supported by psychologists, psychiatrists, social scientists, researchers and social workers.

The perception that the programme is benevolent is considered a critical aspect to its success. The Ministry of Interior also extends the social support programme to a detainee's extended family and tribe as not only will this prevent them from radicalisation but it also helps to secure the family's cooperation to keep the detainee on the right path after his release. During the rehabilitation process, families are offered generous financial and social support. The ministry holds the extended family responsible if the beneficiary commits new offences after his release.

All of these concerted efforts rendered by the Saudi government aim to win the hearts and minds of detainees and their families, and, at the same time, it is hoped that by offering such programme, the detainees will be occupied with activities and appreciate the value of life.

Sri Lanka

According to the Bureau of the Commissioner General for Rehabilitation (BCGR), approximately 12,000 former Liberation Tigers of Tamil Eelam (LTTE) members have been rehabilitated and reintegrated into society since the end of the war in 2009 (Tamils Against Genocide 2014). During their rehabilitation period, they were accommodated at the Protective Accommodation and Rehabilitation Centres managed by the BCGR.

Sri Lanka adopts the '6 + 1 Model' rehabilitation programme, which includes: (1) educational rehabilitation; (2) vocational rehabilitation; (3) psychosocial and creative therapies for rehabilitation; (4) social, cultural and family rehabilitation; (5) spiritual and religious rehabilitation; and (6) recreational rehabilitation; plus (+) community engagement. An aftercare system was put in place for the beneficiaries who required livelihood support once the rehabilitation programme was completed (Hettiarachchi 2013).

Under its social, cultural and family rehabilitation, social and educational tours to different parts of Sri Lanka are provided to gain an understanding of the diversity within the island. These included visits to universities, schools and other developments in Colombo, the ethnically diverse commercial capital of Sri Lanka. These tours are an important eye-opening experience for the former LTTE members as almost 99 per cent of them had never left the conflict area they resided in due to strict LTTE control (Global Cities Research Institute n.d.). With these tours, they are more exposed to the diverse cultures living together as a cohesive society in Sri Lanka.

Visits by family or next of kin are also encouraged. Visits will take place in an atmosphere conducive to rehabilitation. Detainees are also encouraged to write and receive letters, and pay visits to home villages in the event of a celebration, illness or a death in the family.

Challenges

Countries with different political settings have been observed employing family and social rehabilitation programmes as an alternative to combat terrorism and radicalism. Saudi Arabia, for example, a theocratic state that offers the most comprehensive terrorist rehabilitation programme, engages violent extremist offenders (VEOs) using this mode of rehabilitation as one of its approaches and claims a success rate of 80 to 90 per cent (Boucek 2008). Notwithstanding its oppressive junta image, Sri Lanka under the leadership of the Rajapaksa government founded the BCGR for ex-combatants following the defeat of LTTE in 2009. By November 2012, it has since benefited 11,044 ex-detainees (Hettiarachchi 2013). Singapore, a secular state, embarked on the same programme by introducing the ACG in 2002. According to Zaleha Ahmad from the AMP, in addition to home visits counselling, trust-building and emotional support, the association also offers services to the family based on their specific needs such as financial assistance, educational development and economic empowerment (S. Rajaratnam School of International Studies 2009).

While all these success stories deserve the limelight, there are challenges that come with various degrees of intensity and these differ from one country/region to another. This section aims to bring to light issues that could and, in some cases, have challenged the smooth implementation of social and family rehabilitation.

Political willingness

Many governments are continuously being challenged by the threat of extremism and terrorism. Kinetic responses, on the one hand, could only counter the threat partially, but at times were not necessarily effective. Though real and immediate results are achievable through kinetic responses, despite the destruction and disruption to terrorist organisations, the threat continues without the slightest sign of abatement. Kinetic responses also produce significant impact to the defence budget, but governments are willing to commit because they deliver results albeit short-term ones. The key phrase here is 'instant results'.

Rehabilitation, on the other hand, connotes a long-term commitment. In addition to its time-insensitive nature, the approach offers no guarantee of zero-recidivism and acknowledges the absence of a mechanism to measure success. In 2014, Saudi Arabia announced that about 12 per cent of its rehabilitated terrorists had gone back to terrorism (Taylor 2014). The kingdom, however, never disclosed the actual figure of detainees participated in its rehabilitation programme. This, in some ways, casts doubt over its effectiveness and whether it is worth the consideration among politicians. This notion was reinforced by Ali Soufan, CEO of the Soufan Group, as he spoke about obstacles to rehabilitation at the International Conference on Terrorist Rehabilitation and Community Engagement held in Singapore in 2013. He maintained that without political willingness, rehabilitation is 'toothless' and the reason for this is because 'politicians do not see tangible results' in the shortest time possible (Soufan 2013).

Bureaucracy

In many cases, state officials formulate and grant approval for a policy to be implemented. It is also common to see complicated administrative procedures impede the implementation of policies. The terrorist rehabilitation programme is not an exception. Governments usually assign a ministry or a task force to act as the principal coordinating agency for anti-terrorism and/or counterterrorism works. It is not a simple job because the coordinator, in most cases, does not have the capacity to run the show independently. It requires support from multiple units or departments within its ministry or from another. The coordinating agency needs to get all the actors together to address the problems and share expertise and resources.

A consensus is within reach to define the root problem but not necessarily in the case of resource sharing. Each actor is looking at the issue of implementation from a different standpoint. The need to be prudent in tapping available and limited resources has resulted in a bureaucratic environment. Such situations usually occur when an agency is not completely independent and has to rely on another higher organisation that holds the decision-making privilege or has the upper hand in matters related to funding and disbursement of resources. This will then create a non-productive attitude when the agency does not wish to take up an ownership role and waits passively for 'others' to lead and initiate instead. This challenge was observed in some countries in Southeast Asia.[2] Nevertheless, such an issue may not necessarily apply to all governments.

Credible database

One important question to ask is whether the government owns a current and reliable database of VEO addresses, to begin with. In Sri Lanka, the family of VEOs are part of the rehabilitation programme. They participate in activities such as tours to national places of interest including universities and the commercial capital of Sri Lanka. They also visit places conducive to rehabilitation. VEOs are also allowed to visit their hometown in the event of special ceremony or the demise of family members (Hettiarachchi 2013). This is feasible because the families' whereabouts are already on a database in the safekeeping of the relevant agency. Hence, accessibility is not an issue. On top of that, some governments have dedicated a team that is tasked to keep a close eye on the families so as to maintain current information on their whereabouts and activities.

Such an ideal scenario could be beyond accomplishment for certain countries that do not have such databases and also countries with databases that are out of date. In the Philippines, for example, affected families are in hiding or in constantly on the move to avoid government tracking.[3] Also, these families usually live within a like-minded group who are also in the same boat. Thus, it is only natural that each of them is watching each other's back. According to a government official, text messages are an important mode of communication between these families. The presence of an outsider in their neighbourhood, in this case a social worker or case officer, will alarm the entire population. The concerned party will likely be alerted by members of the community to the presence of the 'foreigner' through text messages. The concerned individuals will go into hiding to avoid being located. To top it all, some of them could be living in rural areas or even in the forest where establishing communication with them is challenging, if not almost impossible.

Another reason why a social and family rehabilitation initiative is likely to face a challenge in this setting is because the security and safety of both the authority and the extremist group are likely to be compromised. Locating the wives and uncovering their hideout is as good as stirring up a hornet's nest. For the authority, it is not worth investing in such programme when the safety of its agencies is at stake. To engage in confrontation and the unnecessary exchange of gunfire is the last thing the authority would want.

Trust issues

In the course of the reintegration process, a rehabilitation programme not only provides financial assistance to VEOs and their families but also helps detainees to get a job upon release. Wives are empowered through social assistance until they can stand on their own two feet. For children trapped in poverty, education will be made accessible to them. These are the mechanisms used to boost their morale and ease their resentment over the detention of family members.

The incentives, however, sometimes look too good to be true. The receiving end may perceive it as an attempt to co-opt them to work with the government. It gives rise to two immediate concerns. First, what the government expects from the beneficiaries and whether the beneficiaries can satisfy the government's expectations. Second, whether participation in such programme will compromise their loyalty and association with other individuals in their community. This could be the case when social workers or personnel working on this programme are perceived as agents that provide human intelligence or privilege information to the authority. If this is the case, they will be labelled as traitors and may be boycotted or even exposed to life-threatening danger.

Language barrier

The government should not undermine the role of effective communication, which requires one to master the art of communication and essentially the language itself. Speaking the same dialect and language helps to translate intent in the simplest manner and is a fundamental tool to win hearts and minds.

Tausug, for instance, is a language spoken in three countries though not in its entirety, in the state of Sabah, Malaysia, in North Kalimantan, Indonesia and the province of Sulu in the Philippines. In the case of Philippines, most Filipinos speak Tagalog or one of the seven other major dialects: Bikol, Cebuano, Hiligaynon (Ilonggo), Ilocano, Kapampangan, Pangasinan and Waray. The majority of the Filipino Muslims residing in the Sulu and Mindanao region are Tausug conversant. Therefore, deploying Tausug-conversant social workers could double the chance of effective engagement with the families. Angell and Gunaratna (2011: 355) asserted that this mode of rehabilitation essentially engages the mental and social wellbeing of beneficiaries to avert further escalation of resentment. Hence the government cannot afford to accept the language barrier being added to the already long list of daunting challenges in the rehabilitation programme. Social workers' human-relations skills should be supported with language proficiency to forge a warm relationship with the families and to gain their trust. The ability to communicate using the local dialect symbolises sincerity on the part of the government in attending to the beneficiaries' livelihood difficulties. It strategically indicates that inclusivism is part of the Philippine domestic policy and rules out allegations of the existence of a marginalisation policy against the Muslim population.

If not properly presented, the beneficiaries may develop a belief that participation in family and social rehabilitation programmes is a pre-requisite for the release of a VEO. This justifies the importance of language proficiency as it helps to minimise the likelihood of misunderstanding over the spirit behind this initiative. This is rather appealing to countries that have a penal code that orders arrest and imprisonment for a specific period, and also countries that employ unspecific detention periods such as Singapore, which is exercising its ISA. The ability to convince the beneficiary through common language is a must when initiating the family and social rehabilitation programme so that the beneficiary will have a clear picture of the objective of the programme. It will also help to rule out any false or baseless expectations.

Funding and sustainability

Many governments may have attended regional or international symposiums and conferences on building rehabilitation capability. Many also would have agreed that this subtle approach is worth committing to. The International Conference on Terrorist Rehabilitation, which was held in Singapore in 2009, drew the participation of 12 country representatives from Southeast Asia, South Asia, Central Asia and the Middle East. Today, there is only a handful of systematic rehabilitation programmes out there. A closer observation suggests that the lack or absence of financial support, which could possibly impair the programme, is the cause. Our observations point to two pertinent challenges that need to be addressed by governments.

With regard to sustaining a steady flow of funding, we would argue that governments have to address two types of challenges. First, the absence of funding support from the government could hamper this programme from taking off. For example, in 2013, a group of male Muslim religious clerics founded Salam Engagement Group Philippines Inc. (SEGP). The group was modelled after Singapore's very own RRG. It was supposed to provide religious counselling to VEOs incarcerated in federal prison. The clerics/counsellors had undergone a series of capacity-building training sessions so as to equip themselves with the relevant skills and knowledge. However, the plan failed to materialise due to financial constraints that overshadow the voluntary group that is there to play its part in addressing a national issue. The fund is supposed to help counsellors defray transportation expenses and provide them with minimal allowances as a token for their work. Today, SEGP is almost defunct. Likewise, family and social rehabilitation programmes could share the same fate if government fails to get its act together.

The second challenge is rather hypothetical. We would argue that a programme will have to face the possibility of discontinuation if funding stops flowing. The rehabilitation programme in Saudi Arabia, for instance, is entirely funded by the kingdom. During an official visit to the Mohammed bin Nayef Center for Advice,

Counseling and Care on the outskirts of Riyadh in early 2014, our delegation was briefed that counsellors and social workers are working with beneficiaries throughout the rehabilitation journey. On top of religious guidance undertaken by Saudi clerics and university professors, the families also receive emotional, psychological and financial assistance. Academic and vocational training is being offered at the centre so that beneficiaries could obtain the required knowledge and skill set to join the labour force upon release. Moreover, if they are not married or planning for a marriage in the future, but are financially challenged, the authority will render assistance by providing dowry and a house to jump start their new journey.

This type of intervention demands a generous budget. A steady flow of resources is so important and determines the continuation of the operation. The initiative might send the wrong signals to those who find it attractive to be part of the programme to take advantage of the readily available perks.

Changes in policy

States review and revise their policies from time to time. Political and financial motivation, among others, could produce an unpredictable trajectory of domestic policy relating to a rehabilitation programme. Perhaps Yemen is a good example in this regard.

Yemen was the first country to embark on a rehabilitation programme post-9/11. The four-pronged approach that combined religious dialogue, security, economics, and regional and international cooperation was initiated in 2002, but only lasted three years (International Centre for Political Violence and Terrorism Research 2010a). It received international recognition as a pioneer of employing an unconventional strategic approach to counterterrorism. However, the country, which was under the leadership of President Ali Abdullah Saleh, decided to make a paradigm shift in its policy by putting an end to the programme. Open sources reported that it was a result of its constant domestic 'political disputes and struggles' (International Centre for Political Violence and Terrorism Research 2010a).

In our view, domestic policy could pose a challenge if three different scenarios emerge: first, when there is a change of leadership to someone who favours a different way of dealing with the threat or someone who simply does not trust in the programme; second, when a new government believes that rehabilitation no longer merits a priority status; and third, the nature of the programme, which demands long-term commitment on the part of the government, and its resource-exhaustive nature could be the pitfall eventually.

Conclusion

Saudi Arabia, Yemen, Singapore and Sri Lanka have their own success stories to share in this regard. There are also cases where such programme failed to take off, for whatever reason. The chapter has presented the challenges that have to be recognised and addressed. These challenges could have been the reason for the downfall of the programme. It is important to note that, eventually, it boils down to three important elements of forming and sustaining a rehabilitation programme.

The first element is the provider, which is the government. It is true that state's behaviour reflects its interest. Regardless whether it is a single-party government or a coalition, it needs to get its act together, make an effort to understand the threat landscape, conduct thorough research on available options to solve the issue before finally getting the needed support from every single entity of the government. This should help to avoid the first obstacle, which is lack of political willingness.

The second element is the beneficiary. It is crucial to know and understand the needs and constraints of the beneficiaries. It is equally paramount to identify the right approach and strategy that will bring a government to arrive at the desired outcome, which is to win hearts and minds.

The third and final element is human and financial resources. The programme has to be led by individuals that are knowledgeable, equipped with the right skills, charismatic, resourceful and influential. It needs a persona that asserts the value of life and motivates others to contribute for the betterment of all. Financial resources mean a substantial amount of funding needs to be raised and dedicated to supporting the programme. The government should not shoulder the entire burden alone but should identify strategic partners instead. Local and international foundations, NGOs and regional countries could form options for strategic partnerships.

Notes

1 For examples, see the Singapore case study in this chapter.
2 Author's experience during work to build rehabilitation capability in a Southeast Asian country.
3 Author's interview with Philippine intelligence, August 2014.

Bibliography

Abdul Hamid, Siti Rahmah (2008) 'Caught in a Bad Situation', in Ali Mohamed and Saat A. Rahman (eds) *Winning Hearts and Minds: Embracing Peace*. Singapore: Khadijah Mosque: 154.

Al-Hadlaq, Abdulrahman (2011) 'Terrorist Rehabilitation: the Saudi Experience', in Rohan Gunaratna, Jolene Jerard and Lawrence Rubin (eds) *Terrorist Rehabilitation and Counter-Radicalisation: New Approaches to Counter-terrorism*. New York: Routledge: 59–69.

Alkaff, Sharifah Sakinah Ali (2009) Speaking on YM's programmes and assistance schemes at the International Conference on Terrorist Rehabilitation, 24 February 2009. Available at: www.rsis.edu.sg/wp-content/uploads/2015/04/Report-International-Conference-On-Terrorist-Rehabilitation.pdf (accessed 2 February 2015).

Angell, Ami and Rohan Gunaratna (2011) *Terrorist Rehabilitation: The U.S. Experience in Iraq*. Boca Raton, FL: CRC Press.

Boucek, Christopher (2008) 'Saudi Arabia's "Soft" Counterterrorism Strategy: Prevention, Rehabilitation, and Aftercare'. *Carnegie Endowment*. Available at: http://carnegieendowment.org/files/cp97_boucek_saudi_final.pdf (accessed 24 March 2014).

Breakwell, Tom (2014) 'My Father Was a Terrorist'. *Vice*. Available at: www.vice.com/en_us/article/mv5x4b/my-father-was-a-terrorist-zak-ebrahim-172 (accessed 31 December 2014).

Briggs, Rachel (2012) 'The Changing Face of Al Qaeda'. *Institute for Strategic Dialogue*.

Global Cities Research Institute (n.d.) *Colombo – Sri Lanka*, Global Cities, RMIT Research Institute. Available at: http://global-cities.info/placemarks/colombo-sri-lanka (accessed 30 October 2014).

Gunaratna, Rohan (2009) 'The Battlefield of the Mind: Rehabilitating Muslim Terrorists'. *UNISCI Discussion Papers*, 21: 149, 151. Available at: www.unisci.es/wp-content/uploads/2017/05/UNISCI-DP-21-ROHAN.pdf (accessed 16 May 2018).

Hassan, Muhammad Haniff (2007) 'Singapore's Muslim community-based initiatives against JI'. *Perspectives on Terrorism*, 1(5). Available at: www.terrorismanalysts.com/pt/index.php/pot/article/view/17/html (accessed 17 February 2014).

Hettiarachchi, Malkanthi (2013) 'Sri Lanka's Rehabilitation Program: A New Frontier in Counter Terrorism and Counter Insurgency'. *Prism: Journal of the Center for Complex Operations*, 4(2): 105–107, 112.

Hoffman, Bruce (1985) *The Prevention of Terrorism and Rehabilitation of Terrorists: Some Preliminary Thoughts*. No. RAND/P-7059. Santa Monica, CA: Rand Corp.

International Centre for Political Violence and Terrorism Research (2010a) *Combating Terrorism in Yemen through the Committee for Religious Dialogue: A Report on ICPVTR Visit to Yemen, Yemen, July 2010*. Available at: www.rsis.edu.sg/wp-content/uploads/2015/04/Report-Combating-Terrorism-in-Yemen-Through-the-Committee-for-Religious-Dialogue.pdf (accessed 6 March 2014).

International Centre for Political Violence and Terrorism Research (2010b) *Saudi Initiatives in Countering Terrorism: A Report on ICPVTR Visit to Saudi Arabia, Saudi Arabia, February 6–14, 2010*. Available at: www.rsis.edu.sg/wp-content/uploads/2015/04/Report-Saudi-Initiatives-in-Countering-Terrorism.pdf (accessed 17 February 2014).

Jerard, Jolene (2009) 'International Conference on Terrorist Rehabilitation (ICTR)'. In *Report on a Conference Organized by the International Centre of Political Violence and Terrorism Research (ICPVTR)*. Singapore: Nanyang Technological University.

Kruglanski, A.W., Gelfand, M.J. and Gunaratna, R. (n.d.) 'Aspects of Deradicalization'. *Institute for the Study of Asymmetric Conflict*. Available at: www.asymmetricconflict.org/articles/aspects-of-deradicalization/ (accessed 27 May 2018).

Mathiesen, Thomas (2006) *Prison on Trial*. 3rd edn. Winchester: Waterside Press.

Mohamed, Ali and Saat A. Rahman (2008) *Winning Hearts and Minds: Embracing Peace*. Singapore: Khadijah Mosque.

Rahmat, Hamidah (2008) 'Family Counselling', in Ali Mohamed and Saat A. Rahman (eds) *Winning Hearts and Minds: Embracing Peace*. Singapore: Khadijah Mosque: 122.

S. Rajaratnam School of International Studies (2009) *Report on International Conference on Terrorist Rehabilitation (ICTR)*. Singapore: S. Rajaratnam School of International Studies. Available at: www.rsis.edu.sg/wp-content/uploads/2015/04/Report-International-Conference-On-Terrorist-Rehabilitation.pdf (accessed 24 May 2018).

Sageman, Marc (2008) *Leaderless Jihad*. Philadelphia: University of Pennsylvania Press, Inc.

Shanmugam, K. (2009) 'Inaugural Speech', at the International Conference on Terrorist Rehabilitation, Singapore, 24 February 2009. Available at www.rsis.edu.sg/wp-content/uploads/2015/04/Report-International-Conference-On-Terrorist-Rehabilitation.pdf (accessed 2 February 2015).

Soufan, Ali (2013) 'Challenges of Rehabilitation Initiatives', presented at International Conference on Terrorist Rehabilitation and Community Engagement, Singapore, 26–27, March 2013.

Straits Times (2014) 'Alarming Rise in Support for ISIS in Indonesia, Says Counter-Terrorism Chief', 8 December 2014. Available at: www.straitstimes.com/asia/se-asia/alarming-rise-in-support-for-isis-in-indonesia-says-counter-terrorism-chief (accessed 16 May 2018).

Tamils Against Genocide (2014) *Sri Lanka's 'Rehabilitation' of the Liberation Tigers Tamil Eelam*. Available at: www.tamilsagainstgenocide.org/Data/Docs/TAG-Rehabilitation-Report-January-2014-Final.pdf (accessed 16 May 2018).

Taylor, Adam (2014) 'Saudi Arabia Says 12 Percent of Its "Rehabilitated" Terrorists Have Returned To Terror'. *The Washington Post*, 28 November, 2014. Available at: www.washingtonpost.com/news/worldviews/wp/2014/11/28/saudi-arabia-says-12-percent-of-its-rehabilitated-terrorists-have-returned-to-terror/?utm_term=.81411c289a76 (accessed 16 May 2018).

Wilkinson, Paul (2006) *Terrorism versus Democracy: The Liberal State Response*. 2nd edn. London and New York: Routledge/Taylor & Francis.

7 Psychological rehabilitation for ideology-based terrorism offenders

Zora A. Sukabdi

Introduction

As a means to reestablish human capacity and human function in society, rehabilitation of terrorism offenders is an effort that aims to return terrorism offenders to normal life, improve their self-efficacy, and ensure reintegration so that they have a positive function in society. The offenders indulge in psychological, economic, cultural, educational, social, and human resources activities that are integrated to produce a holistic condition. It is a continuous process through the integrative cooperation of various government institutions and civil society. Specifically, psychological and other forms of rehabilitation for terrorism offenders focus on character building of terrorist offenders to achieve more peaceful states of mind and favorable attitudes so they can contribute to society successfully. Orientation of psychological-development activities gives an opportunity to clients (i.e. former offenders) to solve their own problems in a client-centered fashion by providing direction and assistance. Hence, the nature of the activities does not focus on the ability of the implementers/development team and this approach makes it possible to avoid client dependance on their development facilitators.

At a practical level, there are two types of rehabilitation programs for terrorism offenders. The first includes isolation techniques ('*exclusiveness*') and other applications of discipline techniques. The second includes allowing terrorism offenders to mix with other criminal inmates including other terrorism offenders with different roles, backgrounds, levels in religious groups, and motivation (called '*inclusiveness*') and to meet any visitors. Both exclusiveness and inclusiveness include counseling sessions, assistance (e.g. programs for family), exposure to new learning experiences, dialogues with several 'moderate clerics,' and empowerment facilitation.

The fundamental reason for exclusiveness is related to the prevention of the spread of an ideology that justifies violence. The use of sacred texts (*tafsir*) to justify violence (Venkatraman, 2007; Putra & Sukabdi, 2013) and the wide range of terrorist networks are seen to be hazardous (Shemella, 2011; Gunaratna & Rubin, 2011), hence exclusiveness is seen to be the best option. Another disciplinary technique as part of exclusiveness is the use of rewards (e.g. visiting session, opportunities, and facilities) and punishments (e.g. forced duties, some access limitations, line of marching, and flag ceremonies) during rehabilitation. The purpose is to modify and shape behavior based on a functional conditioning (i.e. instrumental conditioning) technique by behavioralists. Negative behaviors are expected to change in form, frequency, or strength through this process. Moreover, recruitment of other types of criminals and even prison officers by terrorism inmates and the riots in several prisons in Indonesia support the argument that this first type of rehabilitation is needed.

Different from exclusiveness, inclusiveness in the rehabilitation process allows terrorism offenders to blend with other criminal inmates and meet visitors. It is often understood as a cultural approach, even though the term 'cultural approach' essentially has larger and comprehensive meaning than that simply associated with inclusiveness as it involves a high sense of local wisdom and philosophy. This type of rehabilitation has many supporters among the ranks of civil society and human-rights activists, yet it brings with it some risk at the operational level such as tension, recruitment, the potential for riots, or military camps at prisons.

To address whether inclusiveness or exclusiveness is best for application in rehabilitating the psychology of terrorism offenders, this chapter will discuss psychological rehabilitation further using some empirical data to support the explanation. As the discussion about rehabilitating terrorism offenders will always be linked to the motivation of terrorism, this chapter will begin the discussion with a review of the motives of terrorism offenders and some demographical data about perpetrators in Indonesia. Further, the chapter will highlight some principles and steps in psychological rehabilitation and other practically related issues to illuminate how elected facilitators operate in psychological rehabilitation and what competencies and requirements a facilitator of psychological rehabilitation should have in order to treat terrorism offenders.

Psychological motives and causes of terrorism

Many studies indicate that terrorism based on religious ideology engages religious people (Moghaddam, 2006, 2008; Moghaddam et al., 2007; Bandura, 1999, 2004; Kruglanski & Fishman, 2009) and is strongly related to religious fundamentalism (Pech & Slade, 2006; Taylor & Horgan, 2001; Horgan, 2008). Those studies also describe the steps taken by people who gradually become involved in terrorism. It is a complex process comprising the following three simplified phases: (1) joining the terrorist group; (2) staying within the terrorist group; and (3) exiting, quitting, or disengaging from the terrorist group, whether or not that follows a process of deradicalization. Some scholars suggest that what motivates terrorists varies according to their level and role in a terrorist organization or network (Englehart & Kurzman, 2006; Victoroff, 2005). Accordingly, leaders or inner-circle members in a terrorist group or network may have different motives, targets, and strategies from those of ordinary members or field offenders and among each other.

A study in Indonesia by Mufid et al. (2011) points out three roles of radical religious activists: (1) a leader or ideologue (9.1 percent) who creates ideas and concepts; (2) middle management or organizers (10 percent), namely those who are classified into strategist/technocrat, recruiter, trainer/dispatcher, and supplier/armorer roles; and (3) followers (80.9 percent), categorized as foot soldiers/action perpetrators, technicians, researcher/surveyor/errand runners, transporters, and sympathizer/fellow travelers. Further, there is a number of psychological factors that motivates individuals to be involved in terrorist acts according to Mufid et al. (2011). The factors can be classified into six motives: (1) religious-ideological, that is to establish ideals of religion-based government or society (the establishment of *ad-Dawlah al-Islāmiyah*—a state based on Islamic philosophy and rules—or the implementation of *Sharia*—Islamic law based on the Quran and the Sunna) where violent or terrorist acts are considered as a legitimate means to achieve these ideals; (2) solidarity-driven, that is to express empathy or help fellow believers, especially when they are threatened or become victims in a conflict situation; (3) revenge-seeking, that is to join in terrorist acts as an attempt to retaliate against the enemies for losses (lives or property) experienced by offenders or their families; (4) separatist, that is to achieve a political goal of establishing a separate state; (5) mob mentality, that is to spontaneously participate in violent or terrorist acts without having any clear reasons, other than to follow others in such acts; and (6) situational, that is to be involved in terrorist acts by force.

Mufid et al. (2011) prove that related to the association of roles and motives, religious-ideological psychological motives appear in all roles or layers. Moreover, solidarity-driven motivation is found in the organizers and followers. In addition, revenge-seeking motives, mob mentality, and separatist motives are seen in followers. Lastly, situational motives are seen in leaders and followers. The findings showed that religious-ideological motives are found to be the predominant reason that motivates all kinds of offenders to participate in terrorist acts (Mufid et al., 2011). Table 7.1 describes the roles and motives of terrorism offenders in Indonesia.

Table 7.1 Roles and motives of terrorism offenders in Indonesia (Mufid et al., 2011)

		Roles		
		Leader	Organizer	Follower
Motives	Ideological-religious	80	81.8	37.1
	Solidarity-driven	0	18.2	22.5
	Revenge-seeking	0	0	13.5
	Separatist	0	0	2.2
	Mob mentality	0	0	15.7
	Situational	20	0	9
		100	100	100

Note: *n* for each group are 10 (leader), 11 (middle management), and 89 (follower), respectively.

In terms of causes of terrorism, Tore Bjorgo describes the causes of terrorism at several levels, 'with some distantly related and others closely related to terrorism' (Bjorgo, 2005). There are four levels of causes.

The first level is structural causes, consisting of macro factors such as demographic imbalance, globalization, technology, rapid modernization, transitional societies, rising individualism featured with relative deprivation and atomization, class structure, and international inequalities (between Muslim and non-Muslim countries within the broader context of division between the developed and developing world), and others. As causes of terrorism, these structural causes affect the lives of people through a process that might or might not be comprehended by the population. However, terrorist leaders are able to formulate these structural causes in simple terminologies that are easily understood by their followers.

The second is facilitating or accelerating causes, which make terrorism interesting and possible but are not the main drivers. Modern news media, communication technology, transportation technology, weapon technology, weak control of the state over territory, and others make methods and techniques of terrorism possible and easy, even though these factors could not be considered as the main drivers of terrorism.

The third is motivational causes, which motivate action, such as actual grievances experienced at the individual level. These motivational causes can be considered as symptoms of more fundamental causes.

The fourth is triggering causes, which are seen as the direct trigger of terrorist acts, such as provocative events, political turmoil, excessive action of the enemies, or incidences that require retaliation (Bjorgo, 2005).

Related to radicalism and terrorism in Central Asia specifically, Michael Mihalka (2006) notes that never-ending poverty, increasing inequality across national, regional, and ethnic lines, rampant corruption, and the arbitrary nature of the governments in Central Asia are structural factors that lead to crisis in the region and spur recruitment into radical groups. In the context of terrorism in Indonesia, the single variable of economic factors (e.g. poverty and social inequality) is inadequate to be considered as a structural factor that causes the rise of terrorism. Instead, a combination of structural factors at the global, national, and subnational levels could be considered significant for the rise of terrorism in Indonesia (Mufid et al., 2011).

Related to radicalism, a series of interviews and focus-group discussions with 24 senior religious scholars and charismatic icons in Indonesia was held to understand the psychological transformation of faith into violence. All scholars agreed that religion is identified with the purpose of achieving well-being, both physically and spiritually, both in this world and in the hereafter, as well as materially and spiritually. According to them, since well-being always involves other people, it follows that most religions and beliefs have rules that underscore social ethics, namely those that specify how to coexist with other people. When interacting with other people in a context of society, those ethics explain that faith can lead to radicalism due to the norm of the society and due to violence that stems from different expressions of faith.

There are four expression levels of faith according to senior religious scholars in Indonesia. First, is the private or individual level where faith is only expressed by individuals. Second, there is the communal tier where faith is expressed in families, neighborhoods, places of worship, and among close friends. Third, is the public or social level where faith is expressed publicly. At this level, diverse religious believers mix and coexist next to one another. Automatically, certain discussion topics (such as the value of male and female leaders) and certain religious practices (such as loud reminders for *sahur*—breakfast prior to fasting) which were previously socialized and expressed freely at the communal level become limited in the public domain. This is due to the desire to appreciate others who are of a different faith and ideology. As a result, rules that are mutually agreed and 'universally good' are the ones used in the public domain. Criticizing a particular religion in this domain will become a public issue and might result in conflict. Fourth, is when the state expresses faith in public policies such as anti-corruption efforts, single-roof management, professionalism of the cabinet, Islamic banking, *Hajj* (annual pilgrimage to Mecca) quota, and so on. Religion at this level is expressed in a format that can be accepted by the majority of citizens. In a religious state, religious laws are adopted as state laws. This is due to a specific historical condition that causes laws of a certain religion to become part of the customs and traditions of the people. In this case, the resistance level of the people toward religious laws seems minimal because they are used to carrying out the time-honored laws of that religion.

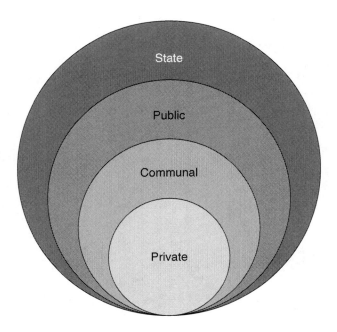

Figure 7.1 Expression of faith

Figure 7.1 describes the expression of faith. According to Indonesian religious scholars, religious violence psychologically occurs when there is a dispute on how to express faith. For example, one religious group or organization agrees to put religious law, practice, and tradition at the state level, while another religious group or organization suggests putting them at the communal level. The dispute arising from differences in opinion may lead to tension, conflict, or violence. In some cases, it may also become a political issue.

Reviewing the findings related to psychological motives and causes of terrorism, one can conclude that rehabilitating ideology-based terrorism offenders is a complex project and concept. It should cover careful individual assessments, parameters of effectiveness, systematically planned programs and steps, high commitment, consistencies, collaborative work, and coordination among entities. Both exclusiveness and inclusiveness approaches may need to be combined and adjusted to fit the context (e.g. causes of each case) and the offenders (e.g. roles and motives) to whom rehabilitation is applied. Hence, the use of the approaches depends on the specific situation.

Steps of psychological rehabilitation

The objective of psychological rehabilitation for religious terrorism offenders, or clients, is to assist them to achieve optimum independence from extremism in mental, social, spiritual, and vocational aspects; achieve their maximum capacity for a better quality of life by acknowledging past mistakes; work to overcome their own personal issues; acquire social, spiritual, and vocational dexterity; and contribute to broader society. Psychological rehabilitation has four functions. The first is the prevention function, which is making clients incapable of falling back into acts of terrorism. The second is the rehabilitation function, which is empowering clients to be useful and able to function in the community. The third is the maintenance function, which provides clients with the capability to maintain the progress that they have achieved. The fourth is the provisioning function, which is equipping clients with the basic spiritual, social, emotional, and economic skills that will become cornerstones in their future lives.

Based on focus-group discussions conducted by nine counterterrorism practitioners who conduct all sorts of rehabilitation programs, including disengagement and deradicalization in Indonesia, there are 15 principles of psychological development for terrorism offenders. The principles are as follows:

1 The principle of humanity where the education and development of religious terrorism offenders are conducted by upholding humanistic principles to maximize human development, building character and positive mindset, and increasing the quality of life as well as physical and spiritual well-being.
2 The principle of creativity where education and development efforts for religious terrorism offenders allow innovation and behavior modification through creative means.

3 The principle of wisdom where education and development are conducted through prioritizing local culture and wisdom so that it is full of social significance for the community.
4 The principle of professionalism where education and development are conducted by professional practitioners with the expertise to achieve the development goals and objectives, upholding the agreed code of ethics, oriented toward quality results, and who have experience that is acknowledged by practitioners in the same field.
5 The principle of empowerment means that education and development involve activists, families, public figures, and all elements of the community.
6 The principle of integration where education and development are conducted thoroughly and cover subjects such as psychology, spirituality, and societal, cultural, legal, and economic dimensions.
7 The principle of effectiveness where education and development benchmarks are periodically assessed for effectiveness with clear parameters and metrics, performed appropriately, on time, with the right measurement, right place, and right target.
8 The principle of appreciation where education and development appraisals constantly recognized all achievements and progress made by all parties involved in the development process.
9 The principle of equality where education and development programs are conducted by upholding values of equality, humility, and simplicity. Hence the facilitators have to present themselves as individuals who are also learning (not placing themselves higher than other people).
10 The principle of integrity where education and development programs are conducted and managed by practitioners with integrity, sincerity, and consistency between words and everyday behavior, and allow for quality control.
11 The principle of politeness where education and development programs are conducted with politeness and in line with local wisdom that does not tolerate any form of symbolic violence such as intimidation, discrimination, threat, bullying, and others.
12 The principle of first care where education and development programs are provided without procrastination as soon as there is demand.
13 The principle of practicality where education or development efforts start from activities that are easily accessible.
14 The principle of staging where education and development initiatives are conducted in sequence from simple beginnings to more advanced curricula.
15 The principle of continuity where education and development are a continuous process with an emphasis on malleability to achieve a continuously evolving business and social environment.

Specifically, according to these practitioners, counselors involved in rehabilitation and aftercare programs for former terrorism activists are divided into six types: (1) mentor; (2) expert; (3) coach; (4) facilitator; (5) counselor; and (6) teacher.

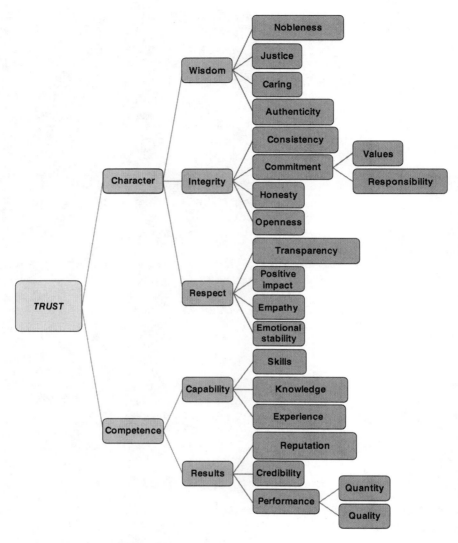

Figure 7.2 Psychological aspects for counselors

Initially, all these counselors must gain the trust of offenders before communicating with them. Without trust between former offenders and educators, behavioral change will not be realized. The trust components are described in Figure 7.2.

As sacred texts are considered to justify the use of violence under certain circumstances, eliminating ideology that advocates violence is unlikely to succeed. Hence practitioners may conduct some critical steps when rehabilitating. These include identifying motives, background, and roles of each perpetrator,

Table 7.2 Development methods for religious terrorism offenders

		Roles		
		Leader	Middle Management	Follower
Motives	Ideological-religious	Religious dialogue, Advocacy	Religious dialogue, Advocacy	Religious education, Advocacy
	Solidarity-driven	Advocacy	Empowerment, Advocacy	Empowerment, Advocacy
	Revenge-seeking	Advocacy	Advocacy	Counseling, Advocacy
	Separatist	Advocacy	Advocacy	Empowerment, Advocacy
	Mob mentality	Advocacy	Advocacy	Empowerment, Advocacy
	Situational	Counseling	Advocacy	Counseling, Advocacy

Note: The methods can be changed for each role and motive if there is valid evidence that the perpetrator or inmate still manage the terror actions outside prisons. Continuous assessment by terrorism experts and law enforcement is recommended.

gaining trust; setting structured rehabilitation process for each perpetrator; and implementing learning materials. The education may include crucial materials such as differences of characteristics between *daar as-salam* (a state of peace) or *daar ad-da'wah* (an area of Islamic peace campaign) and *daar al-harb* (a state of war) according to sacred texts, in order to increase the sense of context or to take the reality of the present situation for the former terrorists into account through interpretation of Islamic teaching. A mix of two types of interventions is needed: peripheral and central routes.

The peripheral route focuses more on improvement in quality of life and well-being (e.g. acceptance, education, social skills, positive emotions, self-awareness, self-regulation, understanding of ethics and norms, thinking skills, etc.). By contrast, the central route focuses on discussion about interpretations of each verse of sacred texts, which is delivered by legitimate clerics through a two-way conversational setting. One-way dialogue is not recommended, as it will provide more proof of dominance and intimidation by authority, magnifying the level of justification for terror attacks. One-way dialogue can also increase hatred and reluctance to work on social issues together with the out-groups. Further, in a situation where the inmate still spreads radical ideology and recruits new members while getting favorable and conducive treatment, exclusiveness may become an option until there is indication of progress. Table 7.2 presents development methods for religious terrorism offenders. Figure 7.3 explains the ten steps in rehabilitating them.

Both exclusiveness and inclusiveness may be applied to fit the purpose of terrorism client rehabilitation, which is to alter negative behavior. For this purpose, the key to a successful rehabilitation process lies in the assessment of clients (e.g. motives, roles, background, progress of behavior modification),

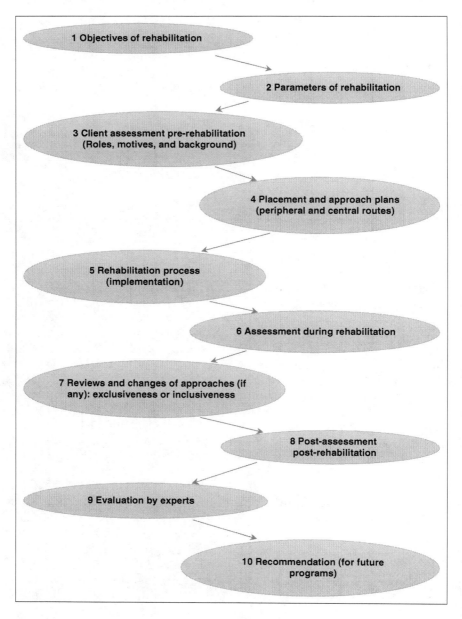

Figure 7.3 Ten steps in rehabilitating ideology-based terrorism offenders

which includes assessments both before and after treatment. Some techniques to collect data in the assessment process such as scales, observation, interviews, qualitative open-ended questionnaires, and product analysis are needed. The parameters of effectiveness need to be clarified accordingly to get detailed information and determine the type of treatment and approach used in each step of rehabilitation.

Regarding preparation before psychological rehabilitation implementation (e.g. Step 2, Step 3, and Step 4), it is important to note that psychologists along with practitioners need to plan in detail the materials, coaches, place, time, approach, and type of facilitations that went through development. Psychologists also need to perform risk analysis. Coordination with related parties, including non-governmental organizations, vocational training centers, agencies related to religious affairs, social institutions, universities, local government, and other stakeholders is recommended. Psychological preparation for coaches or counselors is also critical.

In psychological rehabilitation implementation, development consists of four activities that can be administered: (1) mentoring or coaching (e.g. sessions for motivation); (2) counseling; (3) training or education (e.g. classes for gaining skills); and (4) empowerment programs. This relatively critical stage requires the arts, creativity, and innovation on the part of facilitators. This is to achieve compatibility between facilitators of rehabilitations and dynamics of clients' conditions that may well be erratic or unstable. Further, evaluation of efforts in psychological rehabilitation is needed to get proper feedback and improve the process. The activities of evaluation include assessment whether the development activities achieve the goals set up in the beginning, whether there are changes in cognition, attitude, and behavior of clients, and whether any improvement is needed for future development activities.

Psychological assessment

Initial assessment is required before embarking on psychological rehabilitation. This assessment, called as the client needs analysis, includes a client's background, family background, education, personality, intelligence, role, function in community, service, achievement during imprisonment, strengths, potential, interests, attitudes, skills, resistance, ethnicity, beliefs, environment, and other critical matters. This assessment about a client's psychological needs is performed by psychologists specializing in terrorism or officers who have been previously trained to administer this function.

In terms of reaching well-being in the rehabilitation process, both counselors and practitioners consider character strengths in the psychological assessment during rehabilitation. Peterson and Seligman (2004) define 24 positive character strengths, grouped under six headings, which can be used by psychologists and counselors when assessing clients' progress during psychological rehabilitation. The positive characteristics are listed here:

Wisdom and knowledge: Cognitive strengths that entail the acquisition and use of knowledge.

1 *Creativity (originality, ingenuity)*: Thinking of novel and productive ways to conceptualize and do things; includes artistic achievement but is not limited to it.
2 *Curiosity (interest, novelty-seeking, openness to experience)*: Taking an interest in ongoing experience for its own sake; finding subjects and topics fascinating; exploring and discovering.
3 *Open-mindedness (judgment, critical thinking)*: Thinking things through and examining them from all sides; not jumping to conclusions; being able to change one's mind in light of evidence; weighing all evidence fairly.
4 *Love of learning*: Mastering new skills, topics, and bodies of knowledge, whether on one's own or formally; obviously related to the strength of curiosity but goes beyond it to describe the tendency to add *systematically* to what one knows.
5 *Perspective (wisdom)*: Able to provide wise counsel to others; having ways of looking at the world that make sense to oneself and others.

Courage: Emotional strengths that involve the exercise of will to accomplish goals in the face of opposition, external or internal.

6 *Bravery (valor)*: Not shrinking from threat, challenge, difficulty, or pain; speaking up for what is right even if there is opposition; acting on convictions even if unpopular; includes physical bravery but is not limited to it.
7 *Persistence (perseverance, industriousness)*: Finishing what one starts; persisting in the course of action despite obstacles; 'getting it out the door'; taking pleasure in completing tasks.
8 *Integrity (authenticity, honesty)*: Speaking the truth but more broadly genuinely presenting oneself and acting sincerely; being without pretense; taking responsibility for one's feelings and actions.
9 *Vitality (zest, enthusiasm, vigor, energy)*: Approaching life with excitement and energy; not doing things halfway or halfheartedly, living life as an adventure; feeling alive and activated.

Humanity: Interpersonal strengths that involve tending and befriending others.

10 *Love*: Valuing close relations with others, in particular, those in which sharing and caring are reciprocated; being close to people.
11 *Kindness (generosity, nurturance, care, compassion, altruistic love, niceness)*: Doing favors and good deeds for others; helping them; taking care of them.
12 *Social intelligence (emotional intelligence, personal intelligence)*: Being aware of the motives and feelings of other people and oneself, knowing what to do to fit into different social situations; knowing what makes others affected.

Justice: Civic strengths that underlie healthy community life.

13 *Citizenship (social responsibility, loyalty, teamwork)*: Working well as a member of a group or team; being loyal to the group; doing one's share.

14 *Fairness*: Treating all people the same according to notions of fairness and justice; not letting personal feelings bias decisions about others; giving everyone a fair chance.
15 *Leadership*: Encouraging a group of which one is a member to get things done and at the same maintain time good relations within the group; organizing group activities and seeing that they happen.

Temperance: Strengths that protect against excess.

16 *Forgiveness and mercy*: Forgiving those who have done wrong; accepting the shortcomings of others; giving people a second chance; not being vengeful.
17 *Humility/Modesty*: Letting one's accomplishments speak for themselves; not seeking the spotlight; not regarding one as more special than one is.
18 *Prudence*: Being careful about one's choices; not taking undue risks; not saying or doing things that might be regretted.
19 *Self-regulation (self-control)*: Regulating what one feels and does; being disciplined; controlling one's appetites and emotions.

Transcendence: Strengths that forge connections to the larger universe and provide meaning.

20 *Appreciation of beauty and excellence (awe, wonder, elevation)*: Noticing and appreciating beauty, excellence, and/or skilled performance in various domains of life, from nature to art to mathematics to science to everyday experience.
21 *Gratitude*: Being aware of and thankful for the good things that happen; taking the time to express thanks.
22 *Hope (optimism, future-mindedness, future orientation)*: Expecting the best in the future and working to achieve it; believing that a good future is something that can be brought about.
23 *Humor (playfulness)*: Like to laugh and tease; bringing smiles to other people; seeing the light side; making (not necessarily telling) jokes.
24 *Spirituality (religiousness, faith, purpose)*: Having coherent beliefs about the higher purpose and meaning of the universe; knowing where one fits within the larger scheme; having beliefs about the meaning of life that shape conduct and provide comfort.

Counseling process

Psychological rehabilitation to clients of terrorism cases frequently uses counseling methodology. The counseling aims to facilitate changes in the clients' behaviors, improve the clients' quality of life, and solve the clients' problems. Furthermore, the counseling of religious terrorists consists of four critical stages.

Building a relationship

In this stage, the counselor builds a relationship and trust with a client. The counselor pays attention carefully to the words, body language, facial expression, eye contact, and behavior of the clients. Aloofness, unenthusiastic tonality, and avoidance of eye contact with the counselor or officer are indications that the officer as a counselor is not yet fully accepted by the client. When trust is established, the counselor can have an easier time understanding the client. The client is more open and involved. Hence, the next stage of the counseling process can be conducted with ease.

Identification of problems and exploration

In this stage, the counselor assesses the client's needs, assists in identifying problems, and explores the potential as well as the client's ability in solving problems. The clients must be encouraged to understand any grievances, crises, dilemmas, needs, and problems they face and they should assist finding solutions to the problems with an equal relationship and two-way dialogues. Clients are expected to seek a clearer understanding of themselves. At this stage, the counselor seeks to encourage clients to be open-minded, able to take criticism, and perform critical thinking in finding solutions to their problems.

Problem-solving planning

In this stage, the counselor in psychological rehabilitation and client together plan various problem-solving alternatives. In addition, both parties also formulate the goals they want to achieve, and establish the time period, namely when to start and when to conclude the counseling process.

Applying solutions and closure

In this stage, the client addresses solutions to problems that have been planned together with the counselor, works to develop his/her own capacity, and tries to become independent. At this stage, a strong commitment from both parties is needed. In addition to maintaining the counseling relationship, a counselor's creativity in developing a variety of counseling techniques is required so that the counseling objectives can be reached. Lastly, the counseling process reaches its end, known as closure stage, in which results are observed. The expected results in the closure stage are positive behavioral change in clients, new insights, and step-by-step operational solutions for clients' needs and problems.

Due to the complexity of the terrorism issue, counselors in psychological rehabilitation are suggested to require the following qualities: (1) empathy; (2) genuineness; (3) integrity; (4) responsiveness; and (5) wittiness. Further, it is critical to highlight the use of andragogy during psychological rehabilitation of adult clients with terrorism-related cases. In contrast with pedagogy, which is applied to children, an andragogy approach treats clients as they are independent and able to direct and help themselves in facing reality, conflicting values or attitudes, issues, or even crises. Andragogy allows clients to innovate and think laterally in solving problems. In the independent learning process, adults are seen as active agents who seek the truth and make decisions (learner-centered).

Table 7.3 Differences in pedagogy and andragogy (Knowles 1970)

Aspect	Pedagogy	Andragogy
Learner self-concept	Individuals that depend on their developers	Individuals that are independent and self-directing
Learner experience	Developing; has to be formed rather than used as learning resources	It has been formed, personal experience can be explored as learning materials for themselves and others
Learner readiness of learning	Uniform according to age and curriculum	Evolving, which stems from task and real everyday issues
Learning orientation	Orientation toward learning materials (subject centered)	Task and everyday issues orientation (problem centered)
Learning motivation	With praise, reward, and punishment	Encouragement from within (internal incentives, curiosity)

For children clients, psychological rehabilitation uses educational activities as in pedagogy in which the facilitators teach the clients by placing them in an educational institution within a positive environment. In pedagogy, learning materials and ideas or concepts are introduced by rehabilitation facilitators, while andragogy encourages clients to find and discuss their own learning style, ideas, interests, potentials, and examples. Table 7.3 illustrates the difference between andragogy and pedagogy.

Empowerment process

Similar to counseling, empowerment programs are part of psychotherapies for religious terrorism offenders. The goals of empowerment programs are to restore clients' capacity, disengage clients from destructive behaviors, facilitate adjustments, and prepare clients to reintegrate with their communities as well as in broader society. Empowerment of a client is an attempt to enable the potential within a client's self. Individuals with a high level of self-empowerment tend to see themselves responsible for all the things that occurred in their life or having a high level of internal locus of control. Hence they tend not to blame others when a calamity or grievance happens. These individuals have a high degree of self-introspection and show persistence in self-improvement and positive attitudes toward environments as well as broader society.

The effective empowerment program in psychological rehabilitation to religious terrorism offenders is suggested to meet several internal processes such as reflection of the meaning and purpose of life, self and social context exploration, self-reliance, achievement, accepting criticism, and self-improvement. The steps are illustrated in Figure 7.4. Thoughts about the purpose of life involve both personal goals (subjective) and community or social goals (objective) so that personal

Figure 7.4 Internal processes in effective empowerment programs

goals are in line with social ethics. In this phase, personal goals or desires function to direct behaviors so clients can grow and develop themselves. Otherwise, blind obedience of a client to another person inhibit him/her to grow and may lead to a condition where personal goals are fused with the the goals of others. The congruence among personal, community, and broader societal goals will help to increase contentment within the self and minimize dissonance or crisis.

Self-exploration and social context exploration allows clients to be self-critical and be able to adjust to society. In this phase, clients realize the nature of contexts and behaviors in demand in particular norms, culture, or society. Moreover, the self-reliance phase allows clients to rely on their own capacity and potential. In this stage, they challenge themselves by getting involved in new environments, new learnings, new tasks, new jobs, or new professions. This is also used to examine their endurance in various unpredictable situations, their independence, self-regulation, and potential to survive in real conditions outside of prison.

In the achievement phase, clients meet their needs and show constant positive behaviors and attitudes toward themselves and society. In this phase, they show self-contentment, self-confidence, and self-satisfaction, and are ready to work with various types of people despite differences in ethnicity, religion, personality, and so forth. Clients in this phase ought to show empathy to others outside the militant circle and show positive well-being. In some cases, they show courage in taking risks in various types of work even the toughest, which demands a high level of stress tolerance. Lastly, in the criticism and self-improvement phase, clients examine their own capability to take both positive and negative feedback and perform self-improvement. This evaluation process causes clients to be flexible and sociable, even to blend themselves into unfamiliar environments or situations beyond their comfort zone or regular group.

Subjective psychological transformation in rehabilitation

In some rehabilitation programs, including disengagement and deradicalization, clients are seen to show the behavioral transformation. Disengagement refers to a methodology in empowering the detainees and focusing on constructive behaviors to disengage them from violence or terror activities. It is considered as a neutral method in which the government or any practitioners seek to effect change in religious ideation by addressing what is seen as its material causes without direct reference to or interference in religion or ideology. Deradicalization refers to a methodology for developing equilibrium between the belief system (i.e. ideology) and contexts where the belief system is implemented, by also taking practical issues into account. It is performed through a number of discussions regarding the interpretation of passages and verses of sacred texts. While deradicalization is viewed as a cognitive behavioral therapy, disengagement is seen as behavior modification. Hwang and Villarosa (2011) identify five common drivers toward disengagement: (1) pronounced disillusionment with bombing and other factors (roles, mindsets, and ideology); (2) development of relationships with those outside the jihadi circles; (3) change of priorities; (4) law-enforcement soft approaches; and (5) cost–benefit analysis.

A serial observation of 254 cases of terrorism in Indonesia shows that psychological transformation of ideology-based terrorism offenders is classified into two types of changes: (1) natural (sometimes called 'natural deradicalization'); and (2) designed to change. The first type of change occurs due to maturation or the natural individual growth process, while the second is carried out by social engineering or a designed learning process by others (e.g. government agencies or civil society). In many cases, the natural change of the offender or client is initiated by him/herself (without interference from others) and appears long-lasting as compared to changes initiated by others. The behavioral change process model in Figure 7.5 found in a series of observations of religious militants who experience natural psychological transformation. Context is defined to be the initial condition of a client's background. Crisis is the internal conflict between the client's subjective goals or expectations and realities that cause a feeling of discomfort. Crisis can also be defined as grievances or internal confusion. The quest stage occurs when a client questions his/her strategies or methods, or feels the need to seek any psychological improvement in order to enhance self-development. Encounter provides insights or a series of solutions that can be implemented in responding to questions in the previous stage. Further, behavioral change is initiated by clients, resulting from individual learning that can be observed through actual behaviors.

Figure 7.6 illustrates a client's behavioral transformation process initiated by the environment (e.g. government and other components of society). In this transformation process, the crisis is stimulated by external components or the counselor who aims to challenge the client's view and any kind of rationalization (see Putra & Sukabdi, 2014). Further, in the quest phase, the client raises several fundamental questions about some concepts (e.g. *jihad, darul harb*, and so forth) to any parties who are able to answer them. Encounter is considered as an ultimate point of interaction between counselor and client of the terrorism case. When the counselor is credible and competent in stimulating insights, the following stages are likely to occur. Moreover, interaction allows the client to make contact with the out-group or the ones who were perceived to be the enemy. Bombing victims or other religious believers can be one of these categories. Group counseling in which several clients meet the ones perceived to be 'opposite side' can be facilitated to encourage interaction between the in-group and the out-group. Accordingly, commitment is achieved when there is a change in client's behavior. Finally, the client receives feedback and understands the consequences for the change he/she generates. Hence counselors need to prepare for a client's readiness to accept any feedback.

It is important to note that designed behavior modification that involves the negative type of treatment from the external group (e.g. intimidation, threat, discrimination, and physical attack) and causes trauma may lead to a negative attitude toward 'perceived enemies' by clients and may generate relatively temporary behavioral change in the client. In addition, the presence of denial and forgetting can reduce the effectiveness of any program held in transforming behaviors. Hence psychological rehabilitation to religious terrorism offenders needs to be persistent and long-lasting. It includes seeking help from civil society, not only scholars or practitioners in the psychology field. Facilitators who have qualities mentioned previously (Figure 7.2) can assist psychological rehabilitation for clients of terrorism cases.

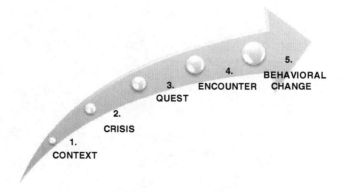

Figure 7.5 Natural behavior transformation process

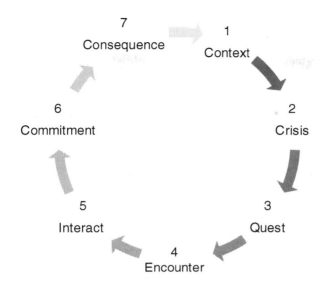

Figure 7.6 Behavioral transformation process initiated by others

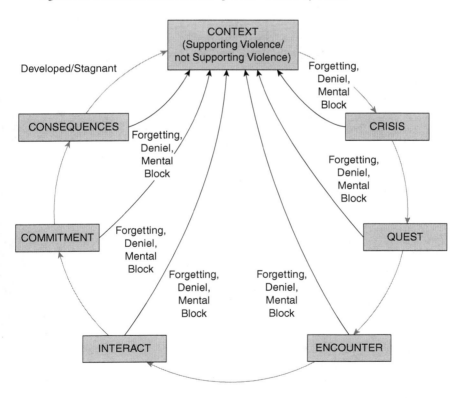

Figure 7.7 How denial and forgetting mechanisms can intervene in the process of psychological rehabilitation

Figure 7.7 illustrates how the denial and forgetting mechanisms can intervene in the process of psychological rehabilitation. In this case, again, practitioners emphasize trust between counselor and client, genuineness and sincerity delivered by the counselor to achieve a successful holistic rehabilitation process.

Conclusion

Rehabilitation of religious terrorism offenders is a means to reestablish human capacity and function in society. It tries to restore a good condition for the former terrorist, including reintegration into the community. Psychological rehabilitation focuses on character building and well-being. Its orientation is to give the opportunity to clients to solve their own problems (client-centered) by providing assistance. Psychological development for religious terrorism offenders facilitates clients to achieve optimum independence in mental, social, spiritual, and vocational facets; achieve their maximum capacity for a better life; have social, spiritual, and vocational dexterity; and be able to contribute to broader society. It has four functions: (1) prevention; (2) rehabilitation; (3) maintenance; and (4) provisioning.

Counselors involved in psychological rehabilitation should have certain qualities and master particular competencies to conduct counseling processes and empowerment programs effectively. Psychological rehabilitation is performed by administering some critical steps including assessment of clients, preparation, implementation, and evaluation of the effectiveness of programs. It is important to emphasize the role of the arts, creativity, and innovation as facilitators for counselors during the rehabilitation process due to the complexity of terrorism issues. Further, psychological rehabilitation requires feedback to improve the process.

Psychological rehabilitation to clients within the context of terrorism cases often uses counseling. Counseling to religious terrorism former offenders itself consists of four critical stages: (1) building relationships; (2) identification of problems and exploration; (3) problem-solving planning; and (4) applying solutions and closure. Moreover, it is also suggested that counselors use the concept of andragogy during psychological rehabilitation to adult clients. The andragogy approach treats the clients as independent agents able to help themselves in coping with crisis. Further, empowerment programs are part of psychotherapy provided to clients. Empowerment aims to support the potential within a client's self.

The behavioral transformation may be generated by both natural processes and designed programs. The natural change process is achieved due to maturation, whereas designed learning programs stimulate a designed change process. The natural behavioral transformation process shows a particular pattern that is different from designed behavioral change. It is important to note that several disruptions such as forgetting, lack of trust, and denial may reduce the effectiveness of psychological rehabilitation.

Bibliography

Bandura, A. (1999). 'Moral Disengagement in the Perpetration of Inhumanities.' *Personality and Social Psychology Review*, 3: 193–209.

Bandura, A. (2004). 'Role of Selective Moral Disengagement in Terrorism and Counterterrorism.' In F.M. Mogahaddam & A.J. Marsella (eds), *Understanding Terrorism: Psychological Roots, Consequences and Interventions*. Washington, DC: American Psychological Association Press: 121–150.

Bjorgo, Tore (2005). *Root Causes of Terrorism: Myths, Reality and Ways Forward*. London and New York: Routledge.

Englehart, Neil & Kurzman, Charles (2006). 'Welcome to World Peace.' *Social Forces*, 84(4) June: 1957–1967.

Gunaratna, R. & Rubin, L. (2011). 'Introduction.' In R. Gunaratna, J. Jerard, & L. Rubin (eds), *Terrorist Rehabilitation and Counter-radicalization: New Approaches to Counterterrorism*. London: Routledge: 1–10.

Horgan, John (2008). 'From Profiles to *Pathways* and Roots to *Routes*: Perspectives from Psychology on Radicalization into Terrorism.' *The Annals of the American Academy of Political and Science*, 618: 80–94.

Hwang, C. & Villarosa, S. (2011). *Counterterrorism Strategy in Indonesia: Adapting to a Changed Threat*. Available at: www.usindo.org/briefs/counter-terrorism-strategy-in-indonesia-adapting-to-a-changed-threat-2/ (accessed 24 May 2018).

Knowles, M.S. (1970). *The Modern Practice of Adult Education; Andragogy versus Pedagogy*. New York: Associated Press.

Kruglanski, A.W. & Fishman, S. (2009). 'The Psychology of Terrorism: "Syndrome" versus "Tool" Perspectives.' In A.W. Kruglanski & S. Fishman (eds), *Psychology of Terrorism: Classic and Contemporary Insights*. New York: Psychology Press: 35–53.

Mihalka, Michael (2006). 'Counterinsurgency, Counterterrorism, State-building and Security Cooperation in Central Asia.' *China and Eurasia Forum Quarterly*, 4(2): 131–151.

Moghaddam, F.M. (2006). *From the Terrorists' Point of View: What They Experience and Why They Come to Destroy*. Westport, CT: Praeger Security International.

Moghaddam, F.M. (2008). *How Globalization Spurs Terrorism: The Lopsided Benefits of 'One World' and Why that Fuels Violence*. Westport, CT: Praeger Security International.

Moghaddam, F.M., Harre, R., & Lee, N. (2007). *Global Conflict Resolution through Positioning Analysis*. New York: Springer.

Mufid, A.S., Sarwono, S.W., Syafii, M., Baedowi, A., Karnavian, T. et al. (2011). *Executive Summary of Research on Motivation and Root Causes of Terrorism*. Jakarta: Penerbit Indonesian Institute for Society Empowerment.

Pech, R. & Slade, B. (2006). 'Employee Disengagement: Is There Evidence of a Growing Problem?' *Handbook of Business Strategy*, 7(1): 21–25.

Peterson, C. & Seligman, M.E.P. (2004). *Character Strengths and Virtues: A Classification and Handbook*. New York/Washington, DC: Oxford University Press/American Psychological Association.

Putra, I.E. & Sukabdi, Z.A. (2013). 'Basic Concepts and Reasons behind the Emergence of Religious Terror Activities in Indonesia: An Inside View.' *Asian Journal of Social Psychology*, 16(2), 83–91.

Putra, I.E. & Sukabdi, Z.A. (2014). 'Can Islamic Fundamentalism Relate to Nonviolent Support? The Role of Certain Conditions in Moderating the Effect of Islamic Fundamentalism on Supporting Acts of Terrorism.' *Peace and Conflict*, 20: 583–589.

Shemella, Paul (2011). *Fighting Back: What Government Can Do about Terrorism.* Stanford, CA: Stanford University Press.

Taylor, M. & Horgan, J. (2001). 'The Psychological and Behavioural Bases of Islamic Fundamentalism.' *Terrorism and Political Violence*, 13: 37–71.

Venkatraman, A. (2007). 'Religious Basis for Islamic Terrorism: The Quran and its Interpretations.' *Studies in Conflict & Terrorism*, 30(3): 229–248.

Victoroff, Jeff (2005). 'The Mind of the Terrorist: A Review and Critique of Psychological Approaches.' *The Journal of Conflict Resolution*, 49(1): 3–42.

8 Assessment and evaluation of terrorist rehabilitation programmes

Malkanthi Hettiarachchi

Introduction

Sri Lanka launched its first terrorist rehabilitation programme with the defeat of the Liberation Tigers of Tamil Eelam (LTTE) in 2009. The presidential directive was clear: 'it's time to launch "humanitarian mission 02", to get them back on track with their normal lives'. The state considered the detainees as 'misled by the terrorist leadership into engaging in terrorist activity' but, nevertheless, 'citizens'. The way forward was to rehabilitate the former 'Tamil Tigers' with a view to reintegration into civil society. The six-pronged multifaceted rehabilitation programme was geared towards supporting the rehabilitees to come to terms with their actions and adopt a non-violent way of life within a safe and secure environment. The architects of the programme studied how terrorists and their leaders denied basic liberties and manipulated their followers during training. The aim was to address these deficits during their period in rehabilitation and facilitate participant re-engagement in civilian life. To move beyond mere disengagement from violence, designing and implementing well-crafted rehabilitation programmes to reverse the process of violent radicalization was essential. Winning hearts and minds was the overarching principle of each rehabilitation centre. To ensure standards of excellence, programme effectiveness was evaluated by the centre and progress made by rehabilitees assessed by independent assessors. Sri Lanka has currently reintegrated 12,206 rehabilitated terrorists into civil society.

Why are assessments important?

Crucial to the success of any rehabilitation programme is assessment and evaluation. Established global rehabilitation programmes have grappled with these challenges for almost a decade and use various measures to assess violent radicalization within their programmes.[1] The many developing rehabilitation initiatives across the globe, while able to learn from existing programmes, continue the search for tools of assessment and evaluation. This chapter will draw from the experience of contemporary rehabilitation programmes and from the material available in the field, so that the least complex to the more complex methods of measurement can be tried out within ad-hoc as well as evolving rehabilitation programmes.

Figure 8.1 Counter, manage and innoculate: a three-dimensional approach to prevent radicalization and re-radicalization

Assessment and evaluation are two distinct processes with some overlap, in terms of observation, data gathering and report writing. According to Baehr, assessment and evaluation complement each other, as they provide two different types of information. The assessment provides information focused on an individual's strengths, difficulties and how to improve functioning for the future. Evaluation provides a judgement on the quality of performance based on an established standard that helps decision making at any given time (Baehr 2010).

Specialists dealing with the rapidly evolving threat of terrorism, through experience, lean towards using *smart power* with the knowledge that both kinetic and soft approaches are required to counter terrorism. Initiatives to combat terrorism, therefore, must focus on the *uphill prevention* using counter/alternative strategies, *downhill management* involving rehabilitation and reintegration, and *community resilience building* to innoculate communities against violent radicalization (Figure 8.1).

The bulk of the proactive work needs to focus on *community resilience building* to innoculate the community against violent radical ideologies. The target groups are the whole of society: school curricula, children and teachers, youth, mothers, religious personnel, community leaders, professionals, educational and vocational institutes, and the private and public sectors. The strategies include reflective and critical thinking, self-reflection, managing emotions, conflict management, peace studies, interacting with the different other, cultural pride and instilling a sense of nationhood and unity among people.

Strategies used to counter radicalization are essential reactive strategies, put into place during the problem period. *Counter radicalization* is about identifying vulnerable communities, picking up early warning signs, countering violence-instigating narratives, delegitimizing the need for violence and the moral justifications for violence, engaging youth, providing alternative and meaningful pathways in life and deterring those moving towards joining radical groups through the judicial and law-enforcement systems.

Rehabilitation to *deradicalize* is about reversing the process of radicalization, post hoc. Rehabilitation therefore focuses on doing everything possible to bring the person back to society by engaging the individual, winning hearts and minds, facilitating alternative pathways to express grievances and an opportunity to become a productive citizen. Deradicalization is a slower but sustained process that includes individual resilience building by developing cognitive resilience through mindfulness training, critical thinking, emotional intelligence, problem solving; interpersonal resilience through conflict resolution, peace building and diversity training; motivational resilience by restoring significance and meaning in life; economic resilience through livelihoods training, education and opportunity for employment; spiritual resilience by working through doctrinal distortions with qualified religious personnel and re-engaging in the faith practice; and social cultural and familial resilience by reconnecting with culture, society, family, as well as diversity training, conflict resolution and peace building. Retraining and re-engagement in the several rehabilitative components help shift the individual away from a violence-justifying ideology and help to prevent relapse or recidivism.

Interventions at every level require state backing and funding through public–private sector partnerships. Funding agencies are heavily outcome driven and require assessments and periodic evaluations to justify investing resources in intervention programmes.

This chapter will focus on the various measures and models used within a rehabilitative environment, whether it is within a custodial, semi-custodial or community setting. Often, the worried, the concerned, the interested, the amateurs, the curious, the critics and the sceptics ask: 'how can you measure the success of a programme?', 'how do you know if a person is deradicalized?', 'human behaviour is complex, how can you measure what a person thinks?', 'our programme works well, why do we want to reduce it to numbers and dilute the value of the programme?', 'we know the programme works, that's enough, why should we prove it to others?!' and 'we see the change, how can a number indicate if something is successful or not?' These are legitimate questions that require robust data-backed responses. The field of terrorism has evolved and engaged social psychologists, forensic psychologists, clinical psychologists, IT consultants, researchers and statisticians with the understanding that measurement is one of the most effective ways in which to know what works and does not work.

Measurement is at the core of any evidence-based intervention programme. Assessments contribute to global knowledge by identifying the relationship between the different variables being assessed. Managers and researchers of creative and effective programmes need to share these efficacious initiatives and their successes with nations that continue to struggle to engage in the process of assessment.

Who and what should be subjected to assessment?

When managing a rehabilitation centre, several types of assessments are required: detainee and inmate assessment; programme assessment; centre assessment; and staff assessment. These assessments inform programme managers and funders about programme effectiveness and where to target resources to improve the service. Assessments highlight potential risks, vulnerabilities and strengths of the individual, the programme, the centre and the staff team. Assessing the various factors of a rehabilitation centre will ensure that the centre achieves a standard of excellence.

The detainee and inmate

Individual assessments facilitate the categorization of intervention groups and prevent the more radical influencing the less radical members. These include a comprehensive assessment and interview process that will inform the staff of the degree of radicalization, level of risk, strengths and vulnerabilities, how prepared the detainee or inmate is to engage, and readiness to change.

The programme

Programme assessments and evaluations allow participants to provide feedback on each activity or session, which promotes a sense of ownership of the programme. Individual programme and overall programme assessments conducted by the centre staff and by external resource persons will help to identify difficulties and improve the practice and service delivery. For example, correlating the feedback forms, internal and external assessments and detainee and inmate deradicalization levels will indicate programme effectiveness. Assessments and evaluations help to improve the implementation of the programme and adjust the programme to improve effectiveness. Programme managers are then able to tailor interventions to suit individual and group needs, identify progress during the period of rehabilitation and conduct follow-up assessments in the community upon reintegration. Periodic assessments can help to assess change longitudinally.

The centre

An assessment of the centre will ensure an adequate staff to detainee/inmate ratio, facilities for educational and vocational training, space for sports and extra-curricular activities, a place for worship, facilities for family visits and medical services. The centre's security assessment is vital, as is the risk assessment to prevent suicide and self-harm. The atmosphere and ethos of the centre needs to reflect a relaxed and respectful environment.

The staff

Staff assessments help to identify strengths and deficits in knowledge, skill and attitude in managing this specific population. One of the primary factors that impacts on reducing levels of violence and aggression is positive staff interaction (Kruglanski et al. 2014). Staff skill in managing detainee and inmate aggression, resistance, non-cooperation and dependency behaviours is vital. Staff capacity to cope with the emotional impact that detainees or inmates may have on the staff, the ability to work compassionately and with forgiveness, and the commitment to support the detainee and inmate to reintegrate are essential aspects when working within a terrorist rehabilitation environment. The frequency of staff supervision, leisure, home leave and health and stress management are features that need to be addressed through the periodic staff assessment framework.

Key tasks in assessment

The assessment process involves the following ten steps discussed here in detail:

First, the assessors within the multidisciplinary team (MDT) need to *collect information* from a range of sources using the five pillars of clinical assessment as a guide (Hecker and Thorpe 2016). The pillars of sound clinical assessment include: interviewing the detainee/inmate and significant others; observation of behaviour in several settings; information through actuarial assessments; information through paper records and reports; and gathering information on the history and background of the individual.

Second, the *recording of information* as soon as it is collected clearly and consistently is vital. This information should be recorded in a manner easily accessible by authorized personnel when required. The information recorded will help to promote accountability within the organization.

Third, the *analysis of information* collected and recorded should be professional and objective. The assessment must go beyond a mere description of facts. A thorough analysis conducted will help to create greater understanding of the person; highlight risks, vulnerabilities, areas to further scrutinize; and also indicate changes in behaviour.

Fourth, *estimate future behaviour* based on the analysis. Statistical analysis needs to point towards predicting potential future behaviour. The likelihood of certain behavioural patterns recurring and contextual variables that may increase or decrease a particular behaviour, are likely to indicate the potential for recidivism.

Fifth, *draw conclusions* from each segment of the assessment and prepare to present the findings. The analysis and predictions need to provide a formal conclusion of findings by all professionals involved in the MDT, on the past, present and future prognosis of the detainee/inmate.

Sixth, *write a report* by drawing together all the information and analyses from multiple sources that outline strengths, vulnerabilities and risks. The report needs to inform the reader about the past, the present and the future risks involved and recommendations for intervention as well as prognosis.

Seventh, *sharing of information* among relevant professionals involved in rehabilitation. If the information gathered is not shared responsibly by all parties in the interest of the detainee/inmate, there is little value in an assessment. The focus of any assessment within rehabilitation should be for the sole purpose of supporting the detainee/inmate to shift away from violent extremist thinking and behaviour, prevent harm by detainee/inmate to another and prevent harm to detainee/inmate from others.

Eighth, *reviewing assessments* to ensure that all staff working with detainee/inmate are able to recognize progress and regression and shift with the changes. Assessment is a process that needs to be ongoing as human beings are malleable and subject to change. The assessment needs to reflect this. Detainee and inmate information should be regularly reviewed during engagement and records updated accordingly.

Ninth, *assessing progress* of the detainee/inmate's readiness for reintegration. The interventions offered, participation in programmes and engagement by the detainee/inmate within the rehabilitation process are all factors likely to indicate the level of progress and risk. Risk assessment is based on the five pillars of assessment discussed. The information gathered will help the management and staff work towards designing the aftercare required by the detainee/inmate in the community and also to liaise with relevant professionals in the community.

Tenth, *maintaining confidentiality and professionalism* is a primary task that will ensure trust and respect of the detainee/inmate as well as the credibility of the programme. Clear protocols should be in place to manage information, how information is shared, when it is shared, with whom it is shared and for what purpose. The progress of the detainee/inmate and the safety of the public are key features when maintaining confidentiality and professionalism.

The process of assessment in itself is therapeutic as it focuses on understanding the individual, the context and the problem, with intervention to improve functioning. Assessors therefore need to be well trained and skilled in using a variety of engagement and interviewing methods together with assessment and evaluation tools that will gather accurate information while helping the detainees/inmates gain insight into their thoughts and behaviours.

How are assessments conducted?

Five pillars of assessment

Jerome Sattler (2001: 5) refers to the four components that form part of any comprehensive assessment. He recommends that an assessment should contain information gathered through interviews; observation; actuarial assessment; and informal assessments. *Interviews* are conducted with the client, family, peers and significant others as required. *Observations* are carried out by the assessor, centre staff and programme facilitators within the centre. Observations made by significant others, educationalists, colleagues and peers within interpersonal and social settings should also be included in this category. *Formal* or *actuarial (statistical) assessments* include the findings from psychometric measures such as the Significance Quest Assessment Tool (SQAT), the Violent Extremist Risk Assessment (revised version, VERA-2R), the Violent Extremism Beliefs Scale (VEBS), the Extremist Risk Guidelines (ERG22+), the Multi-Level

Guidelines (MLG) and other norm-referenced tools that provide statistical information on radicalization, violence, mental health etc. *Informal assessments* provide additional information towards the formal assessments. Informal assessments also include personal, behavioural and social assessments that are not-norm referenced. Hecker and Thorpe (2016: 143) add a fifth component that includes *life records*, which provide vital information on medical, psychiatric, forensic, developmental, educational and vocational history as well as on accomplishments and vulnerabilities.

Assessment interviews

Motivational interviewing (MI) is a technique used to engage the detainee/inmate and gather information, while preparing the detainee for change (Miller and Rollnick 1991). It is an interview technique that helps to reduce resistance and elicit an accurate understanding of the individual. MI is a technique that has four primary components: express empathy as it helps to connect with the detainee and build rapport; develop discrepancy by eliciting the positives and negatives of actions; roll with resistance indicative of respect for autonomy; and support self-efficacy and communicate the ability the person has to make the changes required. The spirit of MI is collaborative as opposed to confrontational. This technique attempts to elicit the responses from the beneficiary instead of telling the beneficiary how to act. The tone of the sessions is autonomous, respecting the detainee/inmate's space and freedom instead of being authoritarian.

Professional and ethical methods of interviewing are likely to generate more accurate information as the detainee/inmate is likely to be more relaxed, feel less anxious and have a lower need to use deception. Using open-ended questions will elicit more information than closed questions. Affirmation and support in recognition of the detainee's efforts to discuss potentially difficult aspects, reflective listening and summarizing what the detainee has expressed help to clarify and gain a better understanding of the detainee narrative, while preparing him or her for change.

What can be assessed?

Detainee/inmate readiness to change

Assessing detainee/inmate readiness to change helps to tailor interventions to minimize resistance.[2] Ongoing assessments using Prochaska and DiClemente's stages of change cycle would indicate the level at which to target interventions during the detainee's period of stay in the rehabilitation centre (Figure 8.2).[3] Some detainees may be resistant and not see the need for change (pre-contemplation). Others may be considering change (contemplation), while still others are prepared to engage in the programme (preparation). Those who are further along the cycle of change would be those actively engaging in the programme (action) and making changes. Finally, there are those who are actively working

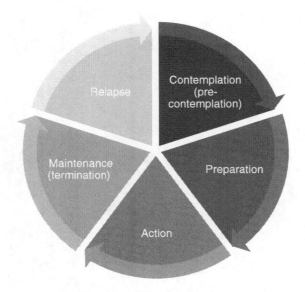

Figure 8.2 Prochaska and DiClemente's Wheel of Change (Prochaska and DiClemente 1982: 276–288)

through potential relapse to maintain the changes (maintenance) and those who have relapsed (relapse). Changes are neither linear nor stepwise. Detainees and inmates move through these stages at various speeds while some continue to experience a level of stuckness. The skill to shift detainees depends on the staff, the centre environment, types of programmes conducted and the level of commitment, enthusiasm and creativity within each centre.

Level of risk

Assessment allows the risk categorization of detainees and inmates. Prison radicalization is often talked about but prison authorities struggle with lack of facilities, space and staff. Prison overcrowding results in heightening the potential for the more radical to influence the less radical, recruit from the criminal population and form a nexus between the underworld and the terrorist networks to transport weapons, explosives, cyanide, suicide bombers and receive hijacked vehicles, illicit and restricted goods. The currency used by the LTTE to pay the criminal network for transport and storage services was illicit drugs. Categorization, therefore, is of primary importance both within a custodial and a rehabilitative environment.

Categorizations are often based on the facilities of the centre and expertise available. The ranges are as follows:

- Alphabetic categories such as A–F (High = A/B; Moderate = C/D; Low = E/F).
- Colour codes such as Red, Amber, Green. For example, Red = 100–75; Amber = 74–25; Green = 24–0.
- Ranges from Normal – Mild – Moderate – Severe, or Low – Medium – High.
- Likert scale ranging from 1–10 or from 1–100.

Finding the cut-off marks is based on assessing a normative sample in the population for levels of radicalization. Others who test only the affected population find a range within that specific affected population.

Sri Lanka used the following scale from A–F to categorize the LTTE terrorists (Table 8.1).[4]

Within rehabilitation centres, categorization of detainees and inmates helps with tailoring the programmes to suit the high, medium and low categories. Those who are highly radicalized are likely to sabotage the programme by preventing others from joining, framing participation in the programmes as betrayal, supporting resistance and encouraging non-cooperation. Staff need to be in control of the rehabilitation centre at all times and not allow the senior or the more authoritative members of the terrorist group to exercise their authority over the junior members of the terrorist group at any time. The moment detainees establish a sense of seniority, the junior members fall into a subservient position and have difficulty making choices and resisting the ideological pressure brought upon them.

In the absence of categorization, the less radical individuals and those who are keen to move on are likely to have difficulty with resisting peer pressure and may find it easier to submit to the attitude of the more radical. Detainees and inmates must be empowered to make independent decisions and not be used by others perceived as senior as they are now not within an environment controlled by the terrorist leadership. Once the assessment indicates the level of radicalization, it is vital that staff continue to observe the participants and continue to assess their level of engagement. Individual programmes, small group programmes and common programmes can be conducted to support the detainees to make maximum gains.

Table 8.1 Categorization of detainees and inmates (Bureau for the Commissioner General for Rehabilitation, Sri Lanka 2010)

A	LTTE frontline leaders (hardcore), regional leaders, political wing leaders
B	LTTE frontline members (hardcore), Black Tigers, suicide cadres, intelligence wing cadres, specially trained cadres who have committed crimes, laid mines and ordered such activities that cause harm
C	LTTE cadres involved in antisocial acts/crimes
D	LTTE cadres involved in recruitment, training and supporting wings
E	LTTE cadres involved in doctrinal, publicity, financial, political wing and vocational activities in supporting acts of terror
F	LTTE cadres trained in weapon handling but not involved in operations or antisocial acts/crimes and other peripheral activities

Interventions

The levels of intervention are based on the individual needs assessment of beneficiaries within each risk category. *Low*-level interventions are building rapport, incentives and privileges, working with family, community interventions, as well as the religious/spiritual, social, cultural and family programmes. *Intermediate* interventions are vocational, educational and religious education programmes. *High*-end interventions are the specialist psychological interventions, using the Socratic method of questioning to challenge moral justifications for violence, facilitate critical thinking, gain insight and consolidate alternative thinking. The timing of the low-, medium- and high-level interventions is determined by the individual's readiness to change, level of insight and progress made within the centre.

Early indicators of radicalization in prisons

Bryans (2012) identifies several early indicators of radicalization in prisons. These include *opinions expressed* in support of violence and terrorism, *material possession* of literature that suggests violence, *behavioural changes* that indicate withdrawal from previous relationships and forming relationships with known violent extremists, *personal history* indicative of engagement with violent extremist groups, *exposure* to extremist ideology and ideologues, *crisis of identity* and seeking to belong, and a range of *perceived grievances* towards authorities and staff. These aspects can be incorporated within a risk assessment in prison so as to steer the detainee away from further radicalization (Bryans 2012).

What are the types of assessment?

The assessments need to be conducted by an MDT that can view the individual from different perspectives. The MDT can involve a social worker, psychologist, faith worker/religious dignitary, community/youth worker, educationalist, medical professional, law enforcement/security and a trained centre staff member. All these individuals will bring their professional perspectives into case management.

A variety of assessments can be conducted based on the particular rehabilitation programme:

- *Initial screening assessment* to explore a broad range of aspects that will highlight particular specialist interventions. The assessment administered initially can also be an *intake assessment*, which can be developed into a comprehensive *360-degree assessment*, further discussed in this paper.
- *Risk assessment* to reduce vulnerability to violence, increase resilience and prevent recidivism including a *radicalization assessment*.
- *Psychological assessment* to identify emotional and behavioural strengths and difficulties including a *cognitive behavioural assessment*.
- *Socio-economic assessment* to facilitate livelihoods.

- *Religious and cultural assessment* to identify spiritual needs and establish a sense of belonging and rootedness.
- *Family and friends assessment* to determine the nature of the support network.
- *Educational assessment* to expand knowledge and confidence through learning.
- *Vocational assessment* to encourage skill building to engage in a mainstream vocation and have an income.
- *Health assessment* to ensure wellbeing.

Assessments have to be timed, and where several assessors and assessments are involved, it is vital to prioritize assessments, giving space to the urgent assessments that will help to ensure the safety and wellbeing of the detainees/inmates and staff. Staggering assessments, based on priority, will prevent the detainee from being exhausted and also provide the opportunity for the various MDT sectors to engage the detainee meaningfully during the assessment process.

Assessments need to be *ongoing* as a person cannot be comprehensively assessed in one single sitting or setting. The accuracy of the assessment increases with greater engagement and rapport. The detainee/inmate needs to be observed and engaged by relevant professionals over time in a variety of settings and situations, and assessment results brought together to plan a way forward.

The detainee/inmate needs to be formally assessed *periodically* to ascertain changes. Assessments that are conducted too frequently may be ineffective, particularly if they are self-report psychometric measures, as the detainee will habituate by getting used to questions, or the aspect of social desirability may affect the assessment. A comprehensive assessment process involves ongoing assessment conducted by the MDT that helps to see the beneficiary from a strengths perspective while addressing the risks and vulnerabilities.

Specific assessments

Initial screening assessment

An *initial screening assessment* with an identified staff member who is skilled with rapport building will help to pave the way for other professionals to conduct their assessments step by step. It is important not to overwhelm the detainee/inmate with assessments. This initial screening assessment will help to identify the problems and risks, whether the detainee needs standard or more specialist assessments, who should conduct assessments as a matter of urgency, and also identify appropriate assessment tools. The conclusions will inform the staff if the detainee is eligible for a particular intervention, his or her ability to access and benefit from the existing interventions and the need to tailor interventions to optimize benefits.

360-degree assessment

This is a comprehensive assessment to obtain a 360 degree understanding of the person. This assessment process needs to be comprehensive and gather information on all aspects in the life of the detainee and inmate. For example:

- Age: 25 (factors relevant to a person aged 25)
- Gender: male or female (factors relevant to a male aged 25 and female aged 25)
- Family: immediate and extended family, significant others, children (who lives at home, influence of family members, their perceptions of detainee involvement in the group, family attitude towards the detainee, family embeddedness related to group activities and ideology)
- Education: level of education, school attended, strengths and difficulties (interests, grades, performance, termination of education)
- Vocation: vocational interests, previous job(s), vocational skills, expectations and interests (reasons for changes in vocation or discontinuing the job)
- Social: skills, interactions, lifestyle (perception of social life in the community, social engagement and reasons for changes)
- Interpersonal: skills, relating styles, interpersonal relationships, childhood relationships, adult relationships, significant relationships (mentors or individuals held in high esteem over time)
- Cultural: practices, participation in events, understanding of culture (value for culture and reasons for rejecting the culture)
- Religious: affiliations, practices, locations of worship, mentors (changes in faith pattern and reasons for changes)
- Political: history of political involvement, views, (changes in political views and reasons for changes)
- Economic: status, methods of income generation, economic requirements (potential economic sustenance avenues in the future)
- Psychological: emotional difficulties, thought distortions, closed mindedness, lack of critical thinking, personality traits (aspects that are resilient and vulnerable)
- Physical/biological: appearance, perception of physical image, physical strengths and difficulties, biological changes due to age or illness (fatigue, tiredness)
- Medical: history of illness, surgeries, significant episodes of illness (medical issues)

Being cognizant of the positives and negatives of each of the above aspects is likely to help the assessor identify risks, deficits, strengths and resilience. This information will help make recommendations on areas of improvement, while reinforcing the positives in each aspect.

Cognitive behavioural assessment

Cognitive behavioural assessments are specifically problem focused. These assessments look at *how the problem developed*, the nature of the problem, the difficulties experienced as a result of the problem, the formulation, how the problem can be managed, the timelines and who is responsible for addressing each aspect of the problem.

The focus of the cognitive behavioural formulation is on what happened *prior* to recruitment, what *triggered* joining the group, what helped to *maintain* the detainee/inmate within a violent extremist framework and what is likely to *protect* the him or her from this predicament.

The aim of the staff is to reduce the detainee's vulnerability to violent extremism and increase the detainee/inmate resilience to violent extremist thinking.

Assessment of the ideology

Deradicalization goes beyond disengagement. Deradicalization is about moving away from a violence-justifying radical ideology. The process of deradicalization requires a shift in thinking (a cognitive shift), away from morally justifying violence, away from legitimizing the need for violence and from seeing violence as the only solution to grievances. Dismantling a violence-justifying ideology involves addressing three aspects that form the ideology. These three aspects involve a grievance, a culprit or target blamed for the grievance and an effective method that is morally warranted (Kruglanski, Gelfand and Gunaratna 2011):

- grievance narrative, actual/perceived;
- target blamed for grievance becomes the focus of hatred and anger; and
- methods or violence morally justified by religious/historical/social narratives.

Assessing radicalizing narratives

Identifying radicalizing narratives helps to prepare counter narratives and alternative narratives. These narratives can help mitigate online radicalization, prevent recruitment from the community and support detainees challenge their thinking:

- Political narratives based on organizational injustice reflecting inequality in distribution of resources, power sharing, discrimination and persecution. Project the state as unjust and the terrorist group as just.
- Moral narratives reflecting moral degeneration of society and corruption as being part of the state machinery. Project moral justification to rescue the community.
- Religious narratives used to justify fighting an enemy of another faith or not of the same religious fervour. Project religious justification to gather recruits and violent legitimize actions.
- Social narratives related to social exclusion, deterioration of social norms and norms of behaviour. Project social justifications as to why communities cannot live together.
- Heroic narratives glamourize and attract the youth to become a rescuer of the people. Project the group as the saviour of the people.
- Historical narratives of communities being persecuted historically or of communities that have fought historically. Project historical justifications to prove that communities cannot live together.
- Separatist narratives of why communities must separate based on discrimination. Project justification to carve out a separate state.

When using counter narratives and alternative narratives, it is essential that detainees are not confronted but supported to question their own narratives and look for alternative interpretations. This method is referred to as the Socratic method, which prevents detainee resistance within a dialogue that fosters the detainee to challenge his or her own thinking.

Radicalization assessments or risk assessments

Radicalization assessments help to identify the intensity of aggression and violence-related thoughts and beliefs. These assessments can be part of the risk-assessment framework, which has a dual function. The assessment can provide a measure of the level of risk posed by the individual to self and others, as well as provide information of therapeutic value. These measures, used over time, can identify changes in levels of radicalization towards violence or away from violence.[5]

Assessment of radicalization

The assessment of radicalization used in Sri Lanka provided information on several aspects.[6] These aspects included, for example: the level of support for armed struggle, general violence, aggression towards a specific group and violence-related views; the presence of meaning and purpose in life; the tendency to hold a grudge against perceived injustices to self and loved ones; the presence of anger, shame, guilt and sense of insignificance; the tendency towards avoidance, benevolence, revenge; community narcissism and martyrdom; the need for closure; the sense of in-group responsibility and attachment to organization; identity fusion; self and family embeddedness in the organization; and attitudes towards staff, the centre and the guards.

Significance Quest Assessment Tool (SQAT)

The SQAT is a self-report measure used to assess the degree of radicalization or violent extremism (Kruglanski, Belanger and Gunaratna 2018: 10–11). The tool provides information on the level of risk and the level of cognitive change in radicalized thinking over time, which helps staff to measure the effectiveness of the interventions conducted within the centres in reducing risk and facilitating cognitive change. Of paramount importance is to understand factors that contribute to the shift in thinking and risk reduction. The SQAT, when administered at baseline and then at periodic intervals, reflects this shift. This tool has been used in Sri Lanka, Indonesia, the Philippines, Spain, Morocco and in the West Bank in Palestine. The SQAT can be administered by researchers, academics, prison staff, supervisors, religious staff or volunteers with appropriate training. It can be filled out by detainees who are literate. The questionnaire is designed to access information related to the quest for significance, acceptance of radical violence-justifying narratives and subscribing to a network and its narratives.

Violent Extremist Risk Assessment (VERA)

Elaine Pressman and John Flockton (2012a) propose the VERA2 protocol, a comprehensive risk-assessment tool.[7] The VERA2 is a psychometric instrument that provides a final violence extremism rating of low, moderate or high, which can be used in conjunction with other assessment instruments and can help with case management in correctional facilities. This instrument requires staff to be trained specifically to administer the assessment protocol. The factors assessed are:

- beliefs and attitudes (7 risk items);
- context and intent (7 risk items);
- history and capability (6 risk items);
- commitment and motivation (5 risk items); and
- protective items (6 mitigating factors).

Mitigating factors are those that would help to reduce the level of risk identified in the first four subsections.

The VERA approach has been updated several times to accommodate new knowledge and different populations, such as the VERA2 and VERA-2R (revised version). Screening versions have also been developed on the VERA2 to address specific needs such as VERA-SV (short version).[8] The most updated version of the VERA-2R includes additional indicators related to mental health and motivational indicators related to women and youth. This tool is in use in many states in conjunction with other assessment tools particularly in North America, Europe, Canada, Australia and Asia.[9]

Violent Extremism Beliefs Scale (VEBS)

The VEBS is a 31-item scale that measures four factors:

- religious violence and extremism;
- extent of positive thinking;
- power politics; and
- risk taking and impulsivity.

This scale is currently used by the Sabawoon Rehabilitation Programme in Pakistan for children recruited by the Taliban (Peracha et al. 2017: 53–62).

The Extremist Risk Guidelines (ERG22+)

The ERG22+ is a violent-extremist risk-assessment tool used within the UK. This tool was developed by the British National Offender Management Service (2011) to assess risk and needs of extremist offenders in the UK. The tool captures 22 cognitive-behavioural factors associated with extremism and the plus (+) captures certain idiosyncratic features associated with violent extremism.

Lloyd and Dean (2015: 40–52) discuss the utility value of the ERG22+, which helps offender management services to assess risk, potential risk and identify the needs to facilitate intervention.

The ERG22+ captures risk and needs based on three dimensions:

- engagement;
- intent; and
- capability.

The ERG22+ does not provide a specific risk-assessment score, but follows a similar model to that of VERA2 (Silke 2014: 117–118).

The Multi-Level Guidelines (MLG)

The MLG is an assessment tool that can be used to assess individual, individual–group, group and group–society dynamics related to violence. The tool defines group-based violence related to terrorism as well as crime and is recommended for use with other relevant risk-assessment tools to evaluate individuals at risk of perpetrating violence or engaging in terrorism-based violence (Hart et al. 2017).

The MLG administration procedure is discussed by Hart and colleagues. It comprises of seven steps:

- Evaluators gather relevant case information (Step 1).
- Consider the presence and relevance of 16 basic risk factors, as well as any case-specific risk factors (Steps 2 and 3).
- Develop an integrative formulation of terrorism risk based on risk factors that are present and relevant (Step 4).
- Develop scenarios of future terrorism based on the formulation, as well as management plans based on those scenarios (Steps 5 and 6).
- Communicate various conclusory opinions about the nature of risks posed by the person (Step 7).

The MLG is based on a nested ecological model of violence where individual and group factors influence each other to enhance or mitigate violence risk (Cook 2014). The MLG is an open-access tool. It is available for purchase by the general public and evaluators are not required to complete a specific training programme prior to purchase or use of the tool. The tool is intended for use by threat-assessment professionals from diverse backgrounds. It may be administered by individual professionals, although administration by multidisciplinary teams of professionals is strongly recommended (Cook 2014: 71–75).

Risk-assessment components

Andrew Silke (2014: 113) proposes seven essential components when conducting a risk assessment. These components are:

- Ideology – the level of adherence to the group's ideological position.
- Capability – the degree of experience and training that increase ability to act on ideology.
- Affiliations – the strength of individual's affiliation to the group.
- Political and social environment – the level of support and encouragement provided by the socio-political environment to engage in violence.
- Behaviour in custody – the degree of participation and cooperation with programmes.
- Emotional factors – the intensity of anger, revenge, grievances and injustices experienced.
- Disengagement factors – ageing, in-group conflict, changed priorities, disillusionment, significant life events such as injury or personal life events, deterred by the thought of future incarceration, time to reflect away from offending, changes in socio-political environment.

Risk-assessment models needs to address the past, the present and the future. An assessment of the individual's past as well as current strengths/vulnerabilities and behavioural patterns is more likely to indicate future behaviour and also identify where to target interventions to minimize future risk. Therefore, when assessing, ensure that the assessor is aware of past and present ideological positions, capabilities, affiliations, interpersonal relations and socio-political contexts, as well as thoughts, emotions and behaviours of the individual.

Conclusion

Disengagement from violence and deradicalization from violent extremism are two processes that involve cognitive and behavioural transformation. In the case of *disengagement*, the cognitive shift will enable a person to decide to refrain from using violence as a method of behavioural expression of discontent, but maintain the ideological or cognitive position of remaining disengaged from the target of blame or perceived enemy. The cognitive shift achieved in *deradicalization* is one that facilitates the individual to abandon the use of violence as a method of behavioural expression of discontent and engage with the target of blame to carve out a future together or arrive at a middle position. The latter position of deradicalization is a more sustained process than disengagement and it allows the person to move on and re-engage with all communities.

Given that both processes primarily involve a cognitive shift or transformation in thinking that will enable the crucial shift in behaviour away from violence, rehabilitation programmes assess this cognitive shift. Assessment remains central in the process of terrorist rehabilitation. Ad-hoc rehabilitation programmes are rapidly formalizing and engaging researchers, statisticians and psychologists to implement evidence-based intervention programmes. The dearth of sound statistical data within country programmes and the hesitation to publish existing data have resulted in a lack of collective knowledge in this field. However, with the new trend in showcasing country programmes, individual programmes take pride in achieving a standard of excellence and have shifted towards including evidence-based interventions within these programmes.

The assessment and evaluation of rehabilitation programmes remain a challenge to programme managers now beginning to implement tools that will provide the statistical evidence on the effectiveness of the programmes being implemented. Currently, effectiveness of programmes is based on recidivism rates. Though recidivism rates are a reflection of effectiveness, they are not necessarily an effective measure of the efficacy of individual programmes due to the several contextual factors that influence recidivism. Assessment of terrorist rehabilitation programmes remains crucial and pertinent to minimizing risk and central in shaping effective interventions, as governments struggle with growing numbers of youth involvement in terrorist groups and returning foreign fighters.

Notes

1 For example, Pakistan uses the VEBS, Sri Lanka uses the SQAT, Singapore uses its own classified measure of risk assessment and Saudi Arabia uses the VERA along with its own country-specific risk assessments. These assessment instruments are discussed further in the 'Specific assessments' section of this chapter.
2 A useful resource on overcoming resistance is Teyber, Edward (2006) *Interpersonal Process in Therapy: An integrative model*, fifth edition. San Bernardino, CA: Thomson Brooks/Cole.
3 A useful resource on stages of change is Prochaska, J.O., J.C. Norcross and C.C. DiClemente (2013) 'Applying the Stages of Change', *Psychotherapy in Australia*, 19(2): 5–15.
4 Also see Hettiarachchi, Malkanthi (2013) 'Sri Lanka's Rehabilitation Programme: A New Frontier IN Counter Terrorism and Counter Insurgency', *PRISM Journal for Complex Operations*, 4(2): 105–121.
5 It is vital that assessment instruments are not used too frequently as participants (detainees/inmates) are likely to habituate to the questions.
6 The battery of assessments used in Sri Lanka was developed and implemented in Sri Lanka, Philippines and Indonesia by a team of researchers with the START Programme at the University of Maryland, USA and the International Centre for Political Violence and Terrorism Research, Nanyang Technological University, Singapore. The measure was designed to capture the rapidly evolving phenomenon of radicalization into violence in the community and in detention centres in Sri Lanka, the Philippines, Indonesia and Spain. The team was led by Professors A.W. Kruglanski, M.J. Gelfand and R. Gunaratna.
7 Also see Pressman, D.E. and John Flockton (2012a) 'Calibrating Risk for Violent Political Extremists and Terrorists: The VERA-2 Structured Assessment', *The British Journal of Forensic Practice*, 14(4): 237–251.
8 On VERA, see Pressman, D. Elaine (2009) *Risk Assessment Decisions for Violent Political Extremism*, Her Majesty the Queen in Right of Canada. Available at: www.publicsafety.gc.ca/cnt/rsrcs/pblctns/2009-02-rdv/2009-02-rdv-eng.pdf (accessed 31 January 2018). On VERA2, see Pressman, D.E., N. Duits, T. Rinne and John S. Flockton (2016) 'Violent Extremist Risk Assessment Version 2 Revised (VERA-2R)', cited in Radicalization Awareness Network Collection of Approaches and Practices, *Preventing Radicalization to Terrorism and Violent Extremism*, European Commission, Radicalization Awareness Network. On VERA-2R, see Pressman, D. Elaine, N. Duits, T., Rinne and John S. Flockton (2016) *VERA-2R: Violent Extremism Risk Assessment-Version 2 Revised*. Netherlands Ministry of Security and Justice, Netherlands Institute

for Forensic Psychiatry and Psychology. On VERA-SV, see Kruglanski, Arie W., Jocelyn J. Belanger and Rohan Gunaratna (2018) *How Radicalization Happens: A Social Psychological Analysis*. New York: Oxford University Press.
9 See above citations on the use of VERA in different countries, as well as Pressman, D. Elaine and John S. Flockton (2014) 'Violent Extremist Risk Assessment: Development of the VERA-2 and Applications in the High Security Correctional Setting', in A. Silke (eds), *Prisons, Terrorism and Extremism*. London: Routledge: 122–143.

Bibliography

Baehr, Marie (2010) 'Distinctions between Assessment and Evaluation', in *Programme Assessment Handbook*. Lisle, IL: Pacific Crest: 441–444.

Bryans, Shane (2012) 'Assessment Frameworks and De-radicalisation Programmes', paper presented at the International Centre for Prison Studies, University of Essex. Available at: www.scribd.com/document/370477456/Bryans-S-2012-Assessment-Frameworks-and-de-radicalisation-Programmes (accessed 31 January 2018).

Bureau for the Commissioner General for Rehabilitation, Sri Lanka (2010) *BCGR Action Plan*, Colombo: Bureau for the Commissioner General for Rehabilitation.

Cook, Alana N. (2014) 'Risk Assessment and Management of Group-based Violence', Doctoral dissertation, Simon Fraser University.

Hart, Stephen D., Alana N. Cook, D. Elaine Pressman, Steven Strang and Yan L. Lim (2017) 'A Concurrent Evaluation of Threat Assessment Tools for the Individual Assessment of Terrorism', *report submitted to the Canadian Network for Research on Terrorism, Security and Society*, final version.

Hecker, Jeffrey E. and Geoffrey F. Thorpe (2016) *Introduction to Clinical Psychology: Science Practise and Ethics*. Abingdon: Routledge.

Kruglanski, Arie W. and Michele J. Gelfand (2010) *Rehabilitation of Former LTTE Cadres in Sri Lanka: A Preliminary Report*. College Park, MD: University of Maryland.

Kruglanski, Arie W., Jocelyn J. Belanger and Rohan Gunaratna (2018) *How Radicalization Happens: A Social Psychological Analysis*. New York: Oxford University Press.

Kruglanski, Arie W., Michele J. Gelfand and Rohan Gunaratna (2011) 'Aspects of Deradicalization', in Rohan Gunaratna, Jolene Jerard and L. Rubin (eds), *Terrorist Rehabilitation and Counter-radicalisation: New Approaches to counter-terrorism*. Abingdon: Routledge: 135–145.

Kruglanski, Arie W., Michele J. Gelfand, Jocelyn J. Belanger, Rohan Gunaratna and Malkanthi Hettiarachchi (2014) 'Deradicalising the Liberation Tigers of Tamil Eelam (LTTE): Some Preliminary Findings', in A. Silke (eds), *Prisons Terrorism and Extremism*. New York: Routledge: 183–196.

Lloyd, Monica and Christopher Dean (2015) 'The Development of Structured Guidelines for Assessing Risk in Extremist Offenders', *Journal of Threat Assessment and Management*, 2(1): 40–52.

Hettiarachchi, Malkanthi (2013) 'Sri Lanka's Rehabilitation Programme: A New Frontier in Counter Terrorism and Counter Insurgency', *PRISM Journal for Complex Operations*, 4(2): 105–121.

Miller, William R. and Stephen Rollnick (1991) *Motivational Interviewing: Preparing People to Change Addictive Behavior*. New York: Guilford Publications.

National Offender Management Service (2011) *Extremism Risk Guidelines: ERG 22+ Structured Professional Guidelines for Assessing Risk of Extremist Offending*. London: Her Majesty's Government.

Peracha, Feriha N., Asma Ayub, Raafia R. Khan, Zaeema Farooq and Andleeb Zahra (2017) 'Development and Validation of Indigenous Violent Extremism Beliefs Scale (VEBS)', *Journal of Psychology and Behavioural Science*, 5(1): 53–62.

Pressman, D. Elaine (2009) *Risk Assessment Decisions for Violent Political Extremism*, Her Majesty the Queen in Right of Canada. Available at: www.publicsafety.gc.ca/cnt/rsrcs/pblctns/2009-02-rdv/2009-02-rdv-eng.pdf (accessed 31 January 2018).

Pressman, D. Elaine and John S. Flockton (2012a) 'Calibrating Risk for Violent Political Extremists and Terrorists: The VERA-2 Structured Assessment', *The British Journal of Forensic Practice*, 14(4): 237–251.

Pressman, D. Elaine and John S. Flockton (2012b) 'VERA: Violence Extremism Risk Assessment (Consultative Version 2)', *Professional Manual Extracts*. Ottawa: Canadian Centre for Intelligence and Security Studies.

Pressman, D. Elaine and John S. Flockton (2014) 'Violent Extremist Risk Assessment: Development of the VERA-2 and Applications in the High Security Correctional Setting', in A. Silke (eds), *Prisons, Terrorism and Extremism*. London: Routledge: 122–143.

Pressman, D. Elaine, Nils Duits, Thomas Rinne and John S. Flockton (2016a) *VERA-2R: Violent Extremism Risk Assessment-Version 2 Revised*. Netherlands Ministry of Security and Justice, Netherlands Institute for Forensic Psychiatry and Psychology.

Pressman, D. Elaine., Nils Duits, Thomas Rinne and John S. Flockton (2016b) 'Violent Extremist Risk Assessment Version 2 Revised (VERA-2R)', cited in Radicalization Awareness Network Collection of Approaches and Practices, *Preventing Radicalization to Terrorism and Violent Extremism*, European Commission, Radicalization Awareness Network.

Prochaska, O. James and Carlo C. DiClemente (1982) 'Trans-theoretical Therapy: Toward a More Integrative Model of Change'. *Psychotherapy: Theory, Research and Practice*, 19: 276–288.

Prochaska, O. James, John C. Norcross and Carlo C. DiClemente (2013) 'Applying the Stages of Change', *Psychotherapy in Australia*, 19(2): 5–15.

Sattler, Jerome M. (2001) *Assessment of Children: Cognitive Applications*, fourth edition. San Diego: J.M. Sattler.

Silke, Andrew (2014) 'Risk Assessment of Terrorist and Extremist Prisoners', in A. Silke (eds), *Prisons Terrorism and Extremism: Critical Issues in Management Radicalisation and Reform*. London: Routledge: 108–121.

Teyber, Edward (2006) *Interpersonal Process in Therapy: An Integrative Model*, fifth edition. San Bernardino, CA: Thomson Brooks/Cole.

Index

ACG (Aftercare Group) 84–6
activists, former terrorism 101
Afghanistan ix, 3, 5–6, 33, 48, 50, 52, 58, 70
Africa viii, 4, 62, 74
agencies ix, 8, 10, 76, 87–9, 105
al-Qaeda 2–5, 33, 36, 64, 79
allegiance 77
anti-terrorism 87
approaches i, xiii, xvi, 7–10, 13, 15–17, 25, 27, 31–2, 38, 41–4, 47, 70–1, 86–7, 104–5
armed conflicts 47–8, 50–2, 54, 57–9
Assessment of terrorist rehabilitation programmes 119, 121, 123, 125, 127, 129, 131, 133–5

behavioral change 102, 112
beliefs xv, 1, 4, 21, 69, 80, 90, 98, 105, 107, 130–1
beneficiaries 8–9, 34, 38, 72, 79, 85, 89–92, 123, 126–7
best practices i, xvii, 71

Calibrating Risk for Violent Political Extremists 134, 136
Canada 31, 131, 134, 136
capacities xv, 6–7, 26, 32, 50, 52, 57, 59, 87, 108–10
Categorization of detainees vii, 125
change makers, positive 71, 73–4
changes, behavioural 15, 126
civil society 73, 82, 95–6, 111–12, 117
clients 69, 95, 100, 105, 107–12, 114, 122
Cognitive behavioural assessments 126, 128
collaboration 6, 8, 38
combat terrorism ix, 20, 86, 118

Combating Terrorism in Yemen 45
commitment xii–xiv, xvi, 11, 57, 102, 112–13, 121, 124, 131
community engagement ix, xi, xiii, 1, 6–7, 38, 86–7, 93
components 37, 41, 112, 122–3, 132
Concurrent Evaluation of Threat Assessment Tools 135
conditions xiv, xvi, 18, 24, 47, 53, 67, 72, 105, 110, 115
conduct 6, 37, 92, 100, 102, 107, 120, 127
conflict ix, 1, 5, 19, 47, 50, 55–6, 58, 62–3, 74, 76, 99–100, 115
conflict resolution 78, 116, 119
constraints, spatial 19–20, 25–6
coordination 65, 100, 105
corrections facility 22–6
Council of Europe 22–3
counseling 91, 105, 107, 109, 114
Counter-radicalisation ix, xi, 11, 45, 76, 92, 135
countering violent extremism xv, 1, 10–11, 46, 61–3
counterterrorism strategy i, 45, 49, 81, 92
country programmes 133
crisis 98, 110–14, 126
culture 29, 33, 86, 110, 119, 128
custody xii–xiii, xv, 9, 11, 17, 20, 29, 133
CVE (Countering violent extremism) xv, 1–3, 10–11, 46, 59, 61–3

DDR (Disarmament, Demobilisation and Reintegration) v, 46–8, 51, 58–9, 61, 63
deradicalisation i, xi, 2, 7–8, 13–15, 44, 46–7, 50, 59, 80

138 Index

detainee classification, comprehensive 23
detainees vii, xvi, 1, 7–8, 11, 13, 17, 23–6, 28–9, 34–41, 43–4, 79–80, 82–7, 120–8, 130
development 3, 7, 16, 27, 49, 63, 76, 86, 100–1, 105, 111, 135–6
dialogue 34–6, 44, 70, 95, 130
difficulties 66, 81–3, 118, 120, 126, 128
dilemmas 46–7, 108
discrimination 65, 67, 101, 112, 129
disengagement vii, 10, 13–15, 24, 47, 50, 100, 111, 117, 129, 133

economic rehabilitation 10, 47–9, 51–3, 55–7, 59–60
education 52, 58, 70, 83, 85, 89, 100–1, 103, 105, 119, 128
effectiveness 6, 17, 87, 100–1, 105, 112, 114, 120, 130, 134
Egypt xii, 36, 45
empathy 70, 97, 102, 108, 110, 123
empowerment programs 105, 109, 114
engagement 11, 15, 17, 29, 56, 59, 79, 82–3, 122, 125–7, 132
Entrepreneurial rehabilitation v, 64–5, 67, 69, 71, 73, 75, 77
ethics 65, 98, 101, 103, 135
Europe's Guidelines 22–3
evaluation 11, 104–5, 114, 117–18, 120, 134–5
exclusiveness 95–6, 100, 103–4
exclusivism 1–2, 5, 9
expertise viii, 6, 8–9, 84–5, 88, 101, 124
extremism xiii, 1–3, 5, 9, 34, 40, 65, 80, 82, 87, 100, 131, 135–6

facilities 13, 19, 23–4, 26, 41, 95, 120, 124
faith vii, 21, 32, 98–100, 107, 129
families, role of 46, 55, 60
family members 37–8, 79, 81–3, 88–9, 128
former terrorists 49, 59, 67–8, 70, 72, 74–5, 103, 114
framework ii–iii, xv, 2, 10, 27, 33
FTFs (Foreign terrorist fighters) 4–5, 11

governments i, xi–xii, xv, 1, 5–10, 18, 20, 27, 34–6, 40–1, 46, 65, 80–1, 87–92, 111–12

grievances 98, 108–9, 111, 119, 129, 133
group-based violence 11, 132, 135

High Security Correctional Setting 135–6
human rights 18–19, 39

ICPVTR (International Centre for Political Violence and Terrorism Research) i, viii–ix, xi, 35, 45, 85, 91, 93, 134
ideology 5, 7, 9–10, 14, 24, 33, 36–7, 44, 46, 70, 79, 82, 111, 128–9, 133
implementation iii, 49, 87–8, 104, 114, 120
imprisonment xii, 7, 16, 46, 79, 90, 105
inclusiveness 95–6, 104
Indonesia terrorist recruitments 65
inmates vii, xvi, 12, 16, 19–21, 23–6, 28, 34, 52, 103, 120–5, 127
Intelligence and Counter Terrorism 31, 61, 75
interaction 17, 25, 53, 55, 112, 128
Internal Security Act (ISA) 84, 90
interventions 8, 48, 59, 61, 69, 74, 103, 115, 119, 121–2, 126–7, 130, 132
Iraq 3–7, 11, 29, 33, 36–7, 44, 48, 50, 52, 79, 92
ISIS (Islamic State of Iraq and Syria) 32–3, 64, 77–8, 80, 84
Islam 4, 32–40, 42, 44, 66, 70, 83
Islamic Fundamentalism 115–16
isolation 21–2, 25–6, 51, 53

Jemaah Islamiyah (JI) 33, 79, 93
jihad 33–4, 43–4, 70, 112

leadership xi, 7–8, 36, 82, 86, 91, 107
legitimacy 36, 39, 71, 74
limitations xiv, 16, 21, 27–8, 74, 96
livelihoods 41, 49, 51–4, 61, 63, 126

madrasahs 66, 70
mad'uw 42
mainstream society 9, 15, 48, 52, 73
Malaysia 20, 38–9, 50, 58, 60, 89
MI (Motivational interviewing) 123, 135
mindsets 43–4, 72, 74, 111
moderate 35, 66, 125, 131
modes 7, 10, 13, 16, 83

motives 33, 69, 96–7, 100, 103–4, 106
movements xiv, 4, 33, 66, 78

Nepal 50, 54, 56–7, 61, 63

offenders xvi, 8, 79–80, 97, 100, 102, 111

Panopticon 12, 16, 18, 29
participation 3, 28, 46, 56–7, 63, 89–90, 122, 128, 133
partners 1, 5–6, 8–9
peace ix, 32, 40, 49–50, 55, 57, 59, 63–4, 70, 73–4, 81, 85, 103, 115
people xii–xiii, xvi, 19–21, 32, 35, 52–6, 69–70, 72–3, 75, 81, 96, 98–9, 101, 106–7, 129
perceptions 12, 20, 29, 66, 69, 85, 128
perpetrators xii, 96, 102–3
Philippines xii, 20, 25, 28–9, 67, 88–90, 130, 134
policy viii, 10, 31, 46, 61, 75, 87, 91
practitioners 7, 13, 17, 32, 41, 101–2, 105, 111–12, 114
principle 12, 16, 22, 35, 96, 100–1
prison facility 20–1, 25, 28
problems, solving 108, 119
process, internal vii, 109–10
programme assessments 120
programme effectiveness 117, 120, 134
propensity 10, 24–5
proposition 46, 51
psychological rehabilitation vi, 7, 39, 47, 95–7, 99–101, 103, 105, 107–9, 111–12, 114–15
psychologists 7–8, 10, 16, 82, 85, 105, 126, 133
Psychotherapy 114, 134, 136
punishment 9, 13, 17, 30, 95, 109

Quran 35, 37, 43, 97, 116

radical ideology v, 25, 32–3, 35, 37, 39, 41, 43, 45, 59–60, 81–2, 103, 118
radicalisation 3, 8–9, 11, 15–17, 19–20, 22–4, 29, 31, 42, 46, 50–1, 60, 62, 85
recidivism 9, 13, 19, 50–2, 60, 79, 119, 121, 126
recruitment 9, 20, 54, 62, 65, 96, 125, 128–9
rehabilitating vii, 11, 30, 58, 81, 96, 100, 102–4

rehabilitation centres viii, 86, 117, 120, 123, 125
rehabilitation process 16–17, 39, 54, 80, 85, 96, 104–5, 114, 122
reintegration vii, xiii, 6, 8, 13–17, 19, 27–9, 40, 48, 51, 61–3, 82, 95, 114, 117–18
religious terrorism 64–6, 72–3, 77, 114
resilience, familial 119
resistance 105, 121, 123, 125, 134
Resolving Conflict 61–2
risk xv, 9, 22–3, 50, 82, 96, 121–2, 124, 127–8, 131–3
risk assessment 120, 122, 126, 130, 132, 134
RRG (Religious Rehabilitation Group) ix, xi, 40, 84–5, 90
RSIS (Rajaratnam School of International Studies) i, viii–xi, 76, 87, 93

Saudi Arabia xii–xiv, 30, 34, 38, 45, 50, 60, 79–80, 85–7, 90–4
security 8, 12, 19, 23, 26, 41, 46, 49, 57, 61–3, 83, 88, 91, 134–6
Singapore's rehabilitation approach 84
social capital 47, 53–4, 56, 60–2, 71
social rehabilitation v, 7, 47, 49, 53–4, 60, 79–83, 85, 87, 89, 91, 93
Somalia 48, 50, 52, 58, 60
Southeast Asia 76, 78, 88, 90
SQAT (Significance Quest Assessment Tool) 122, 130, 134
Sri Lanka viii, xiii–xiv, 37, 45, 57, 86, 88, 93–4, 117, 125, 130, 134–5
strengths 26, 96, 105–7, 120, 128, 133
struggle xii, 33, 38, 119
Syria 4–5, 33, 80

teachings 32, 41–2, 47, 52, 82
terrorism activities 66, 79–80
terrorism offenders 95–6, 100
terrorist detainees vii, 10, 17–18, 21–6, 32, 41
terrorist groups i, 7, 15, 30, 33–4, 38–9, 44, 70, 74, 96, 125, 129, 134
terrorist networks 39, 41, 46, 51, 55, 82, 95, 124
Terrorist Rehabilitation and Counter-radicalisation 11, 45, 76, 135
terrorist threats 6, 18
Thailand 24, 75

tools xvi, 1, 11, 62, 115, 130–2, 134
training 7, 38, 41, 56–7, 66–7, 83, 105, 117, 125, 130, 133
transformation process, behavioral vii, 112–13

UK iv, viii, 131
United Nations (UN) 1, 31, 48, 52, 63

VEBS (Violent Extremism Beliefs Scale) 122, 131, 134, 136
VERA (Violent Extremist Risk Assessment) 122, 131–2, 134–6
vocational rehabilitation 8, 38, 41, 47, 52, 59, 86

Yayasan Mendaki 83–5
Yemen xii, 35–6, 41, 45, 50, 60, 91, 93
youths ix, 73, 118–19, 129, 131